Murderers and Other Friendly People

BOOKS BY DENIS BRIAN

Murderers and Other Friendly People
Tallulah, Darling
The Love-minded
Science of Crime Detection

Murderers and Other Friendly People

The public and private worlds of interviewers

Denis Brian

McGraw-Hill Book Company
NEW YORK ST. LOUIS SAN FRANCISCO
DÜSSELDORF LONDON MEXICO
PANAMA SYDNEY TORONTO

To Martine with love

Copyright © 1973 by Denis Brian.
All rights reserved. Printed in the United States of America. No part of this publication may be reproduced, stored in a retrieval system, or transmitted in any form or by any means, electronic, mechanical, photocopying, recording, or otherwise, without the prior written permission of the publisher.

Library of Congress Cataloging in Publication Data

Brian, Denis.
    Murderers and other friendly people.

    1. Interviewing (Journalism) I. Title.
PN4784.I6B7 1973   070.4'3   73-7547
ISBN 0-07-007690-1

123456789BPBP79876543

Alex Haley interview excerpted from *Playboy* interview: "Malcolm X" (*Playboy*, May, 1963); copyright © 1963 by Playboy. Quotations from *The New York Times* on page 254: © 1967 and 1969 by The New York Times Co. Reprinted by permission.
Lasky, Victor. *Robert F. Kennedy: The Myth and the Man.* © 1968 Trident Press, division of Simon & Schuster, Inc.

Contents

Introduction vii

PART ONE: The Hemingway Hunters   1

    A. E. HOTCHNER   3
    MALCOLM COWLEY   15
    BARNABY CONRAD   25
    GEORGE PLIMPTON   31
    ARNOLD GINGRICH   45
    WILLIAM SEWARD   57
    MARY HEMINGWAY   63
    JOHN HEMINGWAY   77

PART TWO: Truman Capote's Friends and Foes   83

    TRUMAN CAPOTE   85
    LESLEY FROST   117
    DONALD CULLIVAN   121
    DUANE WEST   129

PART THREE: Rex Reed and His Targets   133

    REX REED   135
    JACK THOMAS   161

PART FOUR: Controversial Pair from the World's Greatest Paper   165

    HARRISON SALISBURY   167
    GAY TALESE   183

PART FIVE: Politics Right and Left 201

WILLIAM F. BUCKLEY, JR. 203
BENJAMIN DEMOTT 227

PART SIX: Circling the Kennedys in Search of the Myth Makers, or, How Interviews Set the Record Straight 237

WALT ROSTOW 239
HUGH SIDEY 241
GEORGE REEDY 251
THE LASKY-LONGWORTH
  AFFAIR 253
ARTHUR SCHLESINGER, JR. 261

PART SEVEN: Dangerous Assignments 265

ALEX HALEY 267

PART EIGHT: Everybody's Favorite 285

STUDS TERKEL 287

Introduction

America is the interviewer's paradise. Where else is a murderer's best friend his interviewer? Edgar Smith, found guilty of killing a teenage girl, calls William F. Buckley, Jr., his closest friend. And both Perry Smith and Richard Hickock, hanged for the murder of the Clutter family, thought of their interviewer, Truman Capote, as a friend. The very few people who resist interviews—Greta Garbo, Howard Hughes, J. D. Salinger—are regarded as eccentric, or, like the head of the Central Intelligence Agency, understandably secretive.

Even in freedom-loving Britain interviewers are rarely allowed to speak with prisoners in jail, and it isn't possible to emulate Truman Capote, who took TV cameras and his questions into death rows throughout America, or Peter Maas, who interviewed Joseph Valachi in a maximum security prison.

Presidential press conferences have become the custom in the U.S. since Woodrow Wilson started them on a regular basis. And by February 1973, in addition to press conferences, President Richard Nixon had given nine on-the-record, exclusive interviews; the eighth to Garnett Horner of the *Washington Star-News.* According to an anonymous White House aide quoted in *Time* magazine, the interview was granted to the *Star-News* "to screw *The Washington Post,*" because of the *Post's* attacks on the Administration. In Britain, by contrast, Winston Churchill scattered would-be interviewers with expletives and turned down $100,000 rather than submit to questions from Edward R. Murrow of CBS. Today's rulers in Britain are only a little more cooperative and their instinctive response to "Nice day, isn't it?" is "No comment." And anyone remotely connected with the government is encouraged to keep his mouth shut by the "Official Secrets Act," which could land him in prison for betraying secrets.

France still endures the legacy of de Gaulle, who believed "grandeur needs mystery" and confided in no one, not even his admiring and distinguished biographer François Mauriac. De Gaulle's press conferences were rigidly controlled and all questions had to be approved by him in advance. He had no fear of being caught off guard during a spontaneous interview on French TV or radio—because his government owned them. Japan's Premier Shigeru Yoshida once showed what he thought of an interviewer by hurling water from a glass at him. West Germany is a bright spot for interviewers: its chancellor, Willy Brandt, an ex-journalist, is very accessible, and his spirit is reflected in other West German officials.

But the brightest spot of all is America, where, fortified by two quasi-religious beliefs—"the public's right to know" and "press freedom"—interviewers ask questions of almost everyone and get answers. This freedom to know was enhanced by the Supreme Court decision to allow *The New York Times* and *The Washington Post* to publish the previously secret Pentagon Papers, but threatened more recently by the imprisonment of reporters who refused to reveal confidential sources, the Supreme Court ruled in June, 1972, that newsmen had no First Amendment right to avoid such testimony.

These days, more than at any other time, our most vivid

impressions of our contemporaries are through interviews. Almost everything of moment reaches us through one man asking questions of another. Because of this the interviewer holds a position of unprecedented power and influence. Yet, strangely, he isn't subjected even to the scrutiny that is given a man taking a driving test.

I discovered, by turning the tables on the outstanding interviewers and having them *answer* the questions, that most of them reveal themselves as freely and honestly as they persuade their subjects to. I asked them to assess their fellow-interviewers. And I went a step further by asking the people they had interviewed to assess them.

In ancient times interviewing was a pursuit of wisdom and interviewers were treasure hunters after intangible gems. To that end the wise man was questioned exhaustively. This spilled over in more recent times into hero worship and the urge to get everything on paper: hence Boswell badgering Johnson. Today interviewers still hope to get answers to the riddle of the universe, but settle for less.

Jesus Christ is an enigma because no interviewer got to him. Shakespeare is a mystery, too, having had no Boswell, not even a local reporter, question him. Our loss points up the value of an interviewer: he can penetrate the myths and lies, to reveal the man out of his own mouth.

The style of interviews, particularly on television, at its worst ranges from bear-baiting to gossipy coffee klatsches with celebrities jostling one another to tell all. At best a character comes to life. And when that happens it is likely to be in America.

Sometimes the results, like Lillian Ross's interview of Ernest Hemingway, are shattering. Sometimes the subject blows a fuse and walks out. Burt Lancaster did this when Mike Wallace questioned him and so did Governor Lester Maddox of Georgia, when baited by Joe Pyne. And occasionally the result is almost a masterpiece, like Studs Terkel's *Division Street: America,* a book of interviews with ordinary people in Chicago, or Alex Haley's *Malcolm X.*

I found out how the best interviewers persuade the secretive to talk and the talkative to reach the point. And how they can feel compassion and warmth even for the callous murderers and the fanatics they get to know. I discovered why Truman Capote cried when Perry Smith and Richard Hickock were hanged. And why Alex Haley, a black, exchanged friendly letters with George Lincoln Rockwell after interviewing the black-hating American Nazi leader. I realized that the one quality all the interviewers share is curiosity, and that an interviewer without curiosity is as useless as a seasick sailor. And from people who knew Hemingway, President Kennedy and his brother Robert, I learned about facets of their personalities of which the public are probably not aware. But most of all I got to know the interviewers themselves.

Benjamin DeMott—Amherst professor, novelist, literary and social critic—describes interviewers as "bad men." I set out to find if this is true, if they dip their typewriter ribbons in vitriol, as some critics suspect; and to answer the question, "Should interviewers be called, rather than ladies and gentlemen of the press, offspring of the devil?"

PART ONE
The Hemingway Hunters

MALCOLM COWLEY   A. E. HOTCHNER
BARNABY CONRAD   GEORGE PLIMPTON
ARNOLD GINGRICH   WILLIAM SEWARD
MARY HEMINGWAY
JOHN HEMINGWAY

How well do interviewers succeed in their aim to discover hidden truths and reveal men?

Ernest Hemingway ran for cover when trapped into an interview. He lied, joked, threatened, charmed: as if his life depended on concealment. Perhaps he wanted to do the probing himself, or feared too much exposure might damage his reputation and his creative urges. Weren't his novels full of self-revelation? Why waste time explaining himself to others, when they'd probably paint him as a horse's ass, anyway?

Still three hunters got to him.

Malcolm Cowley, a distinguished literary critic, cornered him first for Life *magazine, in February 1948, and stayed in Cuba two weeks to hear Hemingway confess, off the record, that he loathed his domineering mother and despised his suicide father. The ordeal by interview was so painful for Hemingway, he said it took him a week to recover and return to his own writing. But Cowley got back with an interview that made Hemingway a celebrity in several million homes, showing in words and pictures a tough, brave, friendly, cat-loving man, who pursued the* mot juste *with as much enthusiasm and dedication as he stalked his living prey.*

Two years later Lillian Ross took a stab at recording the true Hemingway for The New Yorker. *In her interview-portrait Hemingway was a man who talked to himself, used semiliterate phrases, carried alcohol with him everywhere, like a baby with a bottle—or security blanket. Hemingway shared his shock (when he read the published interview in* The New

Yorker *of May 13, 1950) with his publisher Charles Scribner, and feared that it would make him plenty of enemies.*

Four years after that, in Paris, George Plimpton, editor of a new literary review, The Paris Review, *approached Hemingway and, after visiting him in Cuba and an exchange of letters, obtained the third substantial interview with Hemingway. This time Hemingway was gun-shy and insisted on seeing the piece before it was printed—so that he could go over it carefully. The result showed a serious, absorbed craftsman, cooperative, but impatient to go back to work.*

I, in turn, interviewed two of these Hemingway Hunters to learn more about them—for they were famous in their own right—and about Ernest Hemingway, as part of my attempt to shine the spotlight on interviewers as they shine it on others. To gauge how much of Hemingway his hunters had come away with and how much of the material was camouflage, I also interviewed one of his biographers, A. E. Hotchner; ex-bullfighter Barnaby Conrad; one of the few professors of English literature who could call Hemingway a friend, Professor William Seward; Arnold Gingrich, publisher of Esquire, *publisher of Hemingway's early works, and his fishing companion; the woman who lived with Hemingway as his wife for fifteen years, Mary Hemingway; and finally, his eldest son, John Hemingway.*

A. E. Hotchner

BORN IN ST. LOUIS, MISSOURI, JUNE 28, 1920

A. E. (Aaron Edward) Hotchner wrote a memoir called Papa Hemingway *about his friend and traveling and hunting companion Ernest Hemingway. Hemingway's widow, Mary, said she suffered a "traumatic shock" when she read the galleys—and unsuccessfully tried to prevent its publication. In the book Hotchner vividly described Hemingway's mental collapse and suicide.*

Brian: You were in the Sherry-Netherland hotel when Lillian Ross was actually taking notes for her Hemingway piece. How was it that she didn't entirely reflect the true Hemingway when she was being as objective as possible and, in fact, just reporting the words that were said and the action that went on?

Hotchner: There were two things involved. One was that in the total reportage it was much more interesting to extract that which served her means and to leave out that which didn't. And secondly she apparently had no insight into the fact that Ernest had been working for a hard, long, arduous time in Havana, on a novel which he had just finished. So he came up to New York and suddenly let loose. When he worked he was like a monk: he didn't drink and he didn't philander, and he stayed right with it. But when he came up here with his manuscript it was a release, and as he told her right off the bat: "I'm so sick of sounding like myself with these interviews, I'm going to have some fun. The thing I like best is to sound like an Ojibway Indian, of which I'm part." So that was part of letting loose. She missed all of that. She missed the fact that he'd finished the book and wanted to have some fun. And she missed the fact that he didn't want to make pronouncements and wanted to put everybody on, which he did. She didn't know much about a guy like Hemingway, that was the problem. She was honest and she reported everything as she saw it, but she just wasn't the person to do it, that's all.

Brian: You think it might have come across if she had known him when he was working and put the two together?

Hotchner: It would have helped, yes. But Lillian was the wrong person to understand anybody out of Hemingway's world. I don't think she'd ever been out of the country and I don't think she'd ever taken a drink in her life. She was the wrong person. A good example of how she really didn't do a very good job on reporting that which was *interesting*, the hell with accurate, *interesting*: Marlene Dietrich had come to the hotel and a group of us, including Lillian, had spent the entire night talking—ten hours or so; the most fascinating and longest part of the discussion had to do with astrology. Dietrich was trying to get Ernest to give his vital statistics to an astrologist named Righter who lived in Hollywood and who ran her life, and still does. This went on for endless hours and Marlene told marvelous stories of how she had tried to save Grace Moore, the celebrated singer, through warnings from this particular astrologer that she shouldn't be in an airplane. And Lillian didn't get any of that, or didn't use any of that. And Ernest commented about how he didn't want to be run by the stars and so forth, and all Lillian reported out of the whole evening was a little reference to the fact that Marlene used towels from the Plaza to clean her daughter's apartment.

Brian: What was Dietrich's reaction to this?

Hotchner: She called me up the day *The New Yorker* came out. She was furious. First of all, she said she hadn't known that Lillian was there in the guise of silent girl reporter sitting in the shadows taking notes. She never would have talked so freely, she said, and certainly no reporter should have taken such advantage of her. It gave her license to kill, she said. She was really furious, an uncontrolled tirade. Her fury was fanned hotter by her estimation of the way Lillian had written about Ernest, a man she had known for thirty years, and loved. She wanted to know how Ernest had ever consented to have a person like that sitting around taking notes surreptitiously. Her anger finally choked her and she rang off. Then a little while later she was back on the phone. She had talked to her lawyers and was going to sue. She had always been a very private person, she said, despite her public life, and she was going to make Lillian and *The New Yorker* pay for this humiliating thing they had done to her. We talked for a long time. Later I went over to her apartment to see her. I told her that in a way it was Ernest's fault for not having told her about Lillian. I also pointed out that a lawsuit would only serve to magnify the whole thing. She finally quieted down, but she said she was going to phone Ernest about it. I don't know if she ever did.

Brian: You said he loved to put people on. A version of that was his lying to you about making love to Mata Hari.

Hotchner: Sure. I mean that was part of the fun of it and you had to understand that. And some of the things that I used in the book (*Papa Hemingway*) were so wildly outrageous that I didn't even bother to point them out or footnote them: like the anecdote that he repeatedly told about meeting Legs Diamond's girl friend in "21," and laying her on the landing after the restaurant had closed for the night.

Brian: This was fantasy, you think?

Hotchner: Oh, it was bullshit, of course. But fantasy and exaggeration were components of the delicate machinery that made Ernest what he was. They were kith to the fiction he wrote. But certain people have said: "My God, you were taken in by that. You're pretty gullible." Or they said: "You're such a sycophant you swallowed everything without questioning it." There's a self-appointed Hemingway expert named Phil Young who teaches English somewhere and who once wrote a book about Ernest that was based on the asinine theory that everything Ernest did and wrote in his life stemmed from a leg wound he received in World War I. Young has complained in print that I didn't footnote those incidents, like the "21" orgy, and explain my skepticism. He has also complained that a few of the things Ernest says in my book are very close to some things Ernest has written. If Young himself had written more he would know that writers often work their good stuff into their conversations. Young had never met Hemingway nor heard him talk nor ever seen him, but he, like so many others, are absolute authorities on how Ernest *really* spoke and what he was *really* like. In writing about him, I wanted to do one thing and one thing only: re-create him as he was with me over the course of the fourteen years I knew him. Let him say the things he said, as he said them. Whoppers and all.

Brian: In other words, he didn't really mind if people took this as the truth and printed it? He got a kick out of it?

Hotchner: Of course.

Brian: Were you aware of anything in the Lillian Ross article that was him kidding, and she didn't know it?

Hotchner: I think the whole thing was kidding. I don't think she got any part of Hemingway. I mean the way it came out he sounded like an old rummy. And she had no perspective, no balance. How can you spend only two days with anyone and represent that as any kind of insight into that person? Lillian then was a naive girl with her nose pressed against the window pane, not seeing what was really going on inside.

Brian: D'you think Hemingway was genuinely upset because so many people objected to the Profile?

Hotchner: Of course. He was upset by the piece itself. Lillian always said that he thought it was marvelous. Well, that's ridiculous. What he really said was: "There's so much here that I don't know what to do with it—so I just said it was okay."

Brian: You mean when he wrote to her saying, "You've got it straight," it was to comfort her, rather than to express how he really felt?

Hotchner: He didn't know what to do about it. I know she says that there was time. There was no time. According to both Ernest and Mary, she sent the galleys and by the time they arrived in Havana, it was the week the magazine was being published, so there wasn't anything to do about the galleys.

Brian: You said Hemingway was sick of being interviewed. But apart from the school interview you report and Lillian Ross, Malcolm Cowley, and George Plimpton, hardly anyone else interviewed him, did they?

Hotchner: He was being interviewed all the time, when anybody could corner him. Harvey Breit did several interviews, good ones, for *The New York Times*. The news magazines, *Time, Newsweek*, others, had several interviews, and *Time* did a long cover story about him when he won the Nobel prize. A *Time* reporter spent several days in Havana with him. When Ernest went abroad, interviewers hounded him constantly, and he often gave in. In *Papa Hemingway* I recount what happened in Spain when two German journalists accosted him.

Brian: His main complaint was that it was taking him away from his work or his entertainment, was it? He didn't want to explain himself to people?

Hotchner: No, he didn't really like any of that—although he liked publicity. He really didn't like the mechanics of arriving at publicity, the interview, the radio microphone, the television camera, the still photographer, whatever it is that achieves publicity. That's what he didn't like. Lillian seems to think that any writer who in any way participates in publicity is a traitor to his art. But you know there were many "public" writers who seemed to do all right—Mark Twain, Dickens, Balzac, Tolstoi—and despite his shenanigans, or I should say as a result of his shenanigans, Mailer has produced *The Armies of the Night*. Who can say Salinger wouldn't be a more vital writer today if he were not such a recluse? Back in the days when we used to play poker down in the village with Don Congdon and others, Jerry was certainly part of the scene, and this was the period when he began writing the first of his short stories.

Brian: Then you don't agree with Lillian that the personal life of an important person is sacrosanct?

Hotchner: Don't you think it incongruous that Lillian is so sanctimonious about her own privacy and that of the "true" artists like Salinger whom she touts so highly, and yet she has made her career and reputation out of invading the privacy of the people she writes about. The Hemingway interview was the result of her pressuring Ernest to allow her to write about him, and he only acquiesced as a personal favor to her. If she is truly such a champion of the uninvaded artist one can only wonder at this schism in her philosophy.

Brian: Did you think that Mary Hemingway's objection to your publishing the book *Papa Hemingway*—that there were things about a man that should be kept from the public—was justified?

Hotchner: Who would determine just what things should and should not be kept from the public? This omnipotent censor of good taste. Who would it be? The author's wife? Well, Mary had her opportunity to set an example for all of us. Ernest had left a collection of chapters about his life in Paris in the twenties. One of those chapters recounted how Scott Fitzgerald had one day come to Ernest and confided to him his anxiety over the size of his penis. The chapter then spelled out how Ernest assured Scott, after inspecting his penis, that it was "normal" by taking him to a museum and showing him the penis on a statue. I was helping Mary with this manuscript at the time, so I can tell you first-hand that the publisher suggested that in the interest of good taste this particular chapter should be eliminated. It was pointed out that this material would be particularly offensive to Fitzgerald's daughter, Scotty, and that it was not integral to the book. Mary was not to be deterred. It was her decision and her decision alone to print this chapter.

Brian: You're saying that she had a different standard of what should and should not be published in regard to Hemingway?

Hotchner: I'm saying it's the widow syndrome, a process I call Widowfication. When Ernest was alive, Mary felt differently. She once wrote an article for a publication called *Today's Woman*, "My Husband, Ernest Hemingway," in which she confided such delicate intimacies as her fondness for kissing the soft place in back of his ear. But now Mary wants to control everything that's written about Ernest. I think her basic objection to *Papa Hemingway* is that I wouldn't let her see my manuscript, and I told about the last tragic years before the authorized biography was published.

Brian: Although, in fact, Baker did reveal that Hemingway killed himself.

Hotchner: Yes, and Baker's footnotes indicate that most of his material came from my book. I had not intended to write about Ernest's last tragic year and death, but Mary came to me in the summer before I started to write my book and said: "Listen, Carlos is doing a book, as you know, and I want him to write the whole thing at the end as it was. And will you tell him everything and get him to talk with the doctor?" I said: "Mary, you mean you've come to the point that you're going to have it told, but you're going to have it told third-hand by somebody who knows nothing about it?" "Yes," she said. That's what really decided me to write my book.

Brian: Did you feel Baker's book had anything of value?

Hotchner: Well, yes, it's a compendium. It's a repository of all the facts, without point of view, interest, or any real insight into the man.

Brian: I noticed that with the Lillian Ross stuff Carlos Baker didn't contact her, he just paraphrased her *New Yorker* article.

Hotchner: Well, that's what he did with everything. He had hundreds of Ernest's letters, lent to him by Mary and by friends, and too much of the book consists of paraphrasing those letters, and sometimes quoting from them. Mary maintains that Ernest prohibited publication of his letters in a written document which she found, and it was one of the reasons she filed suit against my book, yet Baker published a book full of them. If you noticed, in the front of Baker's book Mary is listed as coholder of the copyright. I don't know if that means she's a coholder of the income from the book, but for whatever reason, Ernest's letters suddenly were not so sacrosanct when it came to the authorized biography.

Brian: Malcolm Cowley and Mrs. Hemingway both say you used the contents of Hemingway's letters to you in your book.

Hotchner: Yes, I know. That was an issue in the lawsuit, and by way of response I gave my letters to Mary's lawyers who went through all of them and could find nothing to support her contention. I guess Cowley doesn't know that. Mary also contended that the book was full of errors, but when, under oath, she was asked to enumerate these errors all she could think of was that I had mis-measured their living room by four feet, I called their chauffeur by the wrong name, and I said that on one occasion Ernest came into the Florida bar wearing khaki shorts whereas Mary claims he never wore shorts in Havana. Of course these three items were changed after the first edition but Mary persists in her various aberrations about the book—that I made a million dollars out of it and only did it for the money. (It took me three years to write it on an advance of a few thousand dollars.) Money concerns Mary very much. It probably accounts for her decision to publish things like *Islands in the Stream*, which Ernest had said he had to work on to make publishable. Mary also maintained in her law suit—and she continues to harp on it long after the law suit was lost—that Ernest had no idea I'd ever write about him—an act which she brands a stab in the back. Mary doesn't know much about writers' innards. When Ernest and I were in Spain together in 1959, having a good time travelling the bullfight circuit with matador Antonio Ordóñez, I had an amusing adventure going into the ring, on the occasion of a gala *mano a mano*, dressed as matador. I was billed as Antonio's *sobre saliente*, the formidable El Pecas (The Freckled One) and it was a funny and perilous afternoon. Now I never dreamed at the time that Ernest would ever write about that, but months later there I was in prose and photo, spread across pages of *Life* magazine, my exploits described in detail under the bi-line of Ernest Hemingway. What Mary doesn't seem to realize is that a writer is an undisciplined animal who will write about anything that touches his life. And all writers know that.

Brian: Have you ever discussed this with Mrs. Hemingway?

Hotchner: Mary is not given to discussion. She tends toward pronouncements. I think what bothers her most about my book is what I left out of the book about her.

Brian: D'you think the only genuine way to interview Hemingway was to share his life for some weeks?

Hotchner: At least. I believe implicitly in Mr. Boswell's credo: "Nobody can write the life of a man but those who have eat and drank and lived in social intercourse with him."

Brian: Plimpton told me that when he asked Hemingway about the white birds in *Across the River* that Hemingway almost threw him into the harbor and said angrily: "Could you do any better?"

Hotchner: I was in Madrid when George approached Hemingway and asked him about the interview, but I wasn't present during George's interview with Hemingway. It was a fine interview but the nature of submitting written questions elicits stilted and rather formal answers.

Brian: You think it's good but stilted?

Hotchner: It's stilted because it's edited. It's submitting a list of questions to somebody and then he very carefully thinks about it and writes it all down. I don't think that gets very close to the man. I don't think it would have made Mr. Boswell's book very good. It's an interesting interview in that it elicited very measured and correct responses from Hemingway. But I don't think a writer can honestly portray a person unless he's been around his subject for a length of time, and then carries off—without any kind of editing, censorship, looking over the shoulder, or any kind of interference—his reaction to that person, his memory of conversation, behavior, smells, sights, foods, whatever it is—that's what works.

Brian: D'you have enough for a second book on Hemingway?

Hotchner: Oh yes, and a third.

Brian: Might you bring it out?

Hotchner: No. I've done what I wanted to do—to get Ernest Hemingway, as I knew him, on the page—in moments of good-going and bad, triumph and defeat, killing off old friends, befriending the friendless, working, drinking, joyful and disillusioned. And I'll tell you something: there have been a few times in the years since he died, when I have felt the sharp pang of missing him—a re-visit to our haunts in Spain, a golden autumn day when the pheasants fly—and I have re-read a chapter or two and I have found him there—just as he was. That's all that matters to me.

Malcolm Cowley

BORN IN BELSANO, PENNSYLVANIA,
AUGUST 24, 1898

Although Malcolm Cowley persuaded Ernest Hemingway to be interviewed for Life *magazine in February 1948—an interview which helped to perpetuate the Hemingway legend—he failed to break down William Faulkner, who had an old-fashioned, jaundiced view of personal publicity. But Cowley and Faulkner frequently corresponded and Cowley published the letters in his book* Faulkner-Cowley File: Letters & Memories, 1944–1966. *As a literary critic Cowley had the comparatively rare experience of seeing his subjects in action, of knowing the men and their output. He proved a man with views of his own, one of which was that Ernest Hemingway's official biographer, Professor Carlos Baker, was not sympathetic toward his subject.*

Brian: Were you startled when you read the piece on Ernest Hemingway by Lillian Ross?
Cowley: Yes, I was.
Brian: What was the surprise? How did it fail to show the man you knew?
Cowley: If you take a stenographic account of what a man says at a certain time, that does not necessarily give you the impression of what the man was. Lillian Ross's piece gave much more of the impression of a playboy and a snob than one ever actually got from Ernest.

Brian: And you don't think he had either of those qualities?

Cowley: I don't think it was a true impression. In other words, something much more was there.

Brian: Some people felt that it was the picture of a trivial man.

Cowley: I had the same feeling, because not long before that I'd been down to Havana to do a profile on Hemingway and those weren't the things we talked about at all. As a rule he gave much more perceptive answers to questions than you got in her article.

Brian: When you interviewed Hemingway did you research exhaustively and take a long list of prepared questions?

Cowley: No, but as far as research goes, I'd read everything that Hemingway had written, and had opinions on it. The trouble with most interviewing is that the interviewer doesn't know nawthen for nawthen.

Brian: "Norton for Norton"?

Cowley: He asks questions and the questions don't yield anything because they're not the right questions.

Brian: Oh, naught for naught, you mean. I thought you said "Norton for Norton" and I didn't understand.

Cowley: I was using an old Midwestern statement. "He doesn't know nawthen for nawthen" means "he doesn't know anything at all."

Brian: Oh, I see. Do you feel, then, that the interviewer draws out of the subject largely what the interviewer has to contribute?

Cowley: Yes, very largely, because it's hard to give an intelligent answer to a stupid question.

Brian: But I don't think Lillian Ross was asking him many questions, was she? Wasn't she mostly observing him in action?

Cowley: Yes.

Brian: I understand Hemingway resisted being interviewed. Do you feel that when a writer resists interviews it's perhaps because he wants to use the autobiographical material himself?

Cowley: Sometimes. For example, Hemingway would say to me: "Don't use this. I want to use it myself sometime."

Brian: When he said it made him almost physically sick to talk about himself, did you believe him?

Cowley: He was exaggerating. [Chuckles.]

Brian: In his biography, Carlos Baker says of Hemingway: "He wanted his writing to be judged on its merits rather than anything he said or did as a man. Some of the people who had met him personally were convinced by the experience that his books 'must be, shall we say, shit.'" Did you have a letdown when you met Hemingway, after having read all his books?

Cowley: No, he lived up to his books. This is a very complicated question. He created for himself a persona, like Byron, for example. I never had the pleasure of meeting Lord Byron, but Hemingway was an extraordinary person to meet and I always regarded his persona as something rather different from the books he wrote. There were other interviews with Hemingway, for example Hotchner's whole book, although part of that was faked. You know what he did? I could spot it because [chuckles] I knew the sources. When he said "Hemingway said" actually he was quoting from Hemingway's letters to him. Because Hemingway's will said: "You must not quote from my letters. They're protected by copyright." So Hotchner just put the letters in place of the conversations.

Brian: Apart from that, did Hotchner's book strike you as a vivid, truthful account of Hemingway?

Cowley: Of his last days, I thought it probably was.

The early stuff was ignorant. I mean, I know enough about [laughs] Hemingway's life to know that Hotchner got it all wrong in places.

Brian: Although Hemingway called you the best critic in the U.S. and you spent two weeks in Cuba with him, afterward he's quoted as calling your piece about him as "not awfully accurate." Did he ever tell you what he considered inaccurate?

Cowley: [Chuckles.] Yes, the account of Oak Park, which I got from other sources and which I very much calmed down in the version I used. He didn't want that used at all. The rest of the stuff—what Hemingway did was, he said: "I don't want to talk about myself. But I'll tell you whom to get in touch with." So he gave me a list of people to get in touch with and I used what they told me. So in that respect my piece is extremely accurate in using what other people told me about Hemingway. The one inaccuracy Hemingway picked up against me, according to Hotchner, was that I said he carried one flask of vermouth and one of gin. And Ernest said: "Who would waste a whole flask on vermouth?" But this information came from, I think, Buck Lanham or John Groth, so somebody else made the error and I simply repeated it.

Brian: Hemingway praised your honesty in withholding some material he didn't want used. What was that?

Cowley: He didn't like my saying, which was absolutely true, that at Oak Park he was a literary boy, not a sports boy.

Brian: Did he ever tell you why he hated his mother?

Cowley: I never asked him the question. What would this be? You can see from the story that she made a worm out of his father. She was one of those arty women who ruled the roost.

Brian: You knew Scott Fitzgerald personally. Did you

think Hemingway's portrait of him in *A Moveable Feast* was fair?

Cowley: It was a caricature to some extent, but the whole thing rests, not on Fitzgerald, but on Zelda. Hemingway did not like Zelda and he blamed Zelda for the ruin of Fitzgerald. And, also, to tell the truth, Hemingway was a man who could not bear rivals; essentially couldn't. And, except for Maxwell Perkins, who was out of the field, he very often couldn't forgive anyone [chuckles] doing him a favor. That was the bad side of his character, but too much of the bad side got into the Carlos Baker book. I'll tell you the one thing about the book, since I had also done research on Hemingway's life. At times there were good stories and bad stories about what Hemingway did. And I found Carlos Baker using the bad stories and leaving the good stories out, in cases where I was pretty sure that both were accessible to him.

Brian: Did you ask Carlos Baker why he had done that?

Cowley: No, I never asked him.

Brian: Although some of his critics thought Hemingway wasn't well-read, you thought he was.

Cowley: Tremendously well-read. He was a reader.

Brian: He put on a front then, of being a man of action and not an intellectual?

Cowley: That's exactly it. You ought to see his magazine rack at Finca Vigia, in Cuba. It went the whole range, mostly on the intellectual side.

Brian: Do you think any essential mystery remains about Hemingway?

Cowley: Yes, I think there's an essential mystery about him. Even in Baker's book there are stories that certainly aren't told. I don't intend to tell you about them now. If you ask me the questions . . . No, I won't even give you an example.

Brian: Can you give me a clue without actually stating it?

Cowley: The clue is (actually nobody would know this as far as I know) what happened in Italy between, I think it's July 8, 1918, when he was wounded, and the time when Hemingway went home. Baker doesn't know.

Brian: Arthur Schlesinger, Jr., thought that the Lillian Ross Profile of Hemingway gave a hint of the eventual mental breakdown he suffered.

Cowley: I think the breakdown was in operation at that time.

Brian: Do you think any interviewer has raised interviewing to an art?

Cowley: I think it's beginning to be an art. Studs Terkel's *Hard Times* seems to be a work of art—because think of the amount of selection involved.

Brian: How about Truman Capote's interviewing for *In Cold Blood?*

Cowley: That was quite a respectable job.

Brian: Do you think it was a new genre?

Cowley: No. The nonfiction novel has been around for a long, long time. *Romany Rye. Lavengro.* It's often best in autobiographies. *The Autobiography of Henry Adams* is a nonfiction novel. It's done by selection, you see, instead of invention.

Brian: Did you find any striking weakness in *In Cold Blood?*

Cowley: There's a weakness in the inherent argument of the book. Capote thinks it's an argument against capital punishment. As a matter of fact it's an argument for capital punishment. Did you ever think of that? Here are these two twerps. And their life would have absolutely no dignity or meaning unless they had been executed. That gave their life a certain tragic quality.

Brian: I see your point but it's a rather intellectual one.

Cowley: It's not intellectual. It's esthetic. But esthetics come very close to morals, remember.

Brian: But would any politician be moved by your argument?

Cowley: No, they wouldn't be moved.

Brian: I'll be talking with Truman Capote soon and I'll bring that up.

Cowley: Tell him I said so.

Brian: I will. But you know what I thought was the weakness? I can't believe he got the language of those two murderers. In no case do they use an obscene expression. Can you visualize men like that not occasionally using very obscene language?

Cowley: Sometimes they might. Remember this was a stage where in the face of death they were trying to tell what they were. They would have used a certain amount of obscene language, but I think the story is quite as convincing, if not so fashionable, without it.

Brian: The son of a woman friend of E. M. Forster recently revealed that Forster was a homosexual . . .

Cowley: That was known before in the literary world.

Brian: I wondered if men like Forster and Faulkner are reluctant to be interviewed because they have something to hide, like drinking or homosexuality.

Cowley: With Faulkner, any personal detail about his own life seemed to him an invasion of privacy. He had a very old-fashioned idea of gentility. If you want to get more of the attitude, of the genteel tradition, for that read Henry James's story, which you probably haven't read, called "The Papers." (No, I haven't read it.) Very few people have. But you'll get perfectly Henry James's attitude toward people who get their names and private lives in the papers. It was considered as indecent as eating in public. The Victorians wouldn't eat in public.

Brian: You once called Faulkner the proudest man in the world. Was he the proudest man you ever knew?

Cowley: Absolutely.

Brian: Do you think if one combined your interview with those of George Plimpton, Lillian Ross, and Leslie Fiedler, it might give a fair picture of Hemingway?

Cowley: You know, they might. They'd catch him at different periods and with different feelings. But the most vivid things I've had said to me about Hemingway were by a man now dead, Nathan Asch, who knew him in Paris in 1924-5. And they would have to be thrown in.

Brian: Could you say one vivid thing Asch had told you about Hemingway?

Cowley: Asch's was the picture of a younger man in Paris when Hemingway was already the leader of the young people. And Asch did admire him. Here's something Asch wrote about Hemingway: "Once in Paris he had a dinner-table argument with another young writer"—that was Nathan Asch—"about their respective talents. Later when they were walking toward the Dome for coffee, Hemingway fell into a boxer's crouch and began feinting and jabbing. That was something he often did in those days. The other young writer began shadow-boxing too. He hit Hemingway accidentally and Hemingway hit back, knocking him down. His mouth gritty, tasting bits of teeth, the other picked himself up and stumbled back to his hotel room. Later that night there was a knock at the door. It was Hemingway. 'I couldn't go to sleep until you forgave me,' he said. 'You know of course that I was wrong in the argument. You've got a lot of talent. You've got more of everything than any of us.' . . . It was an event when this towering figure passed the sidewalk tables at the Dome. Arms waved in greeting and friends ran out to urge him to sit down with them. The occasions were charming little scenes, as if spontaneous, although repeated. In view of the whole terrace Hemingway would be striding toward the Montparnasse railroad station, his mind seemingly busy with the mechanics of someone's arrival or departure. And he wouldn't quite recognize whoever greeted him. Then suddenly his beautiful smile appeared that made those watching him also smile. And with a will and an eagerness he put out his hands and warmly greeted his acquaintance, who, overcome by this reception, simply glowed and returned with him to the table as if with an overwhelming prize. . . . Hem wasn't very much around the Dome but I remember one scene that was sort of cute. There was a lousy poet named Cheever Dunning whom nobody could understand why Ford printed in *The Transatlantic Review.* And he took opium and once he decided to have a cure and was sent to the American Hospital in Paris. He couldn't stand it so he tore up the sheets and let himself down from the window in pajamas and hid in a hotel somewhere and let Hem know he had to have opium. I was sitting at the Dome and Hem came up to sit down with me for a moment. He was terribly dramatic. Told me he had a pound of opium in his pocket and did I know that opium generated heat? It was practically burning him up at the moment. . . . No, I have no criticism to make of Hem's conduct. I do think it's a crazy situation, though, that the elimination was so brutal; that, of all the writers in Paris then, Hem was holding the world by the handle and everyone else is either obscure or dead. But you can't blame it on Hem." This may have been from a letter that Nathan wrote me at that time and I collected together when I was preparing for the interview with Hemingway.

Brian: But you didn't use this material in *Life?*

Cowley: No I didn't. You go ahead and use it and credit Nathan Asch.

Brian: Asch wasn't successful, was he?
Cowley: No.
Brian: Did he have talent, as Hemingway said?
Cowley: Yes, he had talent.
Brian: Is there one word you would use for Hemingway?
Cowley: Complicated.
Brian: That's what makes him so fascinating perhaps.
Cowley: A very complicated man. And he was one of the most truly charming people I've ever met. He could charm a brass doorknob off the door.
Brian: I've heard that he was essentially shy and unsure of himself.
Cowley: Yes, he was both.
Brian: Do you feel Carlos Baker was sympathetic toward Hemingway in the biography?
Cowley: Not in the least.
Brian: But you were?
Cowley: I was much more sympathetic to him as a man. I had gone through much the same experience.
Brian: As a writer?
Cowley: No, I mean our boyhoods were in some ways much the same. I was a doctor's son too who really felt at home in the country and not the city. But if you want one word for Hemingway it's "complicated."

Barnaby Conrad

BORN IN SAN FRANCISCO, CALIFORNIA, MARCH 27, 1922

Barnaby Conrad is an expert on bullfighting. In 1947 he was secretary and chess companion to Sinclair Lewis. He was American Vice-Consul in Spain. An artist, nightclub owner, novelist, and bullfighter—he gave up bullfighting after being gored—who has written many books on the subject, Conrad knows of Hemingway through their mutual friend, the Brooklyn-born bullfighter Sidney Franklin.

Brian: As you knew Sidney Franklin, and he was the first subject Lillian wrote about in her *New Yorker* Profiles, I wanted to ask you what you thought about it.

Conrad: I was upset because I thought she was going to do a good article on Sidney. Sidney's got his faults and he's full of bull, if you'll excuse the expression, but he is. For a man that's lived the wonderful life that he's led. And he doesn't have to exaggerate and lie the way he did in his book, *A Bullfighter from Brooklyn*. Just about every other third page of that is true, I think. And I never could understand that, because he's had a fascinating life and he doesn't have to exaggerate.

Brian: Do you have the feeling, then, that he may have talked the same way to Lillian Ross, as he wrote his own book, so that she couldn't help reporting a lot of bull?

Conrad: I think she has a built-in shit-detector, as they say, and she realized a great deal of it was shit. And she didn't like him, I don't think, and she took it from there.

Brian: This shit-detector, I think, was Hemingway's claim. And maybe she appropriated it from him. I remember her mentioning in her article that Sidney Franklin had a big behind and Hemingway suggesting exercises to reduce it, and she pictured him as a man who spoke in thinly disguised clichés, and said he wouldn't marry because he'd seen bulls breeding. She made him out to be a little bit kooky all around.

Conrad: She certainly did and maybe he was, you know. When you read the Carlos Baker biography, he started to go kooky . . .

Brian: No, I'm talking about Sidney Franklin.

Conrad: Oh, you're talking about Franklin. Well, I thought you were talking about Hemingway. She made them both out to be very kooky. I don't think she likes men, especially bullfighting men.

Brian: Did you ever meet Hemingway?

Conrad: I never did. I sat next to Mary Hemingway at a showing of *Applause*. And I started to speak to her and I said to myself: "To what end? What are you going to say in a theater in two minutes?" And I never met Hemingway simply because we were at different parts of the country always at the wrong time.

Brian: You were Sinclair Lewis's private secretary for five months. Did Lewis ever see Hemingway's cruel description of him in *Across the River and Into the Trees?*

Conrad: Where it said Lewis looked like Goebbels being burnt in an airplane?

Brian: That's right.

Conrad: I think Lewis was dead before that came out.

Brian: Do you think Hemingway would have had enough compassion to wait until Lewis died before publishing that description?

Conrad: I don't think Hemingway had much compassion [chuckles], judging from what he wrote about people in *A Moveable Feast.* I have a book out called *Fun While It Lasted* which tells about my experiences with Sidney Franklin and with Sinclair Lewis. And I quote Sidney Franklin about Hemingway's own sexual organs as retaliation for his cavalier treatment of Scott Fitzgerald. (Hemingway had described Fitzgerald's almost neurotic concern that his own sexual organs were undersized and how he, Hemingway, tried to reassure Fitzgerald that he was average by inspecting him in the men's room and by taking him to see male statues for comparison.)

Brian: One theory I read about Hemingway was that he had a great deal of sadism, of violence in him, and that he tried to get rid of it by writing about it. D'you think this is fairly credible?

Conrad: I think it probably is. Getting back to Hemingway a moment ... In my book I tell about a time when Hemingway and Sidney are walking down the main street of Madrid and Hemingway suddenly sees a homosexual and crosses the street and knocks the man down without a word of warning. And Sidney said: "That tells you a lot about Hemingway, doesn't it?"

Brian: It was obvious the man was a homosexual, was it? It wasn't someone Hemingway knew?

Conrad: No, just a peroxide type.

Brian: I remember Hemingway said that in his early days as a boy they used to go about with knives in their pockets, for protection, because of the men who might molest boys. And he later had a strained conversation with Gertrude Stein who said that between women homosexuality was beautiful, but with men it was disgusting and they always hated themselves afterward. Did you discuss the Lillian Ross piece about Franklin with Franklin?

Conrad: Sidney kind of laughed it off. He had kind of a

thick skin. I don't think he was happy but I don't think he brooded on it.

Brian: Have you personally been disappointed as the subject of interviews?

Conrad: Once I was on the Steve Allen show and nobody had prepared him. And he said: "Are you interested in bullfighting? And have you written any book about bullfighting?" Of course I've written sixteen books. And I felt terrible having to toot my own horn. He hadn't read the book or any other book. So I was a little embarrassed.

Brian: What do you think of David Frost as an interviewer?

Conrad: I think he's too effusive. I mean everything is so *wonderful* and he uses the same adjectives towards Sir Laurence Olivier that he uses for some Jewish comic. I think he dissipates his adjectives in his enthusiasm. He's just as enthusiastic for everybody, so you don't believe him really.

Brian: What's his strength then?

Conrad: I think he really cares. I think he really is interested in the people he interviews.

Brian: Then his effusiveness is genuine?

Conrad: I think it is genuine. Then I must think he doesn't have very good taste, if he thinks that some second-rate comic is as important as Laurence Olivier.

Brian: I suppose for Frost, at the time, the comic is as important as Olivier, because it's his show and this must live sort of thing. Have you seen William Buckley, Jr., on his *Firing Line?*

Conrad: I've been on it. I was on it last year. He's an extraordinary interviewer. I think the funniest thing that happened was that, when I was through, he then taped Cassius Clay. And I stuck around because I was going to have dinner with Buckley afterwards, and Clay gave an absolutely wonderful, first-class interview. And afterwards Buckley said: "Would you like to meet Cassius Clay?" And I said: "I certainly would. I'm a boxing enthusiast." So I went up and shook his hand: enormous brute of a man, I didn't realize how big he was. And I said: "Thank you, Mr. Muhammad Ali," that I was very careful to call him. I said: "You were absolutely marvelous." He said: "Well, it did go very well, didn't it? They told me I was up there for an hour. And I couldn't believe it. Now, when you were up there it seemed to take for*ever*." [Laughs.]

Brian: Did Buckley mostly cover your bullfighting, or your writing, or everything?

Conrad: Mostly bullfighting because we had Cleveland Amory on. (Director of Humane Society.) Buckley ended up taking on the bullfighters' point of view. He likes bullfighting. As a matter of fact his brother, Fergus Reed Buckley, has tried fighting bulls in Spain. He lives in Spain.

Brian: How do you feel about Cleveland Amory's point of view—being against bullfighting?

Conrad: I think his point of view is entirely emotional. He drags up all sorts of facts that are simply not true or outdated. It's strictly a gut reaction with him and as such I respect it. But I don't respect his disregard of the facts. He tells about how the bulls are starved and tortured, when in fact they've never been in a bullring before they fight.

Brian: What do you think of the argument that generally people who go in for bullfighting are rather cruel to animals anyway? Do you think that's a valid statement?

Conrad: No, I don't at all. I mean Manolete had pet dogs and kittens.

Brian: I don't mean that any individual bullfighter is personally cruel to other animals. Would you say for example that the Spanish people, the Latin people, are perhaps more cruel to animals than, let's say, the British?

Conrad: I think they are. I think that is a valid statement. I think they're more cruel than Americans who have societies for the prevention of cruelty to animals all over, but they also have societies for the prevention of cruelty to children all over the place. The Spaniards have no need of the latter. They are in fact enormously more kind to their children than the British and the Americans are, I think, in general. They'd never permit any sort of cruelty to children. But they seem to see less well, cruelty to animals, to draft horses and things like that. You see a lot more cruelty and neglect of animals.

George Plimpton

BORN IN NEW YORK CITY, MARCH 18, 1927

At first glance George Plimpton appears to lead everyone's life but his own. As editor and sometime interviewer for The Paris Review, *he pursues literary lights and gets them to describe their working methods. As an author in others' clothing, he briefly lives as a footballer—*Paper Lion—*or professional golfer—*The Bogey Man—*or appears on TV films as a Las Vegas stand-up comic or as a circus trapeze artist. As a friend and admirer of Robert Kennedy, he was on the spot when the Senator was shot by Sirhan Sirhan. Plimpton was one of those who wrestled with the assassin and helped get the gun from him. And in those frantic moments, the reporter in Plimpton noticed how strangely peaceful were the eyes of the killer. But the ever-active Plimpton does find time to pursue his own dreams, and in this interview he spoke not only of his interview with Ernest Hemingway, but of his own life and what it's like to be George Plimpton.*

Plimpton: I was walking down the corridor of the Ritz Hotel in Paris with a number of friends, following the wedding of Ambassador Dillon's daughter. There were about six of us, all joking and laughing, and I looked ahead and there over at the bookstall in the long corridor of the Ritz was a man I recognized as Ernest Hemingway. And he was buying a copy of *The Paris Review*. He was the first man before or since I've ever seen *reading* the magazine, which sobered me up from the effect of the wedding very swiftly.

Brian: You were twenty-eight at the time, I remember. You only knew him through his books until then. Was he in any way a surprise?

Plimpton: I don't know whether it was a surprise or not, but what first pleased me about him so much, was that he would have such an interest in a tiny little magazine which we'd just started. It was 1954, the second year of this very small publication, but his interest was very keen. And that was something at odds with the portrait of the man in the company of Ava Gardner and the glitter world of Madrid.

Brian: Except wasn't he expecting you to interview him for *The Paris Review?* Wasn't he just checking up to see what it was like?

Plimpton: No, I'd never met him before. He didn't know anything about it. And then I was introduced to him that same afternoon in the bar of the Ritz, but he didn't know who I was.

Brian: And then it occurred to you to interview him?

Plimpton: Of course I knew as soon as I saw him that here was a possible chance to ask him if he would submit to this, and I did ask him, very tentatively and nervously. And I was surprised when he said he would. And I think the reason he did was because there must have been a certain *nostalgie* there because that's how he started, of course, with small magazines. And here was the same sort of thing going on twenty years after he'd left Paris.

Brian: In your interview with him he comes across as rather impatient and a little condescending.

Plimpton: A lot of the interview was conducted by letter. It was a difficult time for him. I think he was angry at having to stop his own work to answer questions. Also there are some questions that make writers impatient and unfortunately I asked a number of those. He was very sensitive about discussing technicalities and techniques.

Brian: Mary Hemingway told me that he rewrote some of the questions.

Plimpton: What an odd notion. No, he did not.

Brian: What was one of the questions that made him impatient?

Plimpton: I remember asking him a question that didn't get into the interview because there was never any answer to it: something that always puzzled me; the symbolic white birds that appear in some of his sex scenes, which he was not very good at. In *Across the River and Into the Trees* and in other places, a white bird flies around or appears. We were in Cuba when I asked him about it, on the dock, and he almost threw me into the water. His reaction was one of rage at the notion of my asking. He thought I was being critical. He was very sensitive about things like that. He kept shouting: "Can you do any better?"

Brian: People called Hemingway a "phony" and a "faker" for what they say were his attempts to appear very manly through hunting and fighting.

Plimpton: I've never heard anyone who knew him say that.

Brian: Why do you think the others said it?

Plimpton: I think he was that to people on the sidelines. Gertrude Stein said it of him.

Brian: And Scott Fitzgerald's wife, Zelda.

Plimpton: Well, Hemingway was very uncomfortable in Zelda's presence. He thought she was mad. He was very down on her and thought of Zelda as being a destroyer of Fitzgerald and his artistic capabilities.

Brian: Apparently Zelda accused Fitzgerald of being in love with Hemingway.

Plimpton: Howard Hawks, for example, thinks there is a type of man-love, love that isn't sexual. Hawks' films very often seem to be about very strong relationships between men, not homosexual, but friendships that are based on admiration and appreciations of skills. One can think of so many of the Hemingway stories where this bond does exist, and I think in his own private life he had these strong attachments with a whole succession of males. And then he used to have these almost petulant fallings out with them. Archibald MacLeish was one, Ford Madox Ford another. A lot of them are in *A Moveable Feast.* He seemed to turn on them after a while. And then, later in life, people like Peter Viertel. These friendships finally would break down because the friends were constantly being put to the test for some reason, as if friendship had to be tested. Which made it very awkward for everybody.

Brian: Did you actually discuss this with Hawks or do you infer it from his films?

Plimpton: Hawks does talk about it. All his great films, *Red River, Eldorado,* are love stories between men. In *Red River,* it's between Montgomery Clift and John Wayne. Hawks said he likes to make films about adventurers and since the world of adventure often gets cluttered up with a woman involved, he concentrates on the relationship played off between one man and another—the bond between them almost a love relationship.

Brian: Sidney Franklin, the Brooklyn-born bullfighter, said that Hemingway overreacted to homosexuals, that one time when they were together in Spain Hemingway crossed the road just to knock an obvious homosexual to the ground with a punch. Franklin told this to Barnaby Conrad, who told it to me. Do you credit the story?

Plimpton: No.

Brian: You think Franklin was something of a romancer?

Plimpton: Yes. I sat with Hemingway and Tennessee Williams once. Obviously Tennessee Williams's tendencies are perfectly visible. And I never saw anything but the greatest respect Hemingway had for him.

Brian: Did you use everything Hemingway told you in your *Paris Review* interview?

Plimpton: No, there were things he asked me not to put in.

Brian: Can you tell any of them now?

Plimpton: There were a lot of questions which fascinated him which had to do with genetic possibilities. Why should he be a writer? Where did his ability come from? The whole concept of tradition was very important to him. He talked about: where does the great hunting dog get his honed ability to smell? He couldn't figure it out. His father was a doctor, as you know. So all of this was a sort of puzzle to him, but he felt that it was somehow locked up in genetics. He himself felt this curious affinity with this odd uncle who was an explorer along the Chinese borders and who led very much the life that I think romantically, he imagined himself as following. In Chinese "Hemingway" means something like "hunter of wolves" and he was very proud of that.

Brian: Why would he ask you not to use this in the interview?

Plimpton: I think he felt it was personal and he was unsure of it. Also when he told me that, it was in Madrid, it was after he'd been injured in the two plane crashes in Africa, and he said he wasn't to be trusted at the time. He said he was sort of testing things: it was all right to talk about them but maybe you wouldn't want to have to stand for them if they were down on paper. He went over the interview and wrote a lot of it, so it's a literary document as well as an oral one. He didn't trust his oral senses particularly as he was then in Madrid.

Brian: You record that Hemingway stood to write. Wasn't this because of injuries?

Plimpton: It was just a working habit. If he was injured he'd be easier off sitting down, wouldn't he?

Brian: Unless he was injured in the rear.

Plimpton: You mean if he had boils on his rear?

Brian: Well, he called himself Ernie Hemorrhoid, didn't he?

Plimpton: I never thought of that. I never asked him. Thank God I didn't! But I'm sure he just stood because he liked it and thought it was good exercise.

Brian: You live the life of a football player, a musician, a golfer; and then write about it. Hemingway lived the big-game hunting life and then wrote about it. Any connection?

Plimpton: I don't think so. Another writer who did this sort of thing and then wrote about it was Paul Gallico. It's an old trick but I don't think anyone has done it quite as fully as I have. That idea was my own. Gallico went into the ring with Jack Dempsey—and Dempsey knocked him out. But my notion is to spend months on it, train with boxers. So the book that I do won't be about going into the ring and fighting with a champion, but a survey of the world of boxing. Obviously there are boxing writers who know more about boxing than I ever will. But what I can do is enjoy the understanding of fighters because I've tried to do what they've done. They talk to me slightly differently from the way they talk to reporters. So really the point of the gimmick is to open the door to a kind of relationship with the subject which is a little different from the one they'd have with an ordinary interviewer.

Brian: In your series of living different lives perhaps you should become a medium and try to contact Hemingway. That wouldn't appeal to you?

Plimpton: I don't want to disturb him. I think he's probably fine.... I went to see his grave in Ketchum.

Brian: I gather you were very fond of him.

Plimpton: Yes, I was. I admired him as a man and a writer.

Brian: I have the feeling that although you may not be emulating Hemingway, you are doing the sort of things he would approve of.

Plimpton: Gay Talese wrote an article which appeared in *Esquire* from his book *The Overreachers.* And he tries to make that peg that many of us who started out in Paris, the so-called *Paris Review* group, were all copying Hemingway, which I don't think is right. It's not as simple as that. Of course, I can only speak for myself. I enjoy men of action and activity myself, but that is hardly unusual.

Brian: But how many of them have gone in for lion-taming? Both you and Hemingway have tried it.

Plimpton: I didn't know that he did.

Brian: Yes, he did. And boxing, of course, you both had that interest in common.

Plimpton: Well, he was always interested in people who . . . "grace under pressure" was his famous phrase. I really only knew him in the last few years of his life and then we had a falling out over the interview. He resented the time spent in answering the questions and finally blew up at me. Then we took up again after my fight with Archie Moore. I wrote and asked Hemingway if he'd help me train as a boxer. He liked the whole notion of doing that.

Brian: Is there any event in your life that can't be explained rationally?

Plimpton: When one almost gets killed and one isn't. I nearly got drowned on a trip with Robert Kennedy down the Colorado River.

Brian: Did you feel afterward that you had a charmed life and should do something specifically about it?

Plimpton: I think that things happen from time to time that make you better, that give you a push. And I think most of this comes from other people . . . your family, your father, people like Robert Kennedy, who encourage you to work harder.

Brian: Seriously, you almost drowned on that trip on a rubber raft with Kennedy?

Plimpton: Well, I guess . . . well, I mean, I . . . I think . . . well, fairly close. [Chuckles.]

Brian: How did you feel when you thought you might die?

Plimpton: I think that old saw about your life passing in review is, in a sense, right. Because you'd like your house to be in order. One realizes that those things that are left undone are sloppy, and there is a sort of odd review that goes on.

Brian: As editor of *The Paris Review,* which publishes a lot of interviews, do you have any theory of interviewing? Do you think the mood, time, place, being persistent, having empathy with the subject are important?

Plimpton: Yes, I think all those obvious things: and doing your homework.

Brian: Are *Paris Review* interviewers given carte blanche?

Plimpton: Yes, absolutely.

Brian: How do you decide who is going to ask the questions of a subject?

Plimpton: Now the series is so famous someone will say: "I know John Barth and wonder if you'd like me to interview him?" I try to find out how much he does know about him; then if John Barth would like to be interviewed by him. I tell the interviewer what fascinates me about Barth, then generally leave him alone to do the interview. Primarily I'm interested in how a writer goes about the craft of writing.

Brian: Hasn't *The Paris Review* been satirized for asking the question "Do you use a pen or a typewriter?"

Plimpton: Yes, quite often. Curiously, I find those technical questions fascinating. I'm responsible for that. I remember asking Hemingway and he told me about his habit of standing when he writes.

Brian: And I understand you discourage the use of comments to the effect that the subject laughed or smiled at certain points. Wouldn't this give the impression, for example, that someone was being pompous when he may have been joking?

Plimpton: No, I think you pretty much can tell by the way they say things whether they're being pompous or having fun. When you have to start putting in "he smiled" or "he laughed" or stage directions, or [chuckles] you're not a very good editor [chuckles]. My own feeling about interviewers today is that they rely too much on the tape machine. They don't listen. They don't carry on a conversation, which the machine gives them the chance to do. Then, especially the younger generation are apt to treat the words that come off the machine as Gospel and feel they can't touch them when they transpose them to paper. There are two superb interviews we did with Kerouac and Charles Olson. But the actual transcriptions were absolutely hopeless. In one instance, everyone in the room was drunk, and God knows what was going on in the other. The interviews had to be carefully edited. Kerouac was aware enough of that need; he answered a whole additional group of questions on his typewriter. Of course the hope is to make the final version easy and spontaneous.

Brian: You can't conceive then of ever using interviews verbatim?

Plimpton: Yes, absolutely. There have been some. I would say that a verbatim interview would be Lawrence Durrell's. He speaks superbly and you don't have to change anything: it falls onto the printed page. Two other examples of this are Jorge Luis Borges and, I suspect, Robert Lowell. Some of these are superb, others really thrash around and it doesn't work. That's why, generally, I think an interview should be edited and worked on.

Brian: But so many people have accused interviewers of misquoting them by quoting them out of context and so on. "At the very most I'll correct your grammar but otherwise I'll print exactly what you say"—don't you think that has tremendous appeal?

Plimpton: No. Because most people look at what they've said on the printed page and throw their hands up in dismay. They'd much rather have it good, and accurate, and what they intended to say. That is the point of an interview—not that the fellow is clumsy with words.

Brian: Did you ever try to interview J. D. Salinger for *The Paris Review?*

Plimpton: I wrote him not very long ago. I thought perhaps he'd honor the fact that we'd never bothered him, knowing he doesn't like to be bothered, but since *The Paris Review* had an anniversary issue coming up, I said we'd like to interview him. He wrote back a very nice letter saying I was absolutely right to ask him, but he just didn't want to be interviewed.

Brian: Isn't Salinger unique in his craving for solitude, not to be asked questions?

Plimpton: I think some of the interviews we've done were with people who really did crave it—and we went to a great deal of trouble, or had luck, to get interviews with them. Faulkner only gave in because he was half in love with the woman who interviewed him. I don't think E. M. Forster would have given an interview if I hadn't been a student in his college at Cambridge and knew him.

Brian: Will you keep after Salinger?

Plimpton: Oh, sure. Even if *The Paris Review* quits, I think the series on writing is so important we'll try to continue it.

Brian: Does Vice President Agnew worry you with his threats to press freedom?

Plimpton: Yes. I think the results of censorship are more dangerous by far than the lack of it.

Brian: Do you think he's been stopped by the press reaction?

Plimpton: No. He mesmerizes people. He's awfully good; that's the problem.

Brian: Would you go on a flight to the moon?

Plimpton: Sure.

Brian: It doesn't scare you?

Plimpton: Of course it would. All these things petrify me.

Brian: You're frightened, but you like the challenge?

Plimpton: It's just that I think the astronauts ought to take someone with them who's trained to look at something and describe it. Other than Mr. Armstrong's extraordinary line, "One small step for a man, one giant leap for mankind," there's not one phrase, description, or emotion, really, that one can remember about it, or any of the other space flights. These people are extraordinarily brave, trained technicians, jet pilots. They're not people to tell you what's going on. Nobody expects a jet pilot to do it. I'd think that sooner or later—they'll probably take a doctor next—and way down the line they'll probably take an artist. And way after that, a writer.

Brian: Are you very curious about people generally or only newsworthy people? Does the man next door interest you, for example?

Plimpton: Not the man next door, unless he turns out to be an interesting man. As a writer I'm interested in people who do something to put themselves on the line, people who push themselves to the limit of what they can do. Circus people who do triple somersaults on the trapeze, the juggler who keeps nine things in the air at one time.

Brian: I know of a man who walked a thousand miles in an amazingly short time. All he ate were diet biscuits and he was followed by a car all the time. He was doing it to advertise the diet biscuit. Near the end he was in a terrible state and the people in the car offered him food and drink secretly, but he had such integrity that he wouldn't take it and he refused to give up the walk. That maybe is the kind of thing that would interest you.

Plimpton: No, I don't admire anything in that particular tableau. neither the man walking, nor the advertising agency, nor the idea of the stunt, nor the people behind it, nor the . . .

Brian: How does he differ from the man doing the triple somersault?

Plimpton: Because the man doing the triple somersault has perfected a skill. He loves what he does. He does it with enormous pride.

Brian: So did the walker.

Plimpton: I rather doubt that. I just don't find them comparable. The walker is selling a diet biscuit; the aerialist is demonstrating an enormously difficult skill.

Brian: In your own work what makes you want to try to master things that you admit petrify you? I imagine the lion cage and the trapeze must have been rather scary.

Plimpton: I don't think it's a personal challenge, except in a sense that I have to go through it. I really think the device is that you stand outside yourself and try to see what your reactions are, so that you can sit down and write about it.

Brian: You're not driven to it? You don't feel that "I've got to overcome my fears on every level"?

Plimpton: No. If I weren't a writer, if I were a stockbroker, I sure as hell would not do these things. I might dream of them, but I certainly wouldn't do them. I'd have no reason to.

Brian: Have you turned down many ideas for living different lives?

Plimpton: Oh, sure. Have to be very careful what you accept to do. You have to find something that people are curious about. People say, "Join the Roller Derby or Demolition Derby," or things of that sort, but they have a limited audience and more gimmickry than the great traditional sports.

Brian: Has anyone suggested that you go to prison or work in the Bowery with the Salvation Army?

Plimpton: Oh, sure. All those things, sure.

Brian: Does going to the Bowery appeal to you?

Plimpton: The reason I'm interested in sports is that those guys suffer disciplines which push them to an extreme limit, to the limit of their skills. And I think to watch people and to perform with people who are pushed to the limit of their skills, in a defined time, gives a great deal of material which can be written about. If you go down to the Bowery you're not dealing with that. You're dealing with a sociological phenomenon.

Brian: Do you dream much or have nightmares?

Plimpton: I do a lot of daydreaming, but I don't dream much.

Brian: Walter Mitty daydreams?

Plimpton: Sure. It is usually sports, a pleasant diverting thing. James Thurber once said that 90 percent of the American males at any given time are thinking about striking out the batting order of the New York Yankees.

Brian: What quality do you most admire in people?

Plimpton: Forthrightness. It's refreshing to find people who say what they mean and don't hedge.

Brian: Do you have that quality?

Plimpton: Not particularly, no.

Brian: And what do you least like?

Plimpton: People who cross you.

Brian: Are you like your father?

Plimpton: No, though I do admire him enormously. He's a lawyer, a very brilliant one, a great one. And to be a great lawyer or politician you need a compartmentalized mind, which I don't happen to have—that ability to be able to think of one thing in a crisis and forget about everything else.

Brian: What makes you angry?

Plimpton: At the moment the killing of whales. I sat up last night listening to a record called *The Song of the Humpback Whale,* and thinking about how whales are disappearing. I hope it doesn't sound maudlin, but the desecration and spoiling of art, of mankind, and of animalkind makes me angry.

Brian: How do you reconcile this with your admiration for Hemingway?

Plimpton: The killing instinct is very difficult to talk about. Perhaps the thrill of the chase is an important emotion for some people—a primeval urge that is satisfied in hunting and killing.

Brian: One could say, then, that some men should be allowed to murder other men to satisfy a primeval urge.

Plimpton: Well, that's a strong argument against hunting.

Brian: Are you intrigued by any particular mystery, like Judge Crater's disappearance?

Plimpton: They all intrigue me. I remember an interviewer putting a question to James Thurber, if he could be anyone else who would he like to be? And Thurber said: "I'd like to be the captain of the *Marie Céleste.* So I could find out what the hell happened."

Brian: Do you believe there's an overall purpose to life?

Plimpton: I'm not very good at answering questions like that.

Brian: You'd rather not answer?

Plimpton: I don't quite know how you mean it.

Brian: Malcolm Muggeridge, for example, says that making a million dollars, seducing a beautiful woman, etc., are all second-rate pursuits; that the only worthwhile purpose in life is trying to find out what it's all about and telling people your discoveries. That sort of thing. I wondered if you had a philosophical or maybe religious attitude to life.

Plimpton: My father once said, and I'm inclined to agree: "One lives one's life for the surprises that come along from time to time."

Arnold Gingrich

BORN IN GRAND RAPIDS, MICHIGAN, DECEMBER 5, 1903

Arnold Gingrich has had what I'm sure must be the unique experience of seeing both Ernest Hemingway and Scott Fitzgerald naked. Gingrich knew them and many other writers, as friends and contributors to the magazine he publishes, Esquire. I interviewed him in the garden of his pre-Revolutionary home in Ridgewood, N.J., after first speaking with him on the telephone. A leathery, lean, natural man, he reminded me of photographs of Rudyard Kipling. He agreed with me that my method of interviewing subjects first by telephone and then meeting them in person is probably the most effective method of interviewing. One: Almost everyone is completely at ease on the phone and used to talking freely. Two: It prevents them seeing a tape recorder in action, which can cause even the sophisticated to change gears and begin to orate and talk artificially. Three: The subject is not aware, even by the slightest visual clues, of the interviewer's boredom, embarrassment or indifference, and consequently will talk with the fluidity of a patient on a psychoanalyst's couch.

Brian: I've taken Hemingway as an example of a rather mysterious, complicated man, whom three interviewers tried to get at, Malcolm Cowley, Lillian Ross, and George Plimpton. As you knew him well, as his publisher and friend, I wondered if you had any strong view of why the three of them seem to have such sharply differing ways of seeing him. Cowley reveals him as a fascinating, heroic man, Lillian Ross made him seem almost adolescent and trivial, and Plimpton shows a dedicated, almost ascetic writer.

Gingrich: I think it reflected what each interviewer brought to the interview, except in the case of Lillian Ross. There, just fall back on the fact that the cruelest thing you can do to anybody is to quote him literally, with no selectivity whatsoever, particularly anybody who is prone, as he was, to feeling friendly with somebody, and to relax and let his hair down and talk Indian talk and all that, never dreaming that it would come out any other way than the way he felt about it. And actually thinking it was great when he first read it. He told her he thought it was marvelous.

Brian: I understand Hemingway didn't have time to alter it; that he received the Ross manuscript the same week it was to be printed in *The New Yorker.*

Gingrich: I believe that is true but I think he had no feeling of need to alter it at all. I think he thought, "Well, this girl's marvelous: she got it just the way it was," until afterward he wasn't too sure. When everybody said what a vivisection it was, he still thought, "Hell, they're just jealous."

Brian: D'you remember Hemingway saying to Scribner: "She's making horse's asses out of both of us. This'll make a lot of enemies"?

Gingrich: That's right. It's in the Baker book. Well, I felt of course that the Baker book was the best job. Of course it's hardly fair to compare them. Because you can't compare an interview with a long, definitive labor like the Baker thing. Of the three it seemed to me that Plimpton was perhaps—while it showed an obvious bias in his favor—the least loaded of the three interviews.

Brian: Hemingway said it made him almost physically sick to talk about himself.

Gingrich: Utter arrant nonsense. That's just a little exhibition of being subtle and sensitive. It's a pose, really.

Brian: I had the feeling that one of his motives for trying to avoid interviews was that so many of his novels contain autobiographical material, and that he wanted to keep it for himself.

Gingrich: There's a good deal of truth in that. But he simply shifted completely from one attitude to another. Don't forget the Cowley interview was early ('48) and that's when his pose was to have utter contempt for all the log-rolling, lifted-pinkie, tea-drinking cookie-pushing, café literary society. And then he found himself enjoying it and lapping it up and loving it and becoming an ornament of it. So he came full circle: he became that which he despised. And it was a gradual process. So I think it was just part of the pose. The early pose happened to coincide with the best work. But who's to say which was more sincere, the later pose or the early pose: they're both poses it seems to me, two attitudes.

Brian: D'you think that the real man was essentially hidden?

Gingrich: Oh, sure, yes. I think you had here a terribly, terribly shy person, who in one instance reflects it by being withdrawn and in another turns around and is very boisterous. And both are manifestations of the same thing: a dreadful insecurity.

Brian: You said he became the thing he hated. Weren't there a number of things like that in his life? For example, his despising his father for being a suicide: then becoming one.

Gingrich: Yes, you see in those early years he used to talk at great length about what an incredible thing that was. How could anybody do such a messy thing? How could you leave a mess like that for somebody to clean up, you see? Then goes and does exactly the same thing. He was eloquent about it for years and years, that it was an unthinkable thing to do.

Brian: But he was mentally sick when he did it . . .

Gingrich: Oh, yes. No question.

Brian: And so was his father, I believe.

Grinrich: Quite possibly. And you know the record of other attempts is indicated, both in the Hotchner and the Baker book. I think it must be weighed in that you can't hold him to reason or consistency with something he's earlier said if, in doing this, he's under suspicion of being not rational.

Brian: What do you think of the view by some that Hemingway was a hypocrite in the "he-man" sort of thing? Truman Capote, for example, hated Hemingway for his gratuitous criticism.

Gingrich: My own feeling was that his admiration for other writers seemed to be pretty well in direct proportion to how much they reflected his way of writing. He raved about and went off to an almost ludicrous degree over John O'Hara, because John O'Hara was very much in his vein. And Capote was quite the opposite. Similarly with Saroyan back in that same time. He teed off on Saroyan at one point, doing a character-assassination job on him, for no particular reason, except that he didn't like the Saroyan approach, which was not his approach, or the Robert Nathan approach. He was very apt to be very impatient with people who didn't write his way or see things his way.

Brian: Ironically, he was savage in describing Sinclair Lewis in *Across the River and Into the Trees.* Yet he himself had sensitive skin on his face. And you know Hemingway ridiculed his friend Scott Fitzgerald for worrying about the size of his sexual equipment?

Gingrich: Yes, in *A Moveable Feast.*

Brian: Barnaby Conrad told me he heard from Sidney

Franklin, the Brooklyn-born bullfighter, that Hemingway himself had undersized sexual equipment.

Gingrich: [Chuckles.] I happen to be in a position to give you firsthand, eyewitness observation in both instances and it's true in neither case. They were perfectly normal, ordinary, adequate grown men. I swam with them and fished with them and all that. So, I can actually say that.

Brian: Did Hemingway acknowledge to you that he lied or romanced about his adventures?

Gingrich: He'd never quite come right out and say that something was not true but he would pretty often almost imply that "you have to give them the show they expect." This would be anyplace, no matter whether in a tavern talking to somebody, pulling his leg, or what. A good deal of it was certainly putting people on, indulging in mock modesty, playing things way down in that British way. Or, similarly, the tall tales, all kinds of exaggeration. He was never too concerned with the truth. He loved to arrange it.

Brian: Did you like him?

Gingrich: Very, very much in those early days. I mean the reaction was that of a tenderfoot scout for his scoutmaster, for God's sake. I mean that guy was marvelous at doing all those things one would like to do and doing them supremely well. He was great to fish with and shoot with and do all those things and at that time he was rather impatient of, shall we say, the more social and polite activities. He had a tendency to shun them. I remember his going so far as to show up at the White House with a two-day beard. It was just, again, part of a pose; this rugged, he-man, mountaineer, guide-type character. Well, then he got away from that to some degree, later.

Brian: Was there a strong streak of cruelty in him?

Gingrich: I think yes. In all fairness and trying to be as objective as one can, there was always this attitude really of being the bully of the high school class, the one who insisted on winning and was very, very bad about losing. Yes, he was essentially a domineering, bullying character. And as long as people around him were worshipful and adoring, why they were great—the minute they weren't, why a tendency to find others who were.

Brian: And the picture of Scott Fitzgerald in *A Moveable Feast* was a caricature, you feel?

Gingrich: Ah, well, now that's what's interesting. I think it was essentially only too terribly true. Sure it was malicious. But that trip they made together, he showed Scott at his most irritating and infuriating worst. And did it *marvelously.* Made him come alive as very, very few other things have. That's what's so paradoxical about this. It's a dreadfully unfair thing in many ways and yet there was this masterful characterization. Well, I suppose your word caricature is right: a caricature is something that is almost more like the man than the man is himself. Particularly in view of the fact that Scott never, never lost his first enthusiasm and admiration for Hemingway, in spite of being terribly badly treated by him in return for everything he did for him in the early days, when he was the fair-haired boy and was pushing Hemingway forward. Hemingway later came to occupy the position at Scribners which Scott had when he brought him to Scribners. And the most Scott ever let himself say was: "Ernest was always willing to lend a helping hand to the man on the rung above him." And he certainly had provocation to say worse than that, and that's the worst he ever said. He wrote a letter to him, one of the last letters he wrote before he died, saying how marvelous he thought *For Whom the Bell Tolls* was and how "I envy you like hell,"—he said it and he meant it—but he never in any way begrudged anything that came to Ernest. Whereas Ernest was damned begrudging of anything that came to anyone else.

Brian: In Professor Carlos Baker's book I never found out why Hemingway's marriages failed. Pretty well every novel contains one dead marriage.

Gingrich: You can't literally cross every *t* and dot every *i*, but to a great extent this was true of his life. He wrote things out of his life; got rid of them by writing them. And that included the women.

Brian: Did you feel, too, there was the element of conquest? The hunter's . . . ?

Gingrich: He always had pretty much the collector's attitude, but there was the . . . I always felt fairly phony crocodile tears and the almost excessive protesting about having really loved only one, which grew and grew and grew. It was certainly never so damn evident back in the early days, you know, about his first marriage. Later, particularly in *Moveable Feast*, there's this almost deification of Hadley and of course in this new book, *Islands in the Stream*, even more so, but here again there's no relation, of course, between the character and the woman—the one that purports to be the mother of the oldest boy turns out to be Marlene Dietrich on tour for the USO. Just ridiculous. Just no relation at all. That should be all right for fiction, but with Hemingway I guess you don't know where to draw the line.

Brian: I had a discussion about Hemingway's courage with my brother and I was talking of one of the World War II incidents when Hemingway was sitting at the table when the building was being shelled. And everybody else except Hemingway and Lanham dived for the shelter and later came back to find Hemingway still eating at the table. My brother thought that was an example of a frightened man showing off that he's not afraid; and that normally courageous men would dive for shelter.

Gingrich: I think there is some truth in that. It's part of a pose: a pose that will be maintained even at the risk, even at the price of being scared just literally witless, but still not breaking the pose. As I recall that was in John Groth's thing about the Hemingway Irregulars, and I believe it. First of all I believe John Groth, whom I know very well and I've never known him to lie about anything. And it does pretty well fit the character; this is exactly the role. I compared it to a scoutmaster showing the boys how to behave. And it's one that would be held at all costs. Sure, an imaginative man when he's brave is twice as scared as a clod who isn't bright enough to realize the risk he's running. So I think, on his courage, I can't go along with that yellow streak that Gertrude Stein said he had. I don't think he had a yellow streak. He had the boy's bluff to show off to the neighborhood and do almost anything, no matter what the cost to oneself, just as part of this tremendous pride in showing what you can do. I suppose you've got to say that here again this is part of that shyness and insecurity, an extreme manifestation of it. Don't you think?

Brian: I see your point, yes. Did you feel his anti-Semitism was just typical of his upbringing and the background he came from? That it was fairly light?

Gingrich: Yes, I think it was not really any brooded thing. In that time and place we talked about the hunkies and the polacks and the wops and the greaseballs and everything else. And the kikes and the sheenies were just a part of the language. It didn't mean much. Hemingway had some good Jewish friends. His lawyer, Maurice Speiser, was Jewish, the one before Alfred Rice. I do know it wasn't a thing that was more than superficial.

Brian: There was the occasion when he replied to a Jewish psychiatrist, who had irritated him, "I have sexual intercourse with my cats."

Gingrich: That would be again part of the put-on, of putting people on.

Brian: Did you feel there was an element of masochism in him, in that he took tremendous physical punishment so many times, or d'you think this was just a result of the life he led?

Gingrich: I don't think it was deliberately sought. You might just as well say he was a sadist as a masochist. A great deal of his inflicting of cruelty could come under that heading. But I think those words are both too strong.

Brian: Does Baker's book pretty well cover all you know about him? There's no side to him that you found neglected there?

Gingrich: No, there's nothing Baker doesn't cover. Whether he exhausts everything, who can say?

Brian: Did Hemingway ever discuss with you his loathing of his mother?

Gingrich: Oh God, yes. Of course a good deal of this was that she made him play the goddamned cello and he hated the goddamned cello, it was just as elementary as that [chuckles]. And she just drove him nuts, particularly at that moment when he was writing so regularly for us from faraway places. She was always dying to know where he was and it was difficult because we were in Chicago and she was right there in Oak Park and "What's Ernest doing?" And, God, you know, anything you told her you'd be sorry because he'd be mad. So it was a very difficult spot to be, in the middle. But she had a pretty conventional mother's attitude to her boy, you know. She seemed a very nice, normal mum. But she was determined that they were all going to make music, because music was important to her. And he was going to play the cello. Well, he didn't want to play the cello—as simple as that. There was evidence of a conflict of personalities. She was just a pain in the neck to him, to try to make him do things because she wanted him to do them.

Brian: I felt that they had one thing in common, which

was to freeze people out, to send them to Coventry and never reinstate them, if they'd quarreled or got out of favor.

Gingrich: Yes, I think that is a trait, more from his mother than his father. I didn't know his father. And I only knew her by those long and frequent phone conversations. A [laughing] perfectly normal thing of a mother trying to find out where her boy is and the boy doesn't want her to know.

Brian: He gave the impression he was kicked out of his home.

Gingrich: I think it was a matter of his wanting to get away and get out from under her supervision and a meddlesome, dictatorial relationship.

Brian: So your feeling about the Hemingway interviewers is that they put a lot of themselves into it, rather than the subject?

Gingrich: Oh, yes, completely. Cowley, in my recollection of it, has quite an admiring attitude. Lillian Ross was the little girl commenting on the Emperor's bare behind while everyone else was oohing and ahhing over the cut of his new clothes. And Plimpton, I thought, was being rather elaborately correct with a difficult quarry, trying to bag him for the magazine and not scare him off.

Brian: Did you like the Hotchner account?

Gingrich: I started out to think I wouldn't believe it, if I knew it was so, because I always thought of Hotchner as being around in the phoniest period of Hemingway's life. We had *Papa Hemingway* in the house at Esquire. The boys brought it to me and I said: "Oh God, you don't want me to read this?" "Well, you may find it interesting." So I started out with very, very much a chip on my shoulder, and thought, "Hell, I wouldn't like this." If I liked it I wouldn't like it, don't you know? And then I began reading it and I came across the highly respectful references to *Across the River and Into the Trees,* which I thought was a Christ-awful book, and I thought, "Well, this just shows this guy isn't worth reading." But I kept going. And, by God, I came to scoff and remained to cheer, because it became so evident that the stench of authenticity was all over every page, once the going began to get a little bad. So I just realized that that's the way it had to be. I believed it and found that it was pretty conclusively the truth. By the way, about the visit Leslie Fiedler and a pal of his at Montana, where Leslie Fiedler used to teach: the visit they paid to Hemingway the winter before his suicide, they found him completely *non compos mentis.* It was a dreadfully cruel thing for them to print. It was after he got back from Mayo.

Brian: You think it was a very authentic interview?

Gingrich: Yes, I do. I thought it was terribly indiscreet at the time. But I certainly believe they told it the way it was. Anybody reading that would realize—the man's off his rocker.

William Seward

BORN IN SURRY, VIRGINIA, FEBRUARY 2, 1913

William Seward is one of the few professors of English literature whom Hemingway knew and liked. Seward, professor of English at Old Dominion University, Norfolk, Virginia, first corresponded with Hemingway in 1940, then met him several times. In 1957, their last meeting, they traveled together on a Pullman to Florida. Seward recorded his memories of the writer in My Friend Ernest Hemingway: An Affectionate Reminiscence, *published in 1969.*

Brian: Did you have any strong feelings about the Lillian Ross Profile of Hemingway?

Seward: Frankly I did, yes. I thought it did not depict the man that I knew. In my opinion he was putting on a good act and I would have thought that she would have known that. She probably did.

Brian: I think she played it very straight, recording what she saw and heard, with no editorializing.

Seward: Well, that's what she claims she attempted to do. But even when you do that there is a certain context and a person who's depending simply on a portrait such as that might get the impression that that's the way that he talked constantly.

Brian: I got the impression from her portrait of him that Hemingway was a trivial man.

Seward: I would say that he was exactly the opposite and I think I knew him fairly well, if I may say so modestly. Frankly, nobody saw much of him except Mary, in his later years, in spite of all the talk of Hotchner and people like that. The few times that I saw him he was not on public exhibition and, contrary to the impression, apparently, that you get from somebody like Lillian Ross—and that's one of the quibbles I have with that piece—he was anything but trivial.

Brian: Did you think the Carlos Baker biography was pretty good?

Seward: Factually it was an excellent book. I thought it was tedious reading and I was rather surprised because usually Carlos—and I happen to know him too, incidentally—and let him use a little material. I was doing a book of my own at the time and so I didn't let him use as much as otherwise I would have. His other books struck me as being stylistically a lot more flexible than the biography and perhaps that is to be expected.

Brian: D'you have the feeling that Professor Baker wasn't really very sympathetic toward Hemingway as a man?

Seward: Frankly I don't know. You see he never met Ernest. He had some correspondence. A little of that comes through to me and it's a bit surprising because for years I had the impression that he was, if anything, somewhat sympathetic toward him. I think a little of that does come through.

Brian: That he was sympathetic?

Seward: That he was not. And that surprises me. But factually, from a standpoint of accuracy and so forth, I think it is a very, very good book. The only criticism that I have really, is probably one that you would expect: namely that I don't get any feel of the man. The facts are there but the personality is missing.

Brian: I know you feel very friendly toward Ernest Hemingway. But what do you think of the reports from people that he was very jealous of fellow writers, that he was often cruel to people, and that he was an insatiable hunter?

Seward: You mean a physical hunter?

Brian: Not only that, but quite often he could almost destroy men by what he said.

Seward: I saw him under different circumstances the few times I was with him and I never saw that side of him. My own feeling is that that side of him has been played up over the other side. I knew him as humble and going out of his way not to hurt people. And as an extremely shy person. When he was around photographers and newsmen I think he had a rather suspicious attitude toward them and simply put on a big show. The man I knew was far removed from the portrait in the Lillian Ross piece.

Brian: Your friendship with him developed because you were a professor of English and interested in his writing?

Seward: That's how it began, yes. Which on the face of it was rather unusual because he had perhaps more of an aversion toward professors of English than he did toward news interviewers, if that's possible. Some newsmen he had great respect for. But others, he felt, I think, were trying to trap him and his pose, and—this was only my impression—he was sort of handing them back the sort of superficiality he felt they were dealing out.

Brian: Was he a heavy drinker when you knew him?

Seward: I don't think anyone could refer to him as a teetotaler or even a light drinker.

Brian: He's been described as an alcoholic.

Seward: Oh, heavens no. And that's another aspect of the portraits I've read of him. Our friendship began around 1940. And I have never seen him when you could more than tell slightly that he'd had a drink. I have sat around with him all afternoon and we would sip along— I would not do nearly as much as he did—because I would never attempt to keep up with somebody like that, drinking: but I have never seen him when he gave the appearance even of being slightly intoxicated. He could handle a great deal of consumption. The sort of thing that Scott Fitzgerald apparently couldn't do.

Brian: But in the almost twenty years you knew Hemingway, did you think he was a brave man and admired bravery, or did you think there was a psychological aspect to it?

Seward: Well, of course, that's a very popular theory nowadays. One that I think Philip Young has perpetuated a great deal. I think that, honestly, courage was probably the key word in his vocabulary, both as a man and a writer. I would say, based on my readings of his work and my knowledge of him, that the key words were courage and integrity, both in the work and the man.

Brian: Did you understand why his marriages broke up? Did he ever discuss this with you?

Seward: The only one he ever discussed was the one with Martha Gellhorn and I took that to be confidential. And I passed that off in one sentence in my own book—a generalized reference. My own theory is that if he had married Mary first, I honestly believe he would have had one marriage in his life.

Brian: How does the Hemingway you knew differ from the Hemingway his critics describe?

Seward: He is the only important, so-called great man that I have ever met in whom I was not disappointed. And I have had occasion to meet over the years several U.S. Presidents, which may not be shooting very high, incidentally, but I have never met a supposedly great man in whom there wasn't some disappointment. And I saw Ernest in a number of circumstances and to me he always remained really bigger than life. And I'm not a young kid with a great deal of hero-worship, you know. I never knew Malcolm Cowley as closely as I did Ernest; but I have known Cowley for some years and he's visited in our home and I see him once in a while in New York. And I know Robert Penn Warren. Had lunch with Warren last May. Malcolm Cowley is an awfully nice fellow, but I don't think that we are speaking of people really in the same league when we are talking about Cowley and Hemingway.

Brian: Did you, in all the time you knew Hemingway, detect any signs of his eventual mental breakdown?

Seward: None whatsoever. That's the one serious thing that I do question about accounts. I had correspondence with him practically until a month before he killed himself, and I have combed through those letters to detect anything, but I have been unable to detect anything that indicated even some of the things that Baker suggests. And I think the last few chapters of the last days according to Hotchner's account are apparently very good fiction. I'm not saying that his mind had not been affected some. I mean anybody that had as many accidents and had been as organically beat-up, so to speak ... I am convinced it was much more physical than it was mental. Mary agrees with me. What I think happened was that he'd gotten physically beyond his point of return. He had incipient diabetes among a hundred other things wrong with him and he had lost weight and lost weight. He would apparently persist in drinking against doctor's orders, I think not a great deal, but even any in the shape he was in was bad; and that he could foresee himself as an invalid, lying in bed with people waiting on him, and he just couldn't take it—that's what the evidence points to, to me.

Mary Hemingway

BORN IN WALKER, MINNESOTA, APRIL 5, 1908

Mary Hemingway was, I thought, the key to Ernest Hemingway. She was his fourth wife, their fifteen-year marriage the most enduring of the four. As a journalist working for Time *and* Life, *she met Hemingway through Irwin Shaw in a London restaurant in the spring of 1944. With him she survived two plane crashes and was with him when he killed himself on July 2, 1961. She went to court to try to prevent A. E. Hotchner from publishing his book about Hemingway,* Papa Hemingway, *charging the book invaded her privacy and appropriated her literary property. She failed.*

Mrs. Hemingway lives in a comfortable Manhattan penthouse apartment with an uninterrupted view of New York skyscrapers. I found her smaller than I had expected—barely five feet—but she matched her telephone voice: lively, direct, and friendly. "She doesn't suffer fools gladly," Hemingway wrote. "She does not suffer them at all." Off the record she described to me some of the fools she wouldn't suffer gladly. And considering that my initial unannounced phone call caught her in her bathtub, she proved surprisingly cooperative, when I called again, half an hour later, in talking about her famous husband and his interviewers.

Brian: One of the things I wanted to try and get straight was the Lillian Ross interview and Mr. Hemingway's attitude to it. You were actually with him during the interview.

Mrs. Hemingway: We came up to New York on our way to, I should presume, Spain. I can't even remember the *year*. Anyway you would have that date. (November 1949.) As early as that? Wow! Then we were going to Italy. Well, anyhow, Lillian came to meet us at the airport. She is the most accurate of anyone I ever knew, in interviewers. There is no curtain between her and her subject whatsoever. She's a marvelous interviewer, I think. And she recorded, quite accurately, everything that happened while we were staying, if I recall correctly, at the Sherry-Netherland Hotel. (It was.) We went ashore that evening as it were. And she came the next morning—I was still asleep I think—and she and Ernest had a long chat. And everything she said in that *New Yorker* Profile, Ernest shooting imaginary pigeons . . . no, not imaginary, real pigeons, crossing Fifth Avenue on our way up to the Metropolitan Museum (he pretended his arm was the gun), all of that was entirely accurate.

Brian: What about the comment he was supposed to have made to his publisher, Scribner: "She's made horses' asses of us both"? And that, according to Carlos Baker, Hemingway hadn't time to alter the interview?

Mrs. Hemingway: [Laughs.] I think that it's quite possible if someone is as clear as Lillian and as accurate as she is, everybody is a horse's ass. And what did Carlos say?

Brian: He said that it was a shock for Mr. Hemingway to see the Profile.

Mrs. Hemingway: He may have taken that out of Hotchner's book, which really has a great many errors in it. Hotchner came down, after the thing was published, saying: "YOU ARE RUINED!" [Chuckles.] Idiot things like that. And I remember saying: "No single profile in any magazine, of Ernest, can ruin him." I think that possibly, although of course I don't know where Baker latched onto this, but Ernest, if he did feel that, never gave any impression of feeling it at all. He subsequently wrote to Lillian saying: "You did a good job, daughter." Something of that sort: I'm quite positive about that, that he did write her such a letter.

Brian: I got the comment from the notes at the back of the Baker biography.

Mrs. Hemingway: You know Ernest left a—the only thing I found in the safe in our house in Cuba: the only instructions I found were in a sealed envelope, saying inside that his letters were never to be published. This has caused a great many people lots of confusion [chuckles] and disillusionment and all sorts of things. But for that reason we can't quote him directly—out of his letters.

Brian: D'you know why he would have done that?

Mrs. Hemingway: I've no notion at all. But he wrote it in May 1958 before he had any signs of illness. And the envelope was dated four days later. So he must have had time to think about it.

Brian: Malcolm Cowley said he believed that Hotchner in his book *Papa Hemingway*, when he was theoretically quoting conversations with Mr. Hemingway, was in fact quoting from letters Mr. Hemingway had written.

Mrs. Hemingway: Yes, he did. That's the way he got around the prohibition of publishing letters.

Brian: D'you feel the Carlos Baker biography gives a—are you almost uncritical of it as being truthful of Mr. Hemingway as you knew him?

Mrs. Hemingway: Well, obviously, as you know, Ernest worked at home, so we were always under the same roof. And Carlos Baker never even met Ernest. So obviously his view of Ernest would be different from mine.

Brian: Could you say possibly what's missing?

Mrs. Hemingway: It's not really very easy, especially for publication, it's not easy to say very much about that.

He did the most industrious possible job. And nearly all the facts, not all, of course, but nearly all of them, are absolutely accurate.

Brian: Professor Seward said to me that the man is missing from the book, the living man.

Mrs. Hemingway: I think that would be quite natural, don't you? Since they had never fished together, or hunted together, or chatted together, or any of that sort of thing, Baker did, I thought, a marvelous job of research, but obviously couldn't, didn't know Ernest, and could not view him as a creature.

Brian: I'm thinking back twenty years. And I never recall having seen Mr. Hemingway on a television interview.

Mrs. Hemingway: He didn't like that stuff.

Brian: He tried to avoid it, did he?

Mrs. Hemingway: Always, absolutely always.

Brian: Did he ever go on?

Mrs. Hemingway: Once in Madrid: something about bullfighting. As a favor to some matador friends of his. He thought a writer's job was to write and he hated all the brouhaha which accompanied it, radio and television.

Brian: I had a theory that he avoided interviewers because a lot of the material about himself he would want to use himself. And Mr. Gingrich thought that he was a very shy man.

Mrs. Hemingway: Lots of people, of course, maintain that he was a great bravado boy, boastful, and a big boisterous public figure. That would never be my opinion. You know, sometimes, occasionally in the Floridita bar in Havana, we might have a couple of extra drinks or something and begin to sing along with the conjunta, you know, the guitarists and the maraca, and things like that. But otherwise he was a very private man, really. And wished to be so. That is my opinion.

Brian: Was what people saw as bravado, how he

reacted to the press and the cameras, a cover-up sort of thing? For his shyness?

Mrs. Hemingway: Could well be disguise, an attempt to escape from the shyness. The other thing is of course —both in Havana and New York, in various places, in Paris, you know—he did have friends who were working reporters. And he wouldn't be the kind of man to be rude to friends. So he had problems [chuckles] in all directions.

Brian: Did you ever establish what his attitude to Scott Fitzgerald was? Was *A Moveable Feast* true of his feeling for him?

Mrs. Hemingway: Really, I try never to put myself inside of Ernest's head: I think it's an intrusion. Although, as I said, we lived under the same roof and were very good friends for seventeen years, I think, I feel I have no right to *assume* things which *might* not be true. I think he wrote that piece, especially that funny one about coming up in that car without the top and all that funny stuff, you know, as one sort of crazy memory of his association with Scott. My recollection of their last bits of correspondence before Scott died, and that was quite a lot later, was that they had an exchange of very gentle and sweet letters. Not very many, as I recall, but I certainly didn't count them. He was Ernest's friend and I had never met him and I don't pretend to be an authority on those things.

Brian: I thought Professor Baker's book was a tremendously complete biography but I missed why Mr. Hemingway's marriages had broken up; that although he explained that Mr. Hemingway fell in love with other women he didn't explain why he fell out of love with his wives.

Mrs. Hemingway: The ordinary life of a healthy and honest-to-himself man would probably, in his generation and this generation, include more than one dame. On the other hand, in those days, people were more or less committed to marry the women they wanted to shack up with, somehow that was the custom. *The New York Times*, I see, faithfully records engagements and weddings and all that sort of thing still, pages and pages every Sunday. It would seem to me that a normally healthy fellow would certainly be interested in more than one woman: that is, somebody of Ernest's wide interests and exuberance. He'd naturally have at least two or three girls and the fact that he faithfully got rid of one [chuckles] and married another is just a circumstance of this era, or this recently past era. People don't bother with the wedding ceremony a lot of the time now, you know.

Brian: Arnold Gingrich said: "Ernest buried each wife in a book." You're the exception of course [she laughs], but the previous wives: he wrote them out in books and that was it: when he'd put them in a book he went on to the next.

Mrs. Hemingway: I feel that's really a bit too strong. It's not true. He was disillusioned perhaps.

Brian: And Gingrich said that in *A Moveable Feast* Mr. Hemingway almost sanctifies his first wife, Hadley, and that it wasn't really that way at all.

Mrs. Hemingway: Gingrich, along with a great many people, considers himself *the* final authority on Ernest. Actually Mr. Gingrich knew Ernest for a certain period. But he certainly did not know Ernest during Ernest's marriage to Hadley. It was subsequently, when he was married to Pauline. And so why he makes these vast, authoritative assertions is a puzzle to me. But everybody, and his brother and his cousin and his uncle and his aunt, all think they are the definitive authorities on Ernest. [Chuckles]. It's kind of amusing.

Brian: It is funny, isn't it? Professor Seward had a theory that if Ernest had married you first, that he would have had one marriage. D'you think that's reasonable?

Mrs. Hemingway: Well, that's very sweet of Bill and a compliment to me, of course. But unlikely. Who knows? How would I know? Bill Seward is an extremely nice man. I get letters fairly frequently saying: "Thank God he found you," things like that.

Brian: What did you think of Seward's book on Mr. Hemingway?

Mrs. Hemingway: It was accurate and it was very loving: quite different from Baker's. Bill Seward is a Southern gentleman, and his whole attitude . . . his book is based on really very slight personal acquaintance and a fair amount of correspondence—almost the opposite pole from Baker, who attempted to be entirely objective, sometimes, perhaps leaning backwards.

Brian: Some people thought, from reading the biography, that Carlos Baker didn't like Mr. Hemingway. Truman Capote thought Baker didn't like Hemingway.

Mrs. Hemingway: Neither did Truman Capote.

Brian: Capote told me why he didn't.

Mrs. Hemingway: Yes?

Brian: Because when Nelson Algren's book came out, Hemingway wrote something like "All you Truman Capote lovers can now read a real book by a real writer." And this hurt Capote.

Mrs. Hemingway: [Laughs.] Any comment I could make about that could not be published.

Brian: D'you feel, then, Mrs. Hemingway, that the accounts of bravado were just legends?

Mrs. Hemingway: Sure, they're mostly cartoons.

Brian: It's almost the Errol Flynn sort of thing, the adventurer conquering Burma singlehanded.

Mrs. Hemingway: Yes. They're enormous exaggerations. It would be hard to exaggerate Ernest's own—until he became ill—enormous enjoyment of life, which was so much greater than that of almost anyone . . . really almost anyone, with a couple of possible exceptions. His enjoyment of *everything* and his *zest* for life and his exuberance.

Brian: And did his sense of humor go along with the legends?

Mrs. Hemingway: Oh yes, oh absolutely.

Brian: Somebody told me that there was only one mystery about him, and that was from his wounding in Italy . . .

Mrs. Hemingway: Oh, that's such a lot of . . .

Brian: . . . to his coming home.

Mrs. Hemingway: Oh that's *such* a lot of nonsense, really. Philip Young, he's a professor of English at Pennsylvania State University, he did a whole book based on the fact that Ernest had some kind of terrible psychological wound from having been wounded, and pursued this thing, and he still does. It got him a doctorate or something in literature [chuckles]. And I can say it to you, because I've said it to Philip: I think it's . . . horseradish.

Brian: How does he respond to that—say, "Well, it got me my doctorate"?

Mrs. Hemingway: Philip believes it, sincerely. Obviously he wouldn't pursue the thing to the extent that he has done if he didn't. It's of course true he got wounded, but the pictures we have of those days, he is the same cheerful, happy exuberant self. Everybody has doubts about everything, you know. That's the human condition. *La Condition Humaine.* I couldn't remember who wrote that book. Can you remember?

Brian: It's not André Malraux, is it?

Mrs. Hemingway: Yes, I guess that's who it is. Anyway . . .

Brian: Finally, is the other psychological picture that people have written of Mr. Hemingway's hunting and so on, as revealing a violent man getting rid of his violence by hunting, a true one?

Mrs. Hemingway: We hunted in Africa and we hunted many autumns, many falls, out in Idaho, I mean birds, you know. A great deal of the hunting, both in Africa and Idaho, was the great pleasure of walking through African bush or the Idaho sagebrush. He and I used to hunt ducks and pheasants in Idaho and it was *not* for killing ducks. Frequently the limit would be perhaps six a day and with it one might have twelve in the deep freeze. We'd go and walk four or five miles in the fresh air looking at the country and smelling the wind, and come home with two ducks. It was certainly not the killing that engaged him. We did an awful lot of walking in Africa and of course if we found something that looked remarkably good in the way of a head we might possibly . . . But then we passed up a great many animals who were just too sweet to shoot. I mean both of us did. For example lots of people wondered why he never hunted elephants and Ernest always said they were too important and dignified, too great as living things, to be shot by a man with a gun. So this idea that he was a livid, wild killer, is really truly not so: not truthful.

Brian: And you know for a fact that in the major interviews, with Lillian Ross, Plimpton, and Cowley, he was happy with them and was accurately quoted and pictured.

Mrs. Hemingway: Plimpton only did this thing for *The Paris Review*. I mean that's the principle thing of his. And [chuckles] that's sort of a funny story. George had come down once or twice at least to Havana and hung around with us, you know, we had chatted at various times. And he then sent by mail a list of the questions which would presumably be answered by Ernest for *The Paris Review*. Ernest didn't like the questions very much: he thought they were stupid. So he rewrote the questions. I'm not sure that would be true of every single question, however many there might have been, like thirty or forty, or something. But he thought the questions were stupid, so he redid them.

Brian: That's the way to get good questions.

Mrs. Hemingway: And I'm sure George would agree with that. Ernest rewrote the questions and then, carefully, I think by hand, wrote out the answers. And Malcolm Cowley is really such an extremely nice and thoughtful and understanding man. I remember that Ernest didn't really want to be put in *Life* and he hated to sound boastful or what not, so I remember he put Malcolm on to people like Buck Lanham, General Lanham, and people like that. "You ask him. I don't want to tell you about this." Because it sounded boastful.

Brian: What would have happened if I had managed to get to him by phone and said, "Might I ask you a few questions for an interview?" Can you speculate how he would have responded?

Mrs. Hemingway: Well, I think he would have done his best to put you off. That was his usual practice.

Brian: Did people get through to him a lot, at the Sherry-Netherland for example?

Mrs. Hemingway: We usually got in and out of town fairly quickly. And there was one year when Harvey Breit, who worked at the *Sunday Times Book Review*, very sweetly lent us his house, which was on East 64th Street. And that was *glorious* because nobody knew where we were and we could get around town pretty much with no interference. Most people think of him as being a publicity seeker and I'm afraid Carlos sometimes gives that impression in his book, too. It just could hardly be less true. So it has always seemed to me. For example, when we were in hotels here, we sometimes went out side doors or back doors, things like that. Ernest had people he wanted to see and things he wanted to do here, and he didn't want to waste time with the press.

Brian: I spoke with Hotchner. What about his book?

Mrs. Hemingway: I don't know if you understand; but at no time ever did Hotchner give the slightest hint to Ernest or to me that he was making notes with the idea of producing a book about Ernest.

Brian: No, I didn't know that. But I suppose, in a way, as he was a practicing writer, it might have been expected.

Mrs. Hemingway: No, he always professed himself to like Ernest, you know, just for the fun of it, and all that.

Brian: One of his complaints about the Ross piece was that she left out fascinating material about Marlene Dietrich and Ernest Hemingway discussing astrology, and a tremendous lot of interesting material.

Mrs. Hemingway: I'm sure Miss Ross's idea of what to omit would be very much better than Mr. Hotchner's. He wrote this book and made a great deal of money on it, as a totally traitorous thing to Ernest. If Ernest had known that he intended writing a book, he would never have seen him again, *ever*. This was a knife-in-the-back job, in my opinion. I'm sure Ernest would kill him, would have disposed of him.

Brian: I don't know if it's any consolation, but I think Hotchner was very fond of him.

Mrs. Hemingway: I guess you're always fond of someone who can make you a million dollars; I really don't know about that. But I'm totally, totally alienated by it.

Brian: Did you think his brother Leicester's book, *My Brother, Ernest Hemingway,* was pretty objective?

Mrs. Hemingway: Most of what he talks about is a time when I didn't know Ernest. But I suspected it, for example, because when he was a boy of sixteen he'd go fishing with Ernest off Key West and he purports to remember an hour-long conversation which they had while they were fishing. He was never that bright at the age of thirty or forty, so I don't know how he could have been that bright at the age of sixteen.

Brian: How often did he revert to Indian talk? Was this sort of a joke thing . . . ?

Mrs. Hemingway: Of course it was a joke. He had Bimini talk. For instance our conversation: just for amusement, we'd start out in French, and go into Swahili, and then into Italian and then Spanish and perhaps wind up in English, all in one sentence. You know this is amusing. It brightens your day.

Brian: I think what upset his adherents in the Ross piece was they thought he was being pictured as speaking Indian talk all the time. That it was his normal way of talking.

Mrs. Hemingway: Oh no.

Brian: He was listed in a recent report about Nobel Prize-winners as an alcoholic.

Mrs. Hemingway: I saw that thing. I wrote *Parade* a vehement letter pointing out what a mistake it was and they sent me back . . . Some chicken-shit professor from somewhere or other just grandly decided that this was so, without ever having apparently made very much of an investigation. Somebody who teaches English in Arkansas or Kansas. What can I do? It is *so* mistaken, really.

Brian: Is it true to say he was a man who drank a lot but could hold his liquor?

Mrs. Hemingway: I looked up alcoholism, and that is a disease. Ernest had hepatitis one year and he didn't drink anything for fourteen months. Before that and after that he drank, we almost always had at least one and usually two martinis before lunch and we had two or three martinis before dinner together with at least a bottle of wine, and depending on the number of guests more bottles of wine. Ernest never took anything after dinner, that is, only on the rarest occasions would he take a drink *after* dinner. I'm speaking of our normal life in Cuba. He would go to bed at ten-thirty or eleven o'clock and wake at more or less daybreak without having had anything alcoholic since dinner. We always had, of course, thermoses of cold water beside the bed, because of Cuba's being hot. And the idea that he was alcoholic; I have been told by mutual friends that Faulkner used to go on week-long benders. But I don't know that. I was only told that. But Ernest never did that. I only once or twice saw him a little unsteady on his feet. In seventeen years. Once it happened to be in Cuba. On that particular occasion, we stayed out, which was the *rarest* thing, really the rarest thing. We had gone to one of the most beautiful nightclubs there *after* dinner. We may have gone, in seventeen years, four or five times to nightclubs. But there was a particularly good floor show and we did, in that case, have a few gins and tonics or something like that. And on *one* of those occasions, he was a bit unsteady as we got out of the car. I don't mean he fell down or anything like that, but that's the only time I have seen him that way. I feel terribly offended at that professor who glibly *claims* he was alcoholic. It could not be.

Brian: What was his evidence?

Mrs. Hemingway: The only thing that *Parade* sent me was some kind of review of whatever it was that this professor did. So I don't know what his evidence was. He couldn't know. He had the temerity to publish really with no valid evidence at all.

Brian: When a professor does it everybody believes it must be the truth.

Mrs. Hemingway: They believe the printed word, which is a terrible mistake. [Chuckles.] As anybody who's in the business knows.

Brian: Will you ever write a book of your life together?

Mrs. Hemingway: I'm in the middle of it. But it's a long-haul job, really, because it includes not only . . . it's a whole long thing which begins long before I ever met Ernest. Scribners tells me it puts a great deal more light and shadow, or chiaroscuro, on Ernest as a human being, than has yet been published.

Brian: Here's a Carlos Baker reference to Mr. Hemingway's reaction to his Profile by Lillian Ross. It's on page 651 of the Notes Section: "EH to author, Feb. 24, 1951, stated that the 'thing' was her idea. He was in 'full hold' of a novel and did not give a damn. But when he read it, while continuing to defend her right to say whatever she wished, he was 'shocked and felt awful.'" Do you recall Mr. Hemingway reacting in such terms to the portrait of him?

Mrs. Hemingway: No, but he may have felt so without telling me. Lillian had said that she would send us galley proofs in time for us to make corrections and or suggestions. The proofs arrived so late that there was little time.

Brian: Do you still feel as you did when Oriana Fallaci interviewed you in 1966 and you said: "A writer doesn't belong to the public, only his writing does. Unlike a prima donna or an actress, he has a right to privacy if he wants it. . . . No one should be authorized to tell the dissolution of a man, even less to tell it for money or sensationalism." And do you think a writer should be discouraged from writing all he can find about the truth of a subject, if his aim is to paint a truthful, rounded portrait?

Mrs. Hemingway: I assume this was in reference to Hotchner's book, which cheated all the way, and was full of exaggerations for the sake of sensationalism and royalties. No, I certainly do not think "a writer should be discouraged," etc., if he has the approval of his subject and if, as you say, his "aim is to paint a truthful, rounded portrait." But very, very few of us can do, or *do* do "truthful rounded portraits," made with no motes in the eye, no imbedded preconceptions, no, or even few, possibly unrecognized or identified prejudices. In my experience, and reading, almost nobody achieves it.

John Hemingway

BORN IN TORONTO, CANADA, OCTOBER 10, 1923

John is Hemingway's eldest son by his first wife, Hadley. During World War II he was in command of a platoon of Negro military police. Later he joined the OSS and was parachuted into France to train partisans to infiltrate enemy positions. He was twice captured by the Germans but survived. After the war he tried a career as a businessman but when I spoke with him he was in Sun Valley, Idaho, where he writes articles on hunting and fishing. A direct, outgoing man with a ready laugh, he provided a clear son's-eye-view of his father—and his father's interviewers.

John Hemingway: My own reaction to Lillian Ross's profile of my father was that it was like a tape recorder. While all the things that were said were absolutely accurate, they don't sound the same written out, with the kidding around that was going on—I don't think it was her fault. I think she didn't know how to make it feel the way that it really was then.

Brian: She got it right but missed the fact that he was fooling around?

John Hemingway: Yes, I think that's a fair judgment. Having sort of listened to that kind of conversation and knowing all the people involved—I wasn't around at the time this took place—the funny thing is that if you could place the mood and everything like that, this was the way it was in a nonworking period.

Brian: Do you know what his response to the interview was when it was published? Some say he was shocked, others say he was delighted with it.

John Hemingway: My feeling was that he thought she didn't do a good job because of the fact that she didn't capture the spirit or explain the circumstances, but thought she was a fine girl and in no way blamed her.

Brian: What did you think of the Carlos Baker biography?

John Hemingway: It painted a picture of my father which made him seem like a real son-of-a-bitch, which he wasn't. While strictly accurate it's like taking testimony. Everybody gets to testify and this is the time that all the bastards get a chance to line up and give it to him. [Laughs.]

Brian: Malcolm Cowley, who was very fond of your father, thought that Carlos Baker has taken too many anti things and not put enough pro things in.

John Hemingway: I tend to agree, but I think there were probably plenty of anti guys around. I think Mr. Baker did a very fine research job, but I didn't think there was any warmth in the book. You didn't really catch any feeling of the person at all.

Brian: Your father is said to have had a black temper. Did you ever experience it?

John Hemingway: Yes. What kid hasn't? It could be devastating, but intrinsically he tended not to be. Like everybody else he was made up of many different facets. If somebody got that end of the stick and didn't see the other, I couldn't blame them for getting a bad impression of him.

Brian: Was he ever reconciled to his mother?

John Hemingway: No.

Brian: Was that because she'd bullied him into playing music and leading the life she wanted him to lead, and he resented it?

John Hemingway: I'm not sure it was that so much as the thing of her henpecking his father.

Brian: Did you think A. E. Hotchner's book *Papa Hemingway* was accurate?

John Hemingway: Not accurate. To be quite frank I read the excerpts. My feeling from that was that he caught the character and the way it was to be around him better than any of these other books. But he was sort of placing himself in situations where he wasn't, but he'd heard the details, which appeared to lend more validity to his testimony. And there were a number of inaccuracies, but his wasn't intended, I don't think, to be a scholarly work.

Brian: When did you last see your father for any length of time?

John Hemingway: In April of '61.

Brian: That was shortly before he died (July 2, 1961).

John Hemingway: Right.

Brian: Did you feel that the physical injuries he'd suffered and the illnesses were the causes of his mental breakdown?

John Hemingway: They certainly were contributory factors, or triggered it.

Brian: Was he very sick when you saw him?

John Hemingway: He'd lost a tremendous amount of weight. That was a shock, you know, his appearance. Also his lack of volubility and his normal great good humor. And he was obviously a very ill man and I wasn't aware of the situation or any of the problems that had occurred. I just thought that this was straight physical sickness.

Brian: Were you satisfied with Carlos Baker's treatment of your father falling out of love with his wives and into love with the women he subsequently married?

John Hemingway: He tended to be a man who was very loyal to his women. I think a lot of people stray a little bit and have sort of gotten away and gotten home. I think he felt he was committed when he strayed. That's just my own feeling. I may have it entirely wrong. One doesn't know one's parents really that well.

Brian: Do you think any mystery remains about your father?

John Hemingway: There's a mystery about any person, a full understanding of them, and there always will be. Nobody's going to clear it up.

Brian: Do you think accounts of his drinking are exaggerated?

John Hemingway: He actually could consume a heck of a lot without it appearing to affect him, but it does over the years, you know, more and more.

Brian: Because somebody linked him together with other Nobel Prize-winners, as an alcoholic.

John Hemingway: Oh no, in no way would I consider him as such. He was actually cut off from it to a very considerable extent after having had that bad liver damage in a plane crash. He went for long periods without the use of alcohol, although he wasn't very happy doing it.

Brian: He could hold his liquor apparently. Very few people saw him even stagger.

John Hemingway: No, but your judgment changes nonetheless.

Brian: What do you think of his writing?

John Hemingway: I'm not a critic. I really shouldn't say anything. But I like it.

Brian: I know you write about hunting and fishing. Did he ever see any of your writing?

John Hemingway: No.

Brian: Did he encourage you to write?

John Hemingway: No. He thought it was a very tough racket and no way to make a living.

Brian: I presume you think of your father quite a lot?
John Hemingway: Not as a habit. But I keep thinking what a wonderful old man he would have made if he'd learned how. I don't think he'd faced up to becoming old.

PART TWO
Truman Capote's Friends and Foes

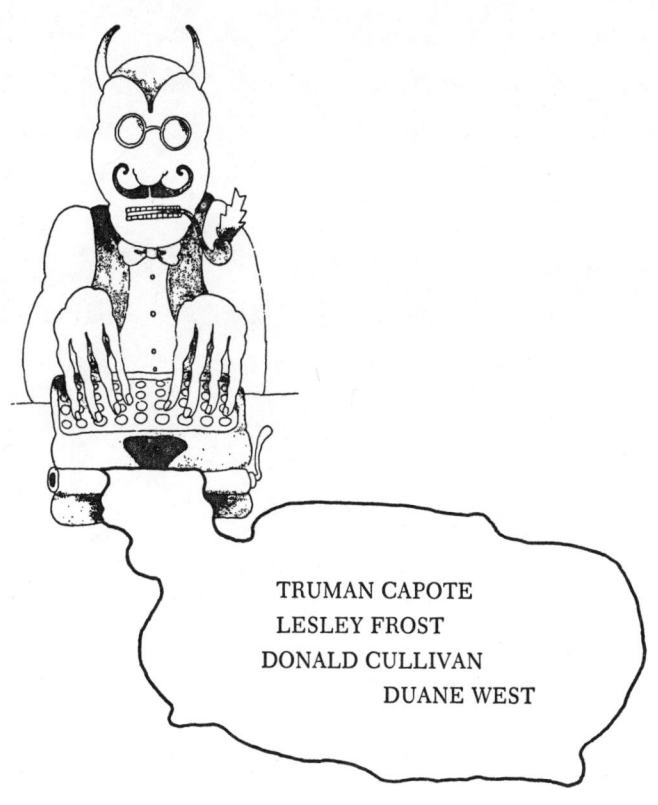

TRUMAN CAPOTE
LESLEY FROST
DONALD CULLIVAN
DUANE WEST

Truman Capote

BORN IN NEW ORLEANS, LOUISIANA,
SEPTEMBER 30, 1924

Truman Capote's early writings were poetic and fictionalized accounts of the terrors and loneliness of his childhood in Alabama. His parents were divorced in 1928, when he was four, and Capote was brought up by elderly aunts and cousins.

Of the few friends he made, one, Martha Beck, grew up to be a murderess and was electrocuted in Sing Sing for her part in the Lonely Hearts killings; another, Harper Lee, became a novelist who portrayed Capote as a child in her To Kill a Mockingbird.

From the beginning Capote the fiction writer showed sympathy for eccentrics and misfits and an interest in the world of outsiders. And when he chose to move from fiction to fact, he turned to the real-life nightmare world of murderers. The result was In Cold Blood. *After that triumph he took a TV camera into prisons throughout America, to interview murderers in death row.*

Until In Cold Blood, *Capote's most spectacular interview had been with friend Marlon Brando. The published account, which Brando resented, revealed an oversensitive, troubled, slightly paranoid man. Brando didn't challenge its truthfulness, but Capote's right to reveal the truth.*

To produce In Cold Blood *Capote lived three years in Kansas, a place as foreign to him, he said, as the moon: where he exhaustively interviewed two murderers, friends and neighbors of the four victims and the lawmen on the case.*

The book (first published in The New Yorker *in 1965) was built out of hundreds of these interviews. To persuade people to recall for him in detail not only their actions but their thoughts, Capote made them his friends. Motivated by curiosity, empathy for outcasts, and a passion for the right word, Capote produced a vivid portrait of one of the killers, Perry Smith. The brutal little man whose unfulfilled dream was to create one work of art at first resisted Capote's efforts to draw him out. But after a year, Smith began to confide in Capote and the result of their alliance was a work of art Smith wouldn't live to see.*

Capote, a lonely, frightened, awkward little mouse of a boy, grew up to be a social lion. When he invited 500 people to a dance at the Plaza Hotel in New York, most of them world-famous, very few declined his invitation, and The New York Times *devoted a page to an account of the party and reprinted the entire guest list. The outsider had become an insider. But even then he spent most of the time just watching others enjoying themselves. "What interests me—what I dwell on and dream of—are not the little nuances of my own life but the lives of people around me," Capote once told Jane Howard of* Life.

Capote told me that he always knows when an interviewer is going to treat him sympathetically or not. The unsympathetic, he said, very early in the piece mention his unusual voice. But I agree with Donald Cullivan that through the fascination of Capote's talk you soon forget the voice—and just listen to the man.

My attempt to test Capote's reputed powers of total recall failed. He wasn't in the mood. But to test his reputed accuracy I interviewed Donald Cullivan and Duane West. Donald Cullivan was an army acquaintance of Perry Smith; Duane West was prosecuting attorney at Perry's trial. Capote wrote of both men in his In Cold Blood. *How accurately? I asked them.*

During my interview with Capote he called poet Robert Frost the meanest man he's ever met and explained why he thought so. I interviewed Robert Frost's daughter, Lesley, to see if there was another side to the story.

Capote spoke to me from his Long Island home, in an all blue room which goes up two floors, mirrors filling one wall and reflecting the blue. It has a winding staircase up to a balcony. And the wall opposite the mirrors has a white fireplace reaching to the ceiling, and floor-to-ceiling bookcases on either side, with a sliding red ladder to reach the topmost books. Capote describes it as the inside of an Easter egg. Glancing out of the window he could see the moors and the ocean. Within stroking distance were his two cats and bulldog.

Brian: It's strange that you should become so involved with murderers. Perry Smith became a close friend. You've made a documentary film about murderers. And even as a small child you ran away with a girl who grew up to become a murderer. (Martha Beck of "The Lonely Hearts Murders.") Did you stay away long?

Capote: No, just overnight. She had an uncle in Evergreen, Alabama, who ran a small hotel.

Brian: Did you lose contact with her after that?

Capote: Oh yes. After that her family took her away. I didn't even realize it was the same person until years later all my relatives in that town said: "Oh that's the girl who was here that summer. She's the one you ran away with."

Brian: Her motive for murder was greed, according to psychiatrist Frederic Wertham.

Capote: Yes, sexual greed on her part and financial greed on the man's part. But I hadn't any particular interest in crime. I wrote *In Cold Blood* by accident. I don't have a particular interest in crime now, except that I know a great deal about it.

Brian: To produce *In Cold Blood* you trained your memory so you could recall accurately almost 95 percent of what you heard. Would you at the end of this interview be able to repeat something I'd said earlier on?

Capote: I don't think I can today because I'm not in a very good mood. I'm not feeling so well. So don't let's try anything tricky . . . [Chuckles.]

Brian: All right. Back to *In Cold Blood*. Did Perry Smith and Richard Hickock lie to you, or try to mislead you, in the early stages of your contact with them?

Capote: I suppose so, inasmuch as Perry Smith had always told me that Dick killed the other two. I mean, that's what he told me earlier on. Then later, he told me the truth.

Brian: What d'you think was his reason for cooperating with you?

Capote: Loneliness. There they were, the first year I knew them, and I knew them almost six years, in this little town in Kansas. Nobody talked to them. Nobody would do anything for them. Nobody had heard of them. Nobody had even heard of their case. You know, there was nothing. I was this person who was there doing this thing and I was very attentive to them. I was drawing them out: out of boredom and out of loneliness, if nothing else. Who else was paying any attention to them? They were very grateful to me, although they were both very suspicious about what I was doing.

Brian: Weren't psychiatrists showing any interest?

Capote: There was only one psychiatrist and I don't think he was interested in them until he found out that I was. And he only saw them once. [Sigh.]

Brian: You say they were suspicious of why you were doing it. Did you ever tell them why?

Capote: Certainly. I told them the truth from the very beginning. But they couldn't understand. I mean, they didn't understand what I was doing. Well, why should they? None of my friends did, either. Nobody could understand what it was that I was doing. They couldn't understand what the end result of it was going to be.

Brian: Did your interviewing technique change over the years you were gathering material for *In Cold Blood*?

Capote: After a bit I wouldn't say it was interviewing in any real sense of the word: it was just talking. I was very, very friendly with them. In fact I was the only friend they had in the world.

Brian: How did you persuade the townspeople to talk about such a tragic and depressing subject?

Capote: It wasn't a matter of my just going in there bang, bang, bang, like some ordinary reporter. I went to that town and I moved into the town. And I began to cultivate people, you know. And on a very friendly basis, they'd introduce me to another person, who introduced me to another person. When I first lived there the case had only just happened. It was a couple of months before it was solved. Nobody had ever heard of Perry and Dick. I didn't know whether I'd have a book or not. I was just sort of experimenting with the whole thing. And so I just cultivated people and by the time the case broke, I was on such friendly terms with the detective in charge of the case (Alvin Dewey), that I was the first person he told.

Brian: You had done this very deliberately?

Capote: Of course. I don't ordinarily go to Sunday school, I can tell you that. The first time I ever went to Sunday school classes.

Brian: Did you enjoy it?

Capote: Not much. [Laughs.] I came to respect all of those people, though.

Brian: You gave $50 apiece to Perry Smith and Hickock to get them to talk with you initially. Could you tell me the gist of your talk then, when you tried to get them to agree to be interviewed—after they'd accepted the money?

Capote: It was very brief, because they had their lawyers in the room and were terribly uptight. They'd only just been caught. This was maybe the day after they were returned to Garden City. They wanted $50. They wouldn't speak to any other reporter and I think that the only reason that the lawyers were able to arrange it was the money. If it hadn't been for that I would never have been able to have spoken, so the whole thing would never have started. I just wanted to establish a contact with them on which I could build. From that point on I supplied them with magazines and writing paper and all the little things that nobody else would think of doing, and they became very dependent on me, you see.

Brian: Did the payments for releases to the others you interviewed amount to a lot of money?

Capote: Oh golly, I've forgotten now. Mostly I tried to get the releases as I went along. But some of them I let go too long . . . and it was all my own money.

Brian: Could you ever feel warmly toward Hickock, knowing that he delighted in killing dogs by hitting them with his car?

Capote: It isn't a question of feeling warmly, but when you get to know somebody as well as I got to know those two boys—I knew them better than they knew themselves—feelings don't enter, of like or dislike. It's some kind of extraordinary condition of knowledge takes place. I found that, of course, appalling and repulsive, you know. (The killing of dogs.) But there it is, it was part of his insensitivity and indifference to life in general.

Brian: Were you serious when you said of the *In Cold Blood* interview that you could tell if people weren't being accurate, by their eyes shifting from right to left?

Capote: I don't know if I said that, but I've often noticed it. When you get right down to hard ground with them, their eyes will start shifting. Shifty eyes [chuckles] is an old phrase.

Brian: Any other clues that indicated to you that people weren't telling the truth?

Capote: You know, all of that's so instinctual. After you get the feel of a person, can't you always tell more or less when somebody's really not leveling with you?

Brian: I think so, yes. The accuracy of *In Cold Blood* was challenged by Phillip K. Tompkins in *Esquire* of June 1966. According to him Mrs. Meier denied that she said she had seen worse men than Perry, denied that she ever heard him cry, denied that he ever held her hand and said: "I'm embraced by shame." And although you say that Perry Smith killed all the victims, Duane West (prosecuting attorney) and Alvin Dewey (chief detective) still believe that Dick Hickock killed the two women. Is this just a difference of opinion: you say it's true and they say it isn't?

Capote: What I wrote in the book was true. It is absolutely accurate. Mrs. Meier, wife of the under sheriff at the jail, turned against me. And Duane West is one of my bitterest enemies. And they were sort of working tooth and tong. As for Alvin Dewey, I don't know why he believed that. He always has and I don't know why he does because it's absolutely untrue. And Mrs. Meier is just not telling the truth.

Brian: Malcolm Cowley said to me that although *In Cold Blood* was meant to be a plea against capital punishment, he felt that it supported it, in that the execution of the two men was the only thing that gave their lives any stature, esthetically.

Capote: Meaning what? Or does he mean in respect to the book? If the boys hadn't been then . . . that was one of Tynan's great things . . . if the boys hadn't been executed then I wouldn't have had an effective ending for the book.

Brian: Tynan's was a snide thing, wasn't it? He was implying that you would have wanted them to die. But Cowley doesn't imply that you wanted that. He says that men like them, who do gruesome things and lead "worthless" lives, can only achieve stature, either as characters in a book or as human beings, by being executed.

Capote: I don't see his point about it in terms of life. The fact of a person being executed—what has estheticism got to do with that? Estheticism is purely something in terms of art.

Brian: Of course executions make heroes and martyrs as well. You're not struck by his comment?

Capote: I've heard variations of it before.

Brian: What surprised me about *In Cold Blood* was that there was no obscene language from either of the men.

Capote: That's what *The New York Times* pointed out. They said: "If these things are absolutely accurate, why is the language so," you know ... As a matter of fact Perry Smith was extraordinarily prissy in conversation. I make a great point of it.

Brian: Did you use any euphemisms for Hickock's language?

Capote: No, I really didn't. The only word that Dick used to say all the time was "shit." But Perry would never say that.

Brian: Was there anything remarkable or moving in the hundred-page farewell letter Perry wrote to you just before he was executed?

Capote: I don't know if I ever said it or not. It was about ... it was about ... Oh my God, I really shouldn't go into all this. It just upsets me so much anyway. [Sighs.] All the time they had been in prison, all those years, they were only allowed to have a certain amount of money. And I always gave them each whatever it was they were allowed to have. Anyway, the thing was that in the letter there was a check for the money. Perry had never spent a penny of it and he was, you know, giving it back to me. I don't know why, but that one thing upset me more than any other thing. It just tore me up. Because

I mean . . . oh God . . . it was touching, as though that all along . . . I can't go into it . . .

Brian: For which of the other murderers you've interviewed have you felt the most empathy?

Capote: A girl called Jeannace Freeman on Death Row at Oregon State Penitentiary. A fantastic story. She's a fascinating girl. She's now had her sentence commuted. But she's been on Death Row at Oregon about five or six years. I just find her a fascinating girl. Strange, curious, a monster. Terribly good-looking. She's not in the film. I went there for that purpose but in the end I edited it out.

Brian: Why, if you felt such empathy for her?

Capote: I liked her personally but my interview with her wasn't any good.

Brian: Did the Edgar Smith case interest you? (He was convicted of the murder of a fifteen-year-old girl in Mahwah, New Jersey, and William F. Buckley, Jr., befriended him and eventually helped secure his freedom.)

Capote: I read his book *Brief Against Death* (Alfred Knopf, 1968). I thought it would have been a much more interesting book if he'd have admitted that he killed the girl. But since he doesn't, I find something about the whole book untrue, and unimpressive, because I'm convinced that he did kill the girl.

Brian: I told Buckley that the only thing that worried me was Smith's lack of memory for the crucial time. Particularly as he was supposed to be a man in control of his emotions. And Buckley said the same thing worried him. But don't you agree that the evidence against the other suspect seemed very strong?

Capote: You can make anything seem very strong. No, I think he did do it. I mean, I'm convinced that he did.

Brian: Whitney in *TV Guide* said that for your TV film about murderers, Prettyman took over much of the interviewing of the murderers because "Capote's high baby voice, seductive in jet set salons, proved somewhat less effective in the yard of San Quentin." Was that true?

Capote: No it wasn't. [Chuckles.] Because, in actual fact, I prepared all of the interviews for the different prisoners. And then, because of the terrible technical difficulties that we had in the prisons sometimes, the lighting was so bad and the lighting currents alternated so much that we worked in such awful conditions that, actually, there were three of us doing the interviews. I mean we would be together and then, as the subject was talking, whichever one of us wanted to, could interrupt and ask something. One was Mary Bailey Gimbel and one was Barry Freeman and one was me. Barry Freeman was really a lawyer, front man for the operation.

Brian: You were almost like friendly detectives.

Capote: Uh-huh.

Brian: You interviewed an ex-convict for *In Cold Blood*. And then he suddenly appeared at your home, stayed all day and got away with some money . . .

Capote: How did you know about that?

Brian: You told Jerry Tallmer of *The New York Post*.

Capote: Well, it happened anyway. I didn't remember that I'd ever told anybody. I mean I told certain friends about it. But I didn't realize I'd ever told the press. It was quite frightening. A bit like *The Desperate Hours*.

Brian: How can you avoid that sort of thing happening again?

Capote: I guess you can't. Something very similar happened last summer. It was similar in the sense that it wasn't somebody that I'd interviewed and met: but it was a psychopath who was out of a mental institution fairly recently, a rather good-looking young man, but so sinister. He just walked in through the lane and through the fields and up to this house and next thing I knew he was knocking at the door. And I went there and there he was. And he was an instantly recognizable psychopath. He began talking to me, in what seemed a normal way and he was in the house before I knew what I could do and it took me forever to get him out of here. And then I had to drive him to the railroad station. And all the way he kept hammering his hand against his fist. He had found out where I was. He had taken a great deal of time and research and located this house out here in the country. I mean, how he found me here is just amazing because I come and go so, you know. It was really frightening. Extraordinary. And afterwards he appeared several times in a building where I live in New York, but I was never there. And finally the doorman there called the police about it. But there's nothing you can do about that. Everybody has . . . I mean, my mail [chuckles] lots of days it would make most people climb the walls.

Brian: But curiosity makes you read it?

Capote: Actually I can tell a lot of times, just by the quality of the handwriting, and I don't bother to read it.

Brian: I imagine all celebrities get that sort of mail?

Capote: But I have the extra burden of receiving an enormous amount of mail from the prison population of the world. They all want to tell me their stories. "If only you could write my story, I know that the world would listen." Or, you know, making me a deal. And if they aren't doing it, their lawyers are. I get tons of letters from lawyers asking me don't I want to write the story of their clients, to have the exclusive rights? Now, for instance, this boy who really committed all those Manson murders, Watson. His lawyer from a little town wrote me this long letter right after they were all caught and in prison and asked me would I be willing to buy the story of this boy's life, exclusive rights to write about him for $50,000. [Laughs.] Can you imagine?

Brian: You've often written about death. Do you believe in life after death?

Capote: Do I believe? No, of course I don't.

Brian: Ever had any extrasensory experiences?

Capote: Just the ones that everybody's had. Thinking about somebody you haven't thought about in months and the phone rings and there they are.

Brian: If Jesus Christ returned to earth and invited you to question him, would there be a question you'd want to ask him?

Capote: No, because I don't believe he ever existed.

Brian: Have you ever heard John Allegro's theory that Christ was a mushroom?

Capote: [Laughing.] No. Whose theory is this?

Brian: Allegro. He's an expert on philology and one of the translators of the Dead Sea Scrolls. And in his book he says that early Christianity was a cult of drug-taking, the mushroom drug, and Jesus Christ was the mushroom.

Capote: [Laughing.] I think that's quite good. I like it.

Brian: When the cultists wrote or talked about the mushroom, they used the word Jesus as a code for mushroom.

Capote: [Laughing.] I think that's pretty good.

Brian: Is there any biggest disappointment in your life?

Capote: Well, I believe people that I shouldn't have believed, that's about what it comes to. I'm very gullible. I'm not gullible at all as a writer, or as an interviewer. But I'm very gullible personally, just in a purely social way. I really and truly believe what people tell me. If I were going to put them in a book or story or an article, I examine what they tell me. But if you say something to me, I just take it automatically and believe it. And then, when it's something important, I get a real sinking feeling. That's happened several times in my life.

Brian: Could you be specific?

Capote: No.

Brian: D'you think of yourself as frank and open?

Capote: Yes.

Brian: Have you ever met anyone you'd call a saint?

Capote: Did you ever read that story of mine called "A Christmas Memory"? In many ways, I suppose, Sook Faulk was a saint. Most people would think of her as a saint. I just think she was a good person.

Brian: Met anyone absolutely evil?

Capote: Absolutely evil? Let me think. I think Kenneth Tynan is absolutely evil, I really do. He's evil because he's the ultimate in hypocrisy and duplicity.

Brian: You never settled the argument where he accused you of not making any effort to prevent Smith and Hickock from being executed?

Capote: Oh, we settled it. I wrote a piece about it in the *Observer* that went on and on for a month. To me it has everything to do with duplicity and what not because he was pretending to be such a friend of mine, and living in my house, and I was so generous to him in every way. And all the time, months before the book came out, he was plotting this attack on me, for no reason, except what he was going to get out of it. It was reprinted everywhere in the world and he made a lot of money out of it. To me, that's really evil.

Brian: And you think his motive was greed?

Capote: Greed and jealousy.

Brian: What makes you cry?

Capote: Oh lord, anything to do with cruelty to animals. Or cruelty in any event. Deliberate cruelty is the only thing I can't forgive.

Brian: What scares you?

Capote: I don't think I used to be scared of anything that I automatically saw, but after doing all the research for *In Cold Blood* and all the murderers that I interviewed, hundreds of them, the very sight of a hitchhiker gives me a shiver. I've driven back and forth across the country several times and the idea of running out of gas in one of those lonely Midwestern places creates a tremendous sense of anxiety in me. And I have a real, true dread of being on some isolated road, depending on the kindness of strangers [chuckles], as Blanche Dubois would say.

Brian: What delights you?

Capote: Oh, I don't know. Unexpected pleasant sexual experience, I suppose.

Brian: Would you be very surprised if Kenneth Tynan apologized to you?

Capote: If I ever see him I'm going to kill him. He'd better stay out of my path. [Laughs.]

Brian: I'll have to record that you laughed when you said that.

Capote: But I usually laugh when I mean it the most. [Chuckles.]

Brian: Did you read the statement by a maid of Mrs. Kennedy Onassis that Jackie was a very selfish and self-centered woman? And a newspaper's comment, that her father having been an alcoholic would explain why Mrs. Kennedy would be more self-centered than for example, Ethel Kennedy, whom they called outgoing and unselfish?

Capote: They're totally different people. I know them both. Jackie Kennedy and her sister are both extremely intelligent, sensitive people. Her sister even more so than she is. They had a difficult childhood. Their father was an alcoholic. That wasn't the problem. They adored their father. His alcoholism was not part of their unhappiness. It was just that their mother and father were separated. Jackie was always a very shy, sensitive, withdrawn person. And through various circumstances and accidents of fate, she feels she's been turned into a permanent freak of some kind. I don't think she's self-centered. That little horror that made the statement! Talk about self-centered people!

Brian: It's always a bit suspect when they're making

money out of their revelations, isn't it? There's always got to be knife in somewhere, or it doesn't sell. I know you don't believe in an afterlife. But do you believe there's a purpose to this life?

Capote: I'm beginning to wonder, let's put it that way.

Brian: You once said: "I developed the muscles of a veritable barracuda, especially in the art of dealing with one's enemies." Are there more, other than Kenneth Tynan?

Capote: Oh, one has many enemies in this world. I'm sure you do, too.

Brian: What is your technique with them?

Capote: I get even with them finally.

Brian: Did you have any frightening or wonderful experiences as a child, that you often recall?

Capote: When I was about four years old, I was in the St. Louis Zoo with some colored woman; I guess she must have been working for my mother. And two lions got loose from a cage. That was frightening. And then I was bitten by a snake when I was twelve years old. Bitten by a water moccasin and nearly died. Spent the whole summer in bed. I quite often recall those experiences in one form or another. Comes back to me as some form of anxiety.

Brian: Do you have a theory of interviewing? Some people think genuine curiosity is essential.

Capote: So do I. And I think you need to know a great deal about the person before you interview them. But the kind of thing I do, they're usually quite anonymous people that I have to get to know: like the book I did about the theatrical company traveling through Russia, *The Muses Are Heard.* The way I work . . . it's rather a tricky thing to do, but nevertheless it always works. If you're having a difficult time with a subject, then you, in effect, change roles. And you, the interviewer, begin by making little confidences of your own that are rather similar to things that you think you will draw out of them. And suddenly they'll be saying: "Ah yes, my mother ran away with five repairmen, too." See what I mean? Or: "Ah, yes, my father robbed a bank and was sent to prison for ten years, too. Isn't it extraordinary we should have those same things happen in our lives?" etc. And then you find you're off to the races.

Brian: You've been the subject of hundreds of interviews. Do you find that you reveal yourself more fully to a peer? Would Norman Mailer, for example, be the ideal man to interview you?

Capote: No. To me it doesn't make any difference. I can tell fairly early on in an interview whether it's going to have any quality or not. It's a question of the person's intelligence. It doesn't matter to me who they are. A man has just written a book about me, Professor William Nance from Texas. I think it's quite an interesting book (*The Worlds of Truman Capote*) and rather well written—but you would think from the first pages of the book and the remarks he makes that he had interviewed me many, many times. In actual fact I met him once in my life and talked for just a couple of hours. He was trying to give an impression that he knew me intimately, when in fact he did not know me intimately.

Brian: In fact he implies that he interviewed you twice, not once. He puts the dates as November 9 and November 10, 1966.

Capote: It's not true, though. I was in Austin, Texas, where the University is, and I gave a lecture there and I saw him just before the lecture and then afterwards he came to the hotel and I was very tired and I got into bed and had myself a drink (Evelyn Waugh was interviewed in bed by a *Paris Review* interviewer) and he sat down in a chair and I talked to him, maybe for an hour and a half, two hours.

Brian: Was it about midnight?

Capote: Yes, it was late.

Brian: Technically he's right, I suppose. He's got the two dates in as before and after midnight.

Capote: Oh, I see. [Chuckles.] Clever. [Laughs.]

Brian: Professor Benjamin DeMott's objection to almost all printed interviews is that the reporter eliminates his own reactions and his own personality from an interview, and so it becomes artificial.

Capote: I know the argument, but I don't agree with it because there's a whole other school where interviewers are constantly putting themselves into the interview and I think that's a thousand times worse, and easier. Rex Reed and all of these young reporters today are continually writing about themselves and the problems they had in getting the interview in the first place, and then their own personal reactions to the person. Anybody can do that. It's wrong. Because the ideal portrait is something in which the interviewer is totally removed and you set the whole thing up so that if it's good, the person that it's about comes across with no distortions on the part of the interviewer—well, of course if he's any good he's an artist, and any artist distorts whatever he touches. But it's not artificial: it's just a form of art. Well, then, all art is artificial. My point is that life is life and art is art. You can't take actual life to make it into art. It's impossible. Given the most careful documentary kind of writing, or filming, it's impossible. Because, by the very nature of what you're doing, framing something, it turns it into an art.

Brian: Do you agree that the First Amendment should be interpreted to mean that there should be no libel law and that one should be able to write or say anything about anyone else without fear of prosecution?

Capote: Yes, I agree with that. I personally don't care what anyone writes or says about me, so I'd just as soon [chuckles] that whole right was given to me.

Brian: As the subject of interviews, is there one that was most refreshing to you in that the questions were bright and unexpected and that you personally found it really interesting?

Capote: Yes, yours is very bright and fresh.

Brian: That's great. But are there any famous ones, for example?

Capote: There was this strange girl called Barbara something who writes for *The Village Voice*, who did a piece about me for *Esquire*. I didn't like the piece but I must say I thought she had a lot of talent. Strange girl. That was a couple of years ago.

Brian: Why didn't you like it, although you liked her?

Capote: I liked her quality. Now there's an interview in which the interviewer's in it completely. It's really much more about her than it is about me. But I think she's an interesting person. There's something fascinating about her: grotesque and weird. Really bright. She could have gone a long way, but I thought there was something quite peculiar about her.

Brian: What do you think of Studs Terkel?

Capote: I just read his book *Hard Times*. I thought that was quite good.

Brian: David Frost?

Capote: I've done his program. I like him. He's a little mechanical. Everything is totally prepared by his staff. And he's simply coming on there, hoping he can keep all those cards ahead, as he's shuffling through. He's thoroughly professional and he doesn't leave you in the lurch, like so many of them do.

Brian: Rex Reed?

Capote: His interviews are clever and amusing. A little too emotional, though.

Brian: William Buckley, Jr.?

Capote: He gives as much as you're supposed to give. It's like a discourse, a debate.

Brian: Mike Wallace?

Capote: He used to beg me to be on his show. And at that time I had never been on any television show. And finally, after months and months, I said I would do it. And then, at the last minute, I called him up and said I was sorry, I'd changed my mind because I'd finally gotten around to seeing his show [laughs] and I just wasn't about to subject myself to any of that nonsense. [Laughs.] He was very upset.

Brian: Which show had you seen?

Capote: I think it was poor Tennessee Williams.

Brian: Have you ever refused to answer certain questions?

Capote: Only if it involved somebody else. I've refused to give interviews quite a lot of times because I've been too busy. I've refused to be on television because the people were boring or I didn't want to be on their program. I never would be on Merv Griffin's program.

Brian: You think he's a bore?

Capote: Well, yes. I like Dick Cavett. I think he's nice. You see, I hardly ever watch, for one thing. I don't have a television in New York.

Brian: After a *Playboy* interviewer interviewed you, you said to Jerry Tallmer: "It's really fun. I'm probably going to have to leave the country." What had you said to the *Playboy* interviewer in 1968 that would cause you to leave the country?

Capote: Undoubtedly it was a reference to things that were taken out of the interview. They took an awful lot of things out, on grounds of libel.

Brian: For example?

Capote: Some of the things I said about Kenneth Tynan were absolutely hair-raising and they took those out because Kenneth Tynan was a great buddy of the *Playboy* people, which I didn't know at that time, in fact, practically an editor [chuckles]. And Hemingway, I said a lot of things about. Oh, Bobby Kennedy, yes. I had quite a lot to say about Bobby. I rather liked Bobby. I think they took the whole thing out.

Brian: Do you imagine you'd give fuller and franker answers to a close friend than to me, for example?

Capote: Well, no. I'm trying to be as frank as I can be.

Brian: I think you are. But I wondered if with a friend you might pull out the stops more. Maybe the reverse would be true.

Capote: I don't know. I'm answering the questions as I feel. So I'm being as honest as I can be.

Brian: I feel you are too. Do you regard the 500 people you had to your famous Plaza Hotel party as friends?

Capote: No, about forty-five of them were friends. But I knew everybody and I more or less liked them for one reason or another, or I wouldn't have invited them.

Brian: If you wanted to interview the entire 500 at that party, in depth, about how many do you think would give you good interviews, be expansive and frank? An educated guess . . . ?

Capote: Anybody can be interviewed if you go about it the right way. If you study the problem, there isn't a single person in the world, from violent prison hermits to chatter-box starlets, that if you really map out the problem you can't get to talk about themselves. If you're talking about interviewing public characters, well that's one problem. What I think is the most interesting and difficult form of interview is with people who don't expect to be interviewed, and in fact don't know that they are being interviewed.

Brian: I think that's Studs Terkel's technique.

Capote: He uses a tape recorder and I feel that's a great mistake, because the moment you introduce a mechanical device into the interview technique, you are creating an atmosphere in which the person isn't going to feel really relaxed, because they're watching themselves.

Brian: You said to George Plimpton: "No one likes to

see himself as he is or cares to see exactly set down what he said or did. I don't like to myself when I am the sitter and not the portraitist. And the more accurate the strokes, the greater the resentment." Was there one particular interview you resented that was very accurate?

Capote: Oh, I don't know. I can always tell in the opening paragraph whether the interview is essentially going to be sympathetic or unsympathetic by the way they describe my voice. They'll go on about my height or something and then they'll have some kind of thing about this funny voice that he has, you know, several different allusions to this strange, funny little voice that Capote has. And I can always tell by where that is placed in the thing and the way the arrangements of adjectives are, whether the interview is going to be sympathetic or unsympathetic.

Brian: What did you think of Gay Talese's book about *The New York Times, The Kingdom and the Power?*

Capote: I thought it was very good.

Brian: Talese apparently tries to discover the thoughts of people. Do you think it comes off?

Capote: Ah, but he stole that from me. That was all my theory and he'll admit it.

Brian: He acknowledges it, does he?

Capote: I don't know that he acknowledges it, but he read the manuscript of *In Cold Blood* long before it came out in *The New Yorker*, and he was fascinated by the whole technique. That was the first time that anybody used that thing of people thinking. They're thinking in there but thinking what they told me they were thinking.

Brian: In *TV Guide* Dwight Whitney describes you as "looks like a small well-bred English bull." How do you react?

Capote: I just felt it wasn't true. Didn't he say bulldog?

Brian: Bulldog, was it? (No, it was bull.) Were you amused by it?

Capote: I just didn't feel he was very accurate. I

happen to have a bulldog [chuckles]. I know I don't look like her. He does that voice description thing too, doesn't he?

Brian: What description by others of yourself most amused you?

Capote: In Harold Nicolson's memoirs there's rather an amusing description of when I was very young. Somebody took me to lunch with him. That was quite good. And then in David Lilienthal's memoirs there's— oh, a very long, quite amusing description of me.

Brian: What description most offended you?

Capote: Well there's a guy that was really . . . I mean it was a hatchet job. It was meant to be a hatchet job. It was meant to be as mean as it could possibly be. At the time I had that big dance at the Plaza, he wrote an outrageous column. You know, he wasn't invited or anything. He was just hanging around outside the hotel and he wrote a really outrageous piece about me. What's his name? (Dick Schaap in *The New York Post*.)

Brian: Didn't he intersperse the dance scene with scenes from the war in Vietnam?

Capote: That's it. It was so corny you couldn't believe it. Terribly corny. William Buckley wrote a very funny piece about it. (Buckley was at the dance and he supported Capote's right to throw a party.)

Brian: You're considered an outstanding interviewer, not only because of the years of interviews you did for *In Cold Blood* but for your *New Yorker* piece on Marlon Brando of November 9, 1957.

Capote: And that was a hatchet job. [Chuckles, mixture of benign and diabolic.]

Brian: There were reports that Brando didn't realize he was being interviewed by you.

Capote: That's not true. Of course he knew it. When I said it was a hatchet job I didn't mean that at all. I was just making a joke. I basically felt the piece was very sympathetic to him. He didn't think so and wrote me the most fantastic letter, which I wish I had kept, just as a souvenir. Originally I was going to do a larger piece about the making of the *Sayonara* film for *The New Yorker*. And in the end I thought it was all a big bore, you know, the whole thing. So I just decided to do this one part of it. But he knew perfectly well he was being interviewed.

Brian: The report that came out was that he told you moving things about his life and you had told him moving things about yours.

Capote: Yes, but I *know* Marlon Brando. And I told you one of the things that I do when I find the subject a little difficult—not that I found him that way—is to become very confidential.

Brian: Do you feel that when he saw what he'd said in print he wanted to take it back, or was upset about it?

Capote: I think they think you're going to edit the whole thing somehow, for them. And then they're shocked when you, according to their lights, didn't have the good taste to leave this out or that out.

Brian: Did you ever meet Hemingway?

Capote: No, but I hated him.

Brian: What did you think of the Lillian Ross piece about him in *The New Yorker*?

Capote: He was such a total hypocrite: he went on pretending to be a friend of hers afterwards. I thought it was rather a good piece, but I didn't like him, so it doesn't matter.

Brian: Do you think from reading his writings and other people's interviews with him, that he was a hypocrite?

Capote: A total hypocrite. And he was mean. I did know Robert Frost and he was about the meanest single man that ever drew breath. But I disliked Hemingway intensely. He was always writing little things about me, when I was very, very young. I was about eighteen or nineteen when I thought: "My God, here's this man fifty years old, this famous man. What the hell does he always want to be knocking me in the teeth about?"—you know. And then, when Nelson Algren's book *The Man with the Golden Arm* came out, Hemingway gave him a quote which the publisher used and the quote said: "All you Truman Capote fans get your hats and coats and leave the room. Here comes a real writer." Well, I thought that, really, I mean, it's really too much. When my *Breakfast at Tiffany's* came out he wrote me a little note telling me how good it was, or how much he liked it. And I thought: "There's more of your hypocrisy for you."

Brian: Mary Hemingway, interviewed by Oriana Fallaci, said: "Unlike a prima donna or an actress, a writer has a right to privacy, if he wants it. People should be prohibited from writing about others' intimate lives." Do you agree?

Capote: Mrs. Hemingway said that?

Brian: Yes. She had wanted to hide the fact that Hemingway killed himself.

Capote: No, I don't agree with what she said.

Brian: According to Hotchner, Mrs. Hemingway wanted to stop him writing a biography of Hemingway because she was cooperating with Carlos Baker.

Capote: And that was a bad book, too. [Chuckles.]

Brian: Because it had no point of view or because it was just facts?

Capote: The Baker book was bad all the way through. It was dull, it was uninteresting, it was badly put together, it had no selectivity, it was an atrocious piece of writing. And then on top of the whole thing [chuckles], considering how much the Hemingway estate backed him up and cooperated with him, it was a piece of duplicity, too. He was shoving the knife in there all the time. I mean, I never read a book in which I came away more with the feeling that the author hated the man he was writing about.

Brian: You said Robert Frost was the meanest man you ever met. Could you give me an example of how he was mean to you?

Capote: When I was about eighteen years old there was a thing called the Bread Loaf Writers Conference. I was invited up there and the great mogul of the thing was Robert Frost. You know, a glob of all these old Midwestern ladies and librarians and what not, oohing and ahhing and carrying on—he was such a ham. Anyway, one rainy day I stepped into this sort of barn—he was in this barn escaping from the rain—and the two of us had a little conversation. And I think he thought that I wasn't particularly awed by Mr. Frost, or something. Anyway, the chemistry was not particularly good. But the next day he had a poetry reading and I had the flu and I said I wasn't going to come. The director of the conference said to me that Mr. Frost was furious and thought I was insulting him. And so I said: "Well, I'll come but I've really got this fever." So I went, and about half way through the thing I felt so badly I thought I was going to faint, because it was terribly hot. So I got up and tried to ease along this aisle to go out this door. And Frost picked up this book and he threw it at me as hard as he could. And [chuckles] shouted, I don't know, something. And he refused to go on with the reading. And I went back to my room and the director of the conference came and asked me would I leave immediately because Mr. Frost was so upset about it. And with the flu and a fever of 103 I had to leave there. And then Robert Frost wrote a letter to *The New Yorker* and got lots of other people at the conference to write, saying how insulting I had been, as though I were representing *The New Yorker*. *The New Yorker* had nothing to do with it, you know, except that I worked there.

Brian: Did he hit you with the book?

Capote: Yep.

Brian: Did you read the recent biography of Robert Frost by Lawrance Thompson?

Capote: No. But I don't have to read. I know he comes out as such a monster. But I know he's a monster [laughs]. I don't have to read it.

Brian: A woman wrote in *The New York Times* book review section, saying he was even more of a monster than the book portrayed.

Capote: [Laughing.] Well, I guess I'll have to add my two bits.

Brian: Do you think it was innate unpleasantness with him? Or do you think it was a result of what he had gone through in life?

Capote: I think he was just a mean man, I really do. There are lots of mean people in the world, you know.

Brian: If you were ever in a position when you thought you were just about to die, could you tell me how you felt?

Capote: Three times. Once was the snake bite when I was twelve years old. I told you about that. Once when I had acute appendicitis and was in absolute agony and nobody could help me. And when I lost control of my car and it hit a tree and I went through the windshield. The tree was coming up and I was going through the windshield and I said: "Well, this is it, buster." [Chuckles.]

Brian: Were you scared or calm?

Capote: When I came to I was incredibly calm. I guess I was in a state of shock.

Brian: As you were flying through the air and saying, "This is it, buster," were you reasonably calm?

Capote: Yep.

Brian: If you could communicate with the world, say on international TV, is there any subject you'd specially want to talk about?

Capote: My mind doesn't work that way. If I said I wanted to talk of the need for peace I'd be a hypocrite, because I don't care about it. I suppose that shocks you. There's no subject I could imagine talking about to an international audience, to try to convince them, that I wouldn't feel hypocritical about.

Brian: I was trying to get at what most concerns you about life, or any aspect of living. If you could appear before people who could change the order of things, what would you ask them to change? For example, pollution might particularly concern you.

Capote: But it doesn't, you see. I really, truly don't *care* enough about any of these subjects to get up and talk about them.

Brian: Do you feel that might be because you haven't any children? Do you think if you had a son of eight and a daughter of six?

Capote: Probably. But I'm not that disconnected. When I think about myself being killed in the automobile accident, I think of certain people and I want to be sure they're provided for, a little bit here and there and what not. I don't feel *totally* disconnected. But I *suppose* if you have children it really does enter into it.

Brian: Do you think your answers to my questions give a fairly good picture of quite a few aspects of you?

Capote: I guess so. I think it's very good what you're doing. But to be perfectly frank with you some of my answers to these questions would be quite different under other circumstances. I've just been in a deep depression for about two months, you know, one of those things that one slides into? So my answers, if I were in a different mood, might be much brighter, more alert, not so "I don't know." So it's really a question of the particular sort of mood that I'm in. But nevertheless I've tried to answer as best I could.

Brian: I was going to ask you why you were depressed

the first time I spoke with you. I had that down as question number one this time but I thought I'd leave it because it might make you more depressed. But it's just general depression, is it?

Capote: Yes. I do, every few years or so, slide into one of these things and it's not at all pleasant.

Brian: I remember you mentioned once that you suffered from severe headaches.

Capote: That's it. It starts that way.

Brian: I know you're very fond of Lee Radziwill, because you told me that although you like Jackie Onassis, or Jackie O as I believe she's called now [Capote chuckles], you think that Princess Radziwill is an even finer person.

Capote: Much. I think there are very few people in the world who are as extraordinary as that girl. She gets no credit for it, of course. She might as well be completely in oblivion. But she's really a brilliant girl and she's got tremendous style and kindness and heart and brains and energy and courage and she's really somebody.

Brian: To the public, of course, she's just a jet setter.

Capote: Well, she's just Jackie Kennedy's sister. I don't even know what a jet setter is. She's a very good mother. She runs a very good house. I suppose, yes, she does travel in those worlds.

Brian: Wouldn't Jackie Kennedy be upset if she knew you thought her sister was much finer?

Capote: She knows it. I've told her. [Chuckles.] I told her in just so many words. She agrees with me about it 100 percent, always has.

Brian: When she wrote to you after reading one of your books and then you had lunch together, do you recall which book it was?

Capote: It was the little book about going to Russia, the Porgy and Bess book, *The Muses Are Heard*.

Brian: Kennedy was a senator then, was he?

Capote: Yes. And she was very attractive and bright and charming and we became very good friends.

Brian: What's your instant reaction to these names: Robert Kennedy?

Capote: He was a friend of mine, you know. I liked Bobby very much. I don't know whether he was . . . Anyway, go on to the next.

Brian: Did you think he was ruthless?

Capote: Yes. He could be quite ruthless. He was most ruthless to the people who were closest to him in a sense. What was that marvelous word he used . . . ? "Hunkers." He used to call various people, who are still weeping and crying over him, you know, those who ran for his clean shirts, to tie up his shoelaces, and who ran after him with a lot of things, he used to refer to them as hunkers. And I said to him: "What is a hunker?" And he said: "A hunker is somebody who rushes ahead of you and sees that the revolving door is spinning by the time you get there." [Laughs.]

Brian: That's an overactive gofor. Norman Mailer?

Capote: Ah, Norman. Well, I've always had the very best possible relations with Norman. He's always been very careful with me, very polite. I used to see quite a lot of him. He used to come and see me quite often and . . . I mean, I've never had any bad experiences with him, like everybody else. And I like him and I respect him as a writer, too.

Brian: Malcolm X.

Capote: Ah, well, he's the only one of the Negro intellectuals, or whatever you want to call them, for whom I have any respect at all. He was quite an extraordinary man and I think that book of his, *Malcolm X*, is the only one of any of those books, and I mean any of them, that's good. I think Eldridge Cleaver's book was one of mind-blowing boredom and talentlessness.

Brian: Vice-President Agnew?

Capote: I think there's something rather beguiling about him. But I wouldn't want to spend any time with him.

Brian: Tennessee Williams?

Capote: We've always been great friends. I feel sorry for him. He's just let something inside get completely out of control. The only thing that really matters to Tennessee is writing and he was always a compulsive writer. He's a compulsive writer like some people are compulsive readers or drinkers or whatever it is. And of course he'll just go on writing and writing and writing and writing, when what he ought to do is not write, and for a long time. And then come back to it with a whole new vision or something.

Brian: John Fitzgerald Kennedy?

Capote: I liked him very much. He was straightforward. He had a nice offbeat smile and an offbeat sense of humor. He was unshockable. You could tell him absolutely anything.

Brian: You heard people trying it, did you?

Capote: I used to do it. I used to tell him all kinds of things about other people or myself.

Brian: He liked gossip, did he?

Capote: Oh yes, loved it.

Brian: Can you give me an example?

Capote: [Chuckling.] I can tell you something I told him in front of about fifteen people at a State dinner. It's a true story. The previous week I had gone to a party that was also attended by a famous designer. He was with a famous actress and they were sitting on a couch, in front of me. And I was having a drink and idly listening to this conversation they were having, or over-listening to it. And the designer was saying: "You know, my dear, the older I become, I find the most extraordinary thing, the most depressing thing is happening: my private parts are shrinking." There was a long pause and then the actress said: "Uh, if ONLY I could say the same!" . . . So anyway, at this State dinner, there were all these people being very quiet, upstairs in the Kennedys' living room. And I just suddenly began telling him this anecdote and after a minute he roared with laughter. But the whole room was completely still until he laughed. They were really shocked that I would have the gall to tell something like that, in front of all those people.

Brian: You had the gall because you knew Kennedy would enjoy it?

Capote: Oh yes. It's a funny story. [Laughs.]

Brian: What was your reaction to the Buckley—Vidal controversy?

Capote: Well, I thought Buckley—you're talking about the *Esquire* pieces?—I thought Buckley was very foolish to have written that article. I mean, why, when he had already had this thing on TV, why drag it all up again? Very questionable, the whole thing. I certainly think he was in the wrong. On the other hand I think Gore was stupid to have answered him. He should have just kept quiet. He shouldn't have bothered to answer it. Neither of their pieces were any good. They were just embarrassing.

Brian: Did you ever know why Gore Vidal was so anti-Robert Kennedy?

Capote: Yes, sure.

Brian: Could you say why?

Capote: Sure, don't you know? Jacqueline Kennedy was wearing an obi. A Japanese dress with an obi. And I think it was the only time they'd ever invited Gore there and he had spent the whole time whispering in her ear. And as he was walking out of the room, he put his hand on her bottom, of this Japanese obi dress. And so Bobby Kennedy walked over to him and grabbed hold of his hand and said: "Cut that out, Gore. That stuff doesn't go around here." The exact quote. And Gore turned on him and told him to take his damned hands off him and said to him: "You Kennedys really think you have it all made, don't you?" And began this crazy sort of tirade . . . (next sentence omitted to avoid libel suit). And after that Gore sat down and wrote that piece for *Esquire* "The Holy Kennedys."

Brian: You got that from an unimpeachable source, did you?

Capote: I sure did.

Brian: You couldn't tell me who?

Capote: If you're not going to print it. [He then tells me.]

Brian: How do you respond to the name Gore Vidal?

Capote: Ah, Gore, poor Gore. [Chuckles.]

Brian: He won't like to hear that, "poor Gore."

Capote: [Laughs.] That's all I have to say. Well, I tell you: you ask him what he thinks of me and that's exactly what I think of him. [Laughing.] You can quote it.

Lesley Frost

Truman Capote had called her poet father Robert "the meanest man I ever met."

Brian: Truman Capote told me that he was at the Bread Loaf Writers Workshop when your father was there. Capote had a fever, and Mr. Frost insisted that he turn up for the reading. And Capote said that in the middle he thought he was going to faint and he started to walk out, and Mr. Frost shouted at him and threw a book at him and hit him. And then he was told he had to leave immediately. And when he got back he found that Mr. Frost had written to *The New Yorker* and persuaded others to write, saying how bad Capote's conduct had been.

Miss Frost: Oh, for heaven's sake. They probably had some quarrels. And after all my father did have somewhat of a temper, too. And a few other people have had tempers. These are things that seem unnecessary even to bother to rake over the coals. I was working with Doubleday when Ernest Hemingway was being published by Doubleday and every few days he'd come storming in and demand more advertising for his books. And one day he said he'd kill John Farrar. So he said he was going out to get a gun. So we barricaded John Farrar in his office and he got under the desk. And Hemingway came back with a great long riding whip which he had bought at

Abercrombie and Fitch next door and said he was going to, you know, have a real . . . Well, we all screamed with laughter, and shut the doors, and slammed doors, and finally he went away. But I think, you know, I think every author and certainly plenty of musicians and painters and artists who live on that ragged edge between genius and what genius does to people . . . You can't go by that. The thing was, my father was one of the most affectionate men, one of the finest friends and one of *the* greatest minds that has come along.

Brian: Am I right in quoting you as saying that your father was on the edge of insanity at times?

Miss Frost: Well, the edge of unreason. I didn't really mean to use the word insanity. Because people look on insanity as something bad. But it isn't bad really, you know. After all, insanity is only unreason, that's all it is. So put it that way, that he was on the edge of unreason once in a while, as genius always is.

Brian: Capote had categorized Robert Frost as the meanest man he ever met. [Miss Frost laughs.] And he felt that after that one encounter.

Miss Frost: [Laughing still, really amused.] Oh yes, on that one encounter.

Brian: I suppose your father wasn't to know that Capote genuinely had flu and really was ill?

Miss Frost: Oh surely. He didn't know he had flu, I'm sure, so he just felt deeply offended that Capote should get up and walk out . . . If you'd seen the quarrels and the jealousies of that group in England around Ezra Pound. It was just wild. They threw each other down stairs and threw things at each other, and all over [chuckles] the wording of a poem.

Brian: You're mentioned in Lawrance Thompson's biography of your father. It reads like this: "She had seen him cause so much injury to the lives of his own children, particularly to Irma, Carol, and Marjorie, that she would not permit him to move into her home."

Miss Frost: Well, this is much exaggerated and all confused. The thing was, when my mother died I was so upset, and my father was upset, too, both of us in the home with her when she died. And the thing was, you know, I just lost my . . . lost control. And it was just one of those things. We got over it, both of us.

Brian: It continues: "She went on to insist that she could not forgive him for having ruined her mother's life . . ."

Miss Frost: Oh, for goodness' sake!

Brian: "'. . . He was the kind of artist who never should have married or, at least, never should have had a family.'"

Miss Frost: I probably said this at the time, but it was a day or two after my mother's death. The thing was that neither the publishers nor Lawrance Thompson allowed me to see any of this. Mr. Edwards said he didn't want me to see it because he didn't want me upset. I know Larry Thompson very well. It's just too bad that he made this mistake about me. I would have let him say quite a lot. But what I said in a moment of terrible grief over my mother's going was quite a different thing from what went on afterwards. I mean, he was one of the greatest men to be with, day and night. Sure he had a temper—like everybody else.

Brian: You were reconciled, then, quite soon after your outburst?

Miss Frost: Oh yes, right away.

Brian: So really, then, the great affection you knew hasn't come across in the book?

Miss Frost: No. And there was a very deep, deep affection . . . I don't think he can be covered by one volume, anyway. And if anyone *really* wants to know about R. F.'s family life I suggest he read my journals, *New Hampshire Child* (written between ages 5-9, and published in facsimile by the State University of New York Press), as well as *The Family Letters of Robert and Elinor Frost*, recently published by the same Press. To these I expect to add a third volume, *The English Years*. I think it's best that a lot of people write about him. And have a shelf full of books about him.... Lawrence Spivak did a lot of interviewing and I heard him say that in publishing books of interviews one book could well be entirely of Robert Frost.

Donald Cullivan

An army acquaintance of and character witness for murderer Perry Smith, Cullivan's religious and moral principles had made him forego a vacation to travel at his own expense from Massachusetts to Kansas to help save Perry's soul, if not his life.

Brian: When did Truman Capote first get in touch with you?

Cullivan: Right after courthouse was out in Kansas. Truman Capote introduced himself as a reporter for *The New Yorker* magazine. And I didn't recognize him physically but I recognized his name. I made some comment like, "Oh yes, you've written such and such a book." I think he was rather pleased to find someone who knew about him. Because I think, out in Kansas, he hadn't run across too many people who did know him. He wanted to know the purpose of my visit and wondered if we could get together. This was just sort of a recess, because I had first gone into the courthouse, I had met Perry Smith's lawyer, before, and he had brought me in so that I was sitting in a place relatively close to Perry Smith, which obviously must have meant something to Capote. So at one of the recesses we made an appointment to get together later on.

Brian: How many times did you meet Perry Smith in prison? When you had dinner with him, was that the most extensive meeting?

Cullivan: Yes. It started off early in the afternoon; we had a long chat. And the dinner was being prepared at that time, by the under sheriff's wife. It went on for about a five-hour period. We talked quite a bit together in the courtroom. Their security conditions were perhaps much less sophisticated than they seem to be these days, so I was able to sit right beside Perry during many of the court sessions. And he'd whisper some remarks to me during the actual courtroom procedures. So we had a chance to chat most every day.

Brian: Did Perry mention Truman Capote and what he thought Capote was doing?

Cullivan: Oh yes, we had quite a few chats about Truman. I think Perry was fascinated by Truman, the difference between Truman's mannerisms and way of speaking, versus a tremendous facility for getting to know you. And there was a way about him, perhaps any good interviewer should have it, in which, shortly after talking to him you're not even aware of how he speaks or in what manner he speaks, he's so fascinating, you're just interested in talking to him. And I think this was certainly noted by Perry. He had quite a few comments about Truman. Some nice. Some not so nice.

Brian: What were the not so nice ones?

Cullivan: I thought this would tickle you. Some of the comments were about the book Truman had given Perry, *Breakfast at Tiffany's,* and he had written a comment in the flyleaf of it. It's sitting in my library right now. Shall I go and get it? [He does.] Right on the inside cover it says: "For Perry from Truman who wishes you well. March 1960." And Perry had the feeling that that was a very cold sort of a thing to write. He was an effusive person himself in many respects. It wasn't the sort of thing he would have written. He expected more. He really felt that was sort of low key. So I remember mentioning this to Truman later on and I think it bothered Truman a little bit that Perry would interpret it this way. He thought it was a very natural sort of greeting. I remember passing Truman's comments back to Perry. And so, following these remarks, Perry then wrote, on the opposite cover, a little note of his own. It's dated Garden City, Kansas, March 28, 1960, and it's liberally sprinkled with quotation marks. And it starts off:

"Capote, you little bastard! I know you went south with the rest of my maps and books from Mexico. I really don't care though. In fact I'm kinda glad you're the one that got 'em. I'm sure you'll put them to good use—

"You're a fool for paying what you did for them. You'd of been better off if you'd of left them there as I first wished. I hope my surprised expression 'Is that all?'"—and now this refers back to the comment on the flyleaf—"reminds you of me. I wanted to call you a name at the time. I was getting angered. It's not too late yet—'You little Piss Pot!' Best of luck and wishes. Your friend Perry." I can see no reason why Perry would choose to write this in the back of a book which Truman gave him and which, as far as I know, he had no intention of giving back to Capote. Perry eventually left it to me, in fact.

Brian: D'you understand what Perry means about Truman having got away with his maps?

Cullivan: Yes. Perry was an incurable romantic and carried maps around with him, everytime there was any sort of an article that he would run across in *True* or *Argosy* on buried treasure or sunken galleons off the Mexican coast—these were things that really reached Perry in a very large sense. He found these things very fascinating. So he collected such articles, picked up maps to give him guidance on how to go searching for this treasure and, as you recall in Capote's book (*In Cold Blood*) at one time Perry and Dick spent some time down in Mexico—this is one of the principal reasons that Perry wanted to go there, to find this treasure. So the maps and books he's referring to, he carried these around with him, in a fairly substantial foot locker. Near the end, after they had to sell their car and were traveling light, he wrapped all the stuff up and stored it somewhere. He gave Truman enough information to find out where it was. And Truman went down and got it out of hock, so to speak.

Brian: A criticism in *The New York Times* regarding the authenticity of characterization in *In Cold Blood* was that there were very few obscenities from Hickock and Smith. Capote said that they didn't use very strong language, in fact the worst thing Hickock would say was "shit."

Cullivan: Yes, this is fairly true. The two expressions in this little note are "Capote, you little bastard" and "you little Piss Pot." You'd think that a fellow with his background could come up with something a lot tougher than that.

Brian: D'you think Capote had become a very close friend of Smith's?

Cullivan: Yes. And he was one of the few people that they would see. And he was one of the few people in a position to do small favors for them.

Brian: Did you feel that Capote's use of all the material you gave him was very accurate?

Cullivan: Considering the nature of the way that he operated, the fact that it was never obvious to me that he was taking notes, I think his characterization of himself as a fellow with a very good memory appears to be accurate.

Brian: What was your reaction to Capote's description of you: "In appearance a cautious bank clerk, with depleted hair and a face rather difficult to recall"?

Cullivan: Oh, well, I'll first give you my wife's [laughs]. She felt it was terribly unfair. And I felt it was reasonably close. I couldn't find any fault. It was fitting.

Brian: Did your wife ever get to understand your going to try to help Perry?

Cullivan: Yes, but very slow in coming. You see, at that time, I was only about three years out of graduate school, struggling along. Here I am taking my vacation time, spending money out of my own pocket because the defense had no money at all. So considering all the normal needs when you have two or three small children, there are lots of things that you've got money to spend for, and it's sort of a reasonable thing for a woman to feel.

Brian: Ironically, you were behaving like a Christian, which so few so-called Christians do.

Cullivan: There were some interesting ramifications, that have come out of this, little things that years later dribble across your path. Some of them comments that were made in local Boston papers. I've just now returned from overseas and we'd been living there for about seven and a half years. Perhaps I was a better Christian in those days than I am now—unfortunately [laughs]. One of the newspaper comments was by a fellow who said: "This was a person who saw something and acted on it." His general comment was that many of us feel strongly about certain things and we nod our head when we see them in the paper, but very few of us normally will take the time or the effort to stir ourselves to do something. I look back at it as something, that at the time and in the particular framework that I was in, my religious experience, social experience, moral feelings about life, that this was something at that time I felt I had to do. If it occurred to me five years ago or right now, God knows what I'd have done, because I'm a different person in many respects.

Brian: Did you feel that Perry had saved his soul?

Cullivan: This became less important to me after I got to know him. I felt that it was really not so much my business, anymore, if it ever was. After I got to see him I felt that perhaps I was doing more good for myself than I was for him. And I certainly have that feeling now. God knows if it was any help to Perry. My testimony was of very little use in helping him out. And he was not interested at all [in saving his soul], and he made it very clear that any of my comments that had any bearing at all on religion were just not within his framework of thinking. Once he made this clear I never brought the subject up. I'm not that heavy-handed.

Brian: Do you agree with Capote that Perry did all the killings? Some people believe Hickock killed two of the Clutters.

Cullivan: No, Perry told me personally that he killed all of them. And I have no doubt at all that he killed them. Because he told it to me over a long period and had no reason to tell me.

Brian: And do you believe, as Capote implies, that Perry's childhood and the battering he'd got from life were largely responsible for the almost conscienceless human being he'd become?

Cullivan: From my own personal experience with him and discussions with him, it seemed as though he did have the feeling that he had had a raw deal in life and that his family background was such that he felt these were mitigating circumstances and since life had treated him badly then life couldn't really complain if he kind of turned and snarled on it.

Brian: As far as you're concerned, then, you feel that Capote didn't leave anything essential out?

Cullivan: I don't really think so. Capote is a very compelling person. In one sense you could say he was perhaps very scheming, attempting to get you in a good frame of mind so that he could pick your brains. On the other hand, as far as I'm concerned, this is no great task. Because I'm always interested in telling people pretty much what I think, regardless of consequences, and without too much incentive. When you talked to him it was quite an experience and so few of the normal people that I run into, engineers and government people, are interesting conversationalists. By and large we're a dull lot. And we don't have too many people who can hold our imagination—Truman could. Shortly after we returned from Brazil, in June of the following year, in which Perry was hanged, Truman invited us to see him in New York. And we happened to be visiting my wife's sister who lived in Long Island at that time, so we drove in to meet him at the "21" Club. And I remember, before we went there, telling my wife—you know, we're middle-class Yankees from the Boston area—not to be taken aback too much by Truman's manner of speech because he does have an odd way of speaking, that you may find unusual at first. And she was saying "Oh my gosh," you know, after I'd mimicked it a little bit, "how shall I stand it?" I said, "I don't think you'll have any trouble." And she admitted later that two minutes after you're talking to him it doesn't make any difference, because he's so interesting to talk to that you get all wrapped up in it. And her sister was telling her to be sure and look around and see who was there at "21" that night, and she said she might as well have been in some little hamburger joint. She never looked around, she was just so fascinated listening to Truman, answering questions and discussing various things about the case. And one of the things to me, and I don't think anyone could fake this: I've always really liked Truman for this, that he's never been afraid to show his emotions. Truman was telling us about the final days and how strong an emotional feeling he himself felt and was literally crying, just harking back to it and I'm sure that he became deeply involved emotionally with Perry and Dick. I think he had really put himself into their lives and had come to know them to a degree that got him highly involved emotionally.

Brian: I entirely agree with you and entirely agree with the fascination of his conversation. Did you give him permission to use the letter that you wrote to Perry? Or did Perry?

Cullivan: I gave it to Truman. He had asked my permission both to use my real name and also to quote from the first letter. I vaguely remember something like a fifty-page contract which said I had absolutely no rights to ever complain about anything, no matter whatever happened to me, and I gave these away for about the sum of one dollar. [Laughs.]

Duane West

Described by Truman Capote as "one of my bitterest enemies." Prosecuting attorney during trial of Perry Smith and Richard Hickock for murder of the Clutter family, about whom Capote wrote his In Cold Blood.

Brian: Do you have very solid reasons for believing that Capote is wrong in his assumption that Perry Smith killed all four of the Clutters?

West: The only thing we went on was what Hickock first said. They made the mistake the first night of putting Smith and Hickock in the same cell block, so they hollered back and forth to one another and decided what to say about the killings.

Brian: I spoke with Donald Cullivan who said that Smith admitted to him that he had committed all four killings.

West: Well, that might be the case. I don't know.

Brian: Did you read *In Cold Blood?*

West: No.

Brian: Did you read any of the reviews?

West: Oh yes.

Brian: Did you feel, in any respect, that Capote might have glamorized the killers, particularly Smith? Or do you think it's accurate?

West: He spent an awful lot of time with those two fellas. And I know he's interviewed more condemned men for a film. But he hasn't got it on TV yet. I suggested he also do a show about the victims of the twelve people.

And I wrote a letter to *Newsweek* about it. And I got a letter after that from a lady who claimed she was one of the victims who had been raped by one of these guys.

Brian: Did Capote interview you extensively?

West: Oh, he talked to me. Of course this whole thing, this reportage . . . that's a laugh. Capote didn't take any notes, but Harper Lee was right along with him and of course she took notes. She was out here about every time he was.

Brian: Did you think his description of you was fair? He described you as looking older than your age. He wrote, "the county attorney, Duane West, an ambitious, portly young man of twenty-eight, who looks forty and sometimes fifty . . ."

West: [Chuckles.] Well, I tell you there were times during that when I felt a lot older than my age. I wasn't one of Truman's bourbon buddies, you know. Of course a book can be misleading by what it leaves out. I prepared all the trial briefs and gave the opening argument to the jury. I examined over half the witnesses and I also gave a hand with the closing statement. Truman took my closing statement and attributed it to Mr. Green and that was a part I didn't appreciate at all. So, I don't know . . . and I couldn't care less. And he left our Mr. Rohleder out of the book too and Mr. Rohleder was the man who really got the evidence that pinned down the conviction. He's our chief of police. And, from what I understand, Truman made Mr. Dewey (chief detective on the case from the Kansas Bureau of Investigation) out to be a hero.

Brian: Capote was very friendly with Mr. Dewey.

West: Well, that was because Mr. Dewey let him look at the diary.

Brian: To be frank with you, Mr. Capote told me he regarded you as an enemy. Can you credit that at all?

West: I don't necessarily feel that we're enemies. As a matter of fact he was very nice to us. Treated my wife and me to seats for *Hello, Dolly* in New York. And we had a very nice time. And just a few days after we got back one of the local attorneys came over and wanted me to sign a release that I wouldn't write anything about the Clutter case. This was before the book came out. And I made an impish remark that this was *quid pro quo* for the nice time we had in New York. And Truman wrote a hurtful note saying: "My, my, how terrible to feel that!"

Brian: Capote feels the Meiers have turned against him, because Mrs. Meier reportedly said he misquoted her.

West: If Mrs. Meier said she didn't say something and Truman said she did, I'm inclined to believe Mrs. Meier.

Brian: But don't you think it would be unlikely for Capote to be inaccurate when attorneys and other newsmen were covering the trial and would know the facts?

West: Well, he took some license with the actual facts of the trial, taking my closing remarks and attributing them to the other counsel. Now there's that. Perhaps you won't believe me when I say that, but it's nevertheless what happened.

Brian: I don't disbelieve you.

West: So when he does something like that and attempts to make a hero out of Mr. Dewey who was not the hero of the piece at all, why should I doubt that he should go ahead and misquote someone else or several others?

PART THREE
Rex Reed and His Targets

REX REED
JACK THOMAS

Rex Reed

BORN IN FORT WORTH, TEXAS, OCTOBER 2, 1940

Rex Reed's interviews revealed that a slob in movie star's clothing is still a slob and a star who's had too much booze is no more endearing than the tipsy lady down the block. Reed arrived on the scene from a lonely Southern childhood (shades of Truman Capote) at a time when the power of the big movie studios to protect their contract stars was waning. No longer was the threat of a blacklist inhibiting to a writer with the urge to tell the truth as he saw it about the Hollywood population. And Reed had such an urge.

Reed was an only child, and lived as a boy in Louisiana and Mississippi, too. Before his success as an interviewer for The New York Times *and* Esquire, *Reed worked as a jazz singer, a pancake cook on an oil rig in the Gulf of Mexico, and a record salesman at Bloomingdale's. After his success as an interviewer Reed played the part of Myron in the movie version of Gore Vidal's novel* Myra Breckinridge. *The movie opens with Reed having himself castrated.* Time *magazine reported: "His debut as an actor is on a par with the best line the scriptwriter could give him to scream: 'Where are my tits?' " But Reed, anxious to be truthful, had beaten all the critics of the film to the punch. "It stank!" he said.*

Reed says: "I don't know where people get this idea I'm a destroyer, or tear people apart. I've written many interviews where I've liked the people and have done what I thought was a nice job with them."

Playwright Robert Anderson (Tea and Sympathy *and* I Never Sang for My Father) *and his actress wife, Teresa Wright, were* well treated by Reed when he interviewed them. Says Anderson: "We feel, in reading other people's interviews, that he has an uncanny ear. He picks things up. And he doesn't carry a notebook around at all, doesn't take things down, yet in terms of other people—it's hard to judge in terms of us—he picks up things and you can see and feel the people."

When I spoke with Reed he was exhausted from overwork, much of which was beginning to bore him. He no longer found the movie star personality piece much of a challenge. My interviews with him were entirely over the telephone. I asked the questions from my home in New Jersey and he answered from his home, an apartment in The Dakota on the west side of Central Park, New York City.

It began like this, after I'd explained I was interviewing interviewers for a book . . .

Brian: Is it convenient to talk now?

Reed: No, I have a dinner party tonight and I've got people on their way here. I just think the best thing for us to do, if you're interested in talking to me about this, we'll just have to make some arrangements to get together or something. Do you think it'll take very long, what you need to ask me?

Brian: What I hoped to do was a couple of phone calls and then meeting you after that. There'd be no chance of talking with you tomorrow morning, say?

Reed: I'll be in Bucks County all day tomorrow. D'you have a telephone number there that I can reach you?

Brian: Yes. You can call me collect any time.

Reed: It's just that I have very little time for this sort of thing. I mean, I've got my own work to do, that, you know, that's just coming out of my ears here. And with this movie thing, too—it's just been impossible for me to ever sit down for thirty minutes at my own typewriter, much less give time to other people. It's been awfully hard for me. It's just hard. So all I can do is promise you that whenever I get a minute I'll call you and see if you're there, and we'll talk, you know.

Brian: The best time for me normally is the evening or weekends, but if the daytime is better, I'll . . .

Reed: Well, that's usually better for me too, the evenings. It's really the only time I'm ever here. I've got so many movie screenings during the day (he is movie critic for *Holiday* magazine), and I've been doing all of these interviews. What kind of book did you say it was going to be?

Brian: It's going to be interviews with outstanding interviewers.

Reed: I'm really afraid I'm not much good at talking about interviewing, because I don't know how to interview anybody. I don't have any kind of technique at all.

Brian: You said in the preface to your book (*Do You Sleep in the Nude?*) that you got into it by accident by interviewing Buster Keaton and Belmondo. What was strange to me was why you did that in the first place.

Reed: To make some money so I could have enough money to get out of Venice and get back to America. I was bankrupt.

Brian: Did you tell Keaton and Belmondo that you were a free-lance?

Reed: No, I told them I was from *The New York Times*.

Brian: You needed a bit of chutzpah to say that.

Reed: Yeh, I lied, you know. It was one instance in which lies paid off.

Brian: I've got a tremendous number of questions and if you feel you don't want to answer them or feel they won't be productive you can just say "skip that" or "nothing to say" or "not interested"—so we could probably come down eventually to about twenty questions that might interest you.

Reed: I'll be very happy to cooperate with you. I'm just so sorry I have so little time. I'm supposed to go to Robert L. Green's annual bash tomorrow in Bucks County: everybody's going to that. And if by any chance I don't go, I'll call you tomorrow. If I do go though, of course, I won't get back until late. Maybe I can even call you tomorrow night: we'll see. And I'm going to Chicago Monday, I'll be back on Tuesday. I won't put this off. I will try to, you know, call you . . .
Brian: That's great. Thank you very much.
Reed: . . . just as soon as I can.
Brian: That's great.
Reed: Okay.
Brian: 'Bye.
Reed: Thank you.
Brian: Thank you.
Reed: 'Bye.
Two weeks later Reed left a message at my home asking me to call him back.
Reed: Hello.
Brian: Denis Brian here, Mr. Reed.
Reed: Who?
Brian: Denis Brian.
Reed: Yes, hello. How are you?
Brian: Do you have a few minutes?
Reed: Yes.
Brian: When you did the original Belmondo and Keaton interviews were you just there as a tourist and film buff?
Reed: Well, I was a film buff. I had been the movie critic for *Cosmopolitan* for about six months and had left the job when Helen Gurley Brown came in and became the editor. And I took the money I had saved and just went to Europe as a tourist and when the money ran out I ended up in Venice as a film buff at the time of the Venice Film Festival.

Brian: What would you have done if *The New York Times* and *The Herald Tribune* hadn't bought those interviews from you? How would you have got back to the States?

Reed: I would have wired my family for money, but I didn't want to have to do that.

Brian: You told me that you said you were from *The New York Times* and that it was the only time lying paid off. Were you nervous doing it, or did you feel reasonably confident because you needed to do it?

Reed: I was just hopeful, let's put it that way. It wasn't really confidence.

Brian: I mean when you were actually interviewing the two men?

Reed: Well, I had done a few interviews before that. I mean, that wasn't the first thing that was ever published. I had done a few things for *Cosmopolitan,* and I had interviewed people before.

Brian: Do you think that if you were interviewed exhaustively by a close friend, you would truthfully answer every question that he or she asked?

Reed: Yes, because I like to be treated that way when I do an interview with somebody. And I think that the only way to do a good interview is to try to do an honest one.

Brian: Have you ever had a subject you thought had truthfully answered every question you asked?

Reed: Ye-es, I've had subjects like that. I can't think of anybody right off. . . . Bette Davis I suppose was probably the most honest.

Brian: Jane Fonda, perhaps?

Reed: Yes, Jane is very honest. But I often think that too many people in show business bend over backwards not to have . . . they want to be loved so desperately that they don't want anyone to be offended by anything they say. And so, I think, sometimes they think they are being honest, but they're holding things in because they don't want anyone to be mad at them. So they cease to be opinionated.

Brian: Are the biggest evasions about sex, or money, or religion, or ... ?

Reed: No, I find that people are very happy to discuss all of those things. They just don't want to ever say anything bad about anybody else in the business. Nobody wants to express an opinion about another professional. That's the hardest thing to get anybody to do, and people work with real bastards all the time but they'll never admit it.

Brian: Why d'you think that is?

Reed: Well, they want another job, you know. They also want to be liked. I mean, these people all want to be liked. Everybody, I think, wants to be liked.

Brian: You think this strong motive with actors and actresses to be liked, this is part of their thing?

Reed: It's part of their hesitancy in being totally honest with themselves and their public.

Brian: I remember you said the director of your film, *Myra Breckinridge*, was a—monomaniac, was it?

Reed: I might have said that, yes. I said all kinds of things about him. Megalomaniac might have been the word.

Brian: That's it. That was the word you said. Of course you're not worried about working for him again?

Reed: Well, no. I wouldn't work for him on a bet.

Brian: Recently you interviewed Mastroianni. He was very frank though a little evasive about his love life. Did you speak through an interpreter?

Reed: No, he spoke English.

Brian: Did you prod him to answer questions, or was he talkative?

Reed: He wasn't talkative at first, but then he ended up liking me, I think. He talked more than he did at first.

Brian: Did you take shorthand notes?

Reed: No, I don't take any shorthand. I just write constantly until my arm drops off, while they're talking. And I used most of it, nearly everything, in that interview.

Brian: One of the fascinating things was the sketch Mastroianni got from Fellini when he asked for a screenplay of the proposed movie, or at least a description of his role. Did he show you the sketch?

Reed: No, he was on the set so he didn't have it with him. But I'm sure he's kept it. (Fellini sent a cartoon showing a man on the sea with his sex organ going down to the ocean floor and mermaids swimming around it.)

Brian: I've heard it said about Tennessee Williams, for example, that the best interview he ever gave, to Mike Wallace, was the day after his father died—when he was in an emotional state, off balance. Have you ever found that with people, if they were a little bit drunk or . . . ?

Reed: Yes. Oh, it's marvelous. Catching people at off-moments is the dream of any interviewer. Ava Gardner, for example, was quite loaded when I interviewed her. It was the most honest interview she ever did. And later she told a very close friend, Terence Young, as a matter of fact, when he was directing her in *Mayerling* . . . you know she was quite angry about the piece, I think, at the time, and later they were talking about it on the set of *Mayerling* and she said, "That son-of-a-bitch knows me better than I know myself." And I would never have gotten that interview that way, unless she had been in an off-moment.

Brian: Did you have any disastrous interviews that were either dull or impossible?

Reed: I don't think I ever had an interview that I didn't use. But I have had disastrous interviews that I've put to my own advantage. I mean, my interview with George Sanders was a disaster.

Brian: That was very funny. Did he ever react to it?

Reed: No, I never heard from him.

Brian: He sounded quite sick.

Reed: But he was really impossible. He wouldn't answer anything. And he wouldn't get into any subject. He was just rude, so I used all of that as part of the piece.

Brian: Did he reluctantly give you the interview in the first place?

Reed: No, it was all set up, all arranged. But when I got there he seemed terribly irritable and anxious to leave and didn't want to talk about anything. I kept wondering, well, why did I waste my time? And I couldn't decide whether to use any of it or not. And then I decided, well, I'll just write it exactly the way it happened instead of trying to make it into some depthy analysis of this man.

Brian: Did any interview stand out for you in that you personally found the subject fascinating?

Reed: Nine times out of ten I find the person fascinating. I end up almost always being much more fascinated than I thought I would when I got there. That's why I think people shouldn't really be reluctant to do interviews, because, although you don't know what you're going to say, after you get there sometimes the person makes the interview for you.

Brian: Anybody you wanted to get very much who refused and still refuses?

Reed: Yes, Katharine Hepburn, but she never did refuse. She just never could arrange her schedule to see me, so it never came off. I was supposed to interview her when she opened in *Coco* and she asked for me, as a matter of fact, and it was all arranged and then she canceled the interview because she was going somewhere. And then we set it again, and she was going away for the weekend. It just got to be one postponement after the other and finally it was too late to do the interview, the show had been running too long. So . . .

Brian: Would you still try?

Reed: Yes, I'd love to do an interview with her. But I haven't asked her again.

Brian: Are you naturally curious about everyday people or just extraordinary people?

Reed: I'm curious about everybody. I think a good journalist is always a voyeur and a Peeping Tom.

Brian: Would you like to get away from actors and directors and interview politicians and scientists and so on?

Reed: Yes. And I probably will. I have done some of that. I did a piece on Lester Maddox, the governor of Georgia, and it's still my favorite of all the pieces I've done. It was in *Esquire*.

Brian: Do you have a vivid memory of your childhood, either frightening, exciting, romantic, or traumatic, that you quite often think back to?

Reed: Uh . . . nothing really frightening that I can remember. I remember . . . the most . . . I was very close to my family. We were extremely close. My mother and father were my best friends all my life. The most terrible thing that I can remember is the time my father got angriest at me. And it was all my fault. And of course I felt terribly guilty about it for years [chuckles] after that. It's probably not of too much interest to people, except that I was reading a book at the kitchen table and he asked me to go and get his house slippers, and it made me so angry that he would *dare* to ask me to leave my book instead of fetching them himself, that I went and I got the house slippers and I spat in his house slippers. And when I brought them back [chuckles] to him, he put them on and he said: "These slippers feel wet." And of course I became *terribly* . . . er . . . Well, I knew that I couldn't possibly ignore it, because they were wet. So I said, "I sneezed on them." And I remember I got . . . it's the only real thrashing that I can ever remember getting. And he always said he did it, not so much because of what I did, but the fact that I lied to him about it. So that is ... I've always remembered that for some silly reason.

Brian: What sort of boy were you? Were you bullied or did you bully?

Reed: No. I had a very lonely childhood, really. I wasn't ever in the position of being bullied because I didn't know anyone my own age. My father worked for an oil company, we moved around all the time. And I was always the new kid in school. I went to thirteen schools before I ever graduated from high school. There was never any time to make lasting friendships or anything. So I was terribly lonely. I had no brothers or sisters. And I was always with older people. So I sort of gravitated towards books and movies and things because there was never any time to join in any of the local ... You know, I wasn't terribly athletic because I didn't have time to get to know the kids long enough to belong to any of their teams or anything. I mean, it was just a very lonely kind of life.

Brian: Is there any quality that you recognize in yourself that you've inherited from your father?

Reed: Er ... oh, yes, a lot of them. I'm not sure that any of them are particularly literary, or flattering. I think that my ability to save money I got from him. He was always very frugal and he always had money in the bank and money put away for a rainy day and I've always been conscious of that. And he was always a very fair man and I've always thought that I had a lot of compassion. He and my mother were not especially opinionated types. I mean they never got involved in issues, and I don't know where I got that. That seems to be something that I picked up [chuckles] on my own.

Brian: Do either of them say what they really think of people as you do?

Reed: No, not really. My father was always very

outspoken about people, but always behind their backs. [Chuckles.]

Brian: You had a lot of chutzpah to do those interviews for *The Times,* saying that you were from *The Times* when you weren't. Do you have a lot of nerve? Would you approach the so-called unapproachable people?

Reed: I don't know if I would or not. Some of the people I have approached are pretty unapproachable. George C. Scott is certainly not easy. There have been several.

Brian: Did you have any boyhood heroes?

Reed: I'm sure I did but I can't remember who they were. As I became a young man I began to admire writers more than anybody else. James Agee has always been a great idol of mine. The Southern writers like Truman Capote are my favorite writers.

Brian: Do you have strong opinions about other interviewers?

Reed: I thought Lillian Ross was wonderful and I think Gay Talese is brilliant and those are probably my two favorite interviewers.

Brian: Do you believe that a public figure is entitled to keep some areas of his life private?

Reed: I think he's entitled to do whatever he wants to do, but then I think that reporters are also entitled to try to find out. [Chuckles.]

Brian: Could I have your reaction to these names? Ted Kennedy.

Reed: I think he's been a political disappointment, but personally I admire him very much. I admire people who show that they're human, you know. But I think that maybe politically he's harmed himself.

Brian: Chappaquiddick didn't disillusion you?

Reed: No, no. Because I think he's one of the few politicians that we know who is human. The others do terrible things behind everybody's back and hide them. At least we know about Teddy Kennedy. It makes him a little more likable and human to know that he's fallible.

Brian: Tennessee Williams?

Reed: I think of Tennessee Williams as an injured, bruised, gentle kitten. A gentle kitten that's been bruised by inhumanity and maltreatment. And I think he's the greatest poet who's ever written for the theater.

Brian: Elizabeth Taylor?

Reed: Um . . . I think she's the American dream gone sour.

Brian: Nixon?

Reed: I think Nixon is truly one of the . . . I don't know how to word it exactly, but he epitomizes everything I loathe and distrust. I think he's like a wiley animal. I wouldn't trust anything he did.

Brian: Does the same go for Agnew?

Reed: No, I trust Agnew to be always true to his own boorishness, his own narrowmindedness. Agnew is right out in the open saying it like he feels it is, even when it isn't. But Nixon is worse because he's a tester. He's the one who sends Agnew out to test the water first, before he goes in. He's like the pariah legend, you know, who lets his side-kick taste the food to see if it's been poisoned by the cook.

Brian: Ernest Hemingway?

Reed: I was never a great admirer of Hemingway's. I never liked his writing very much. It was too simplistic. And I've always felt that he was a bit of a hypocrite. I mean his ethical code that he always advocated for a man's man to follow was the very thing that he was never able to follow himself. So, in retrospect, I think his writing is not to be taken too seriously.

Brian: As a man, have you ever been really scared?

Reed: I guess not. I guess I've been very lucky. I've

never been, you know, threatened by a street gang. I've never actually encountered the horrors that I know exist in New York. I've never been faced with any kind of physical threat. My apartment has never been robbed. I've never . . . No, I guess I really don't know anything about that, but I'm probably the most vulnerable person in the world since almost everything scares me. You know, to get a traffic cop, I have to practically go to bed for three days with tranquilizers because it upsets me so much.

Brian: You mean if they stop you?

Reed: Yes.

Brian: Why? Do you speed?

Reed: No, but I mean I have been stopped for turning left from a righthand lane and there's always that feeling [chuckles], when a traffic cop walks up to your car, you want to say: "Yes, officer, I'm guilty. Please let me go. I'm sorry." A guilt for everything else we do in life, I guess, always comes out when we're faced with a policeman.

Brian: You share that with Alfred Hitchcock, that fear of policemen.

Reed: Yes. I'm terrified of policemen. I've never felt safe with policemen.

Brian: Have you ever been really angry, really lost your temper? Perhaps you did it with the director of *Myra Breckinridge*.

Reed: No, I never really lost my temper on the set. I guess not. I'm pretty good at holding things in.

Brian: What makes you cry? Do you cry easily?

Reed: No, I don't cry easily and I don't laugh easily either. But I cry sometimes at very silly things, you know—I saw a Pluto cartoon once that made me cry for two days.

Brian: Could you explain why?

Reed: It had something to do with the ill-treatment of a tiny animal. And I cry in old Margaret O'Brien movies a lot. I cry almost always if a child is mistreated. Anything to do with children makes me cry.

Brian: Although you weren't mistreated, apparently, as a child.

Reed: No, but I wasn't really a happy child either.

Brian: Because you were lonely?

Reed: Yes. And anything about orphans or children being mistreated or children losing their parents or things like that. I remember a picture called *All the Way Home,* which was really, you know, the book that James Agee wrote. It was based on *Death in the Family.* I've never been quite the same since that film, it moved me so much.

Brian: As it's so hard for you to laugh, who or what does make you laugh?

Reed: Well, I find that very subtle things are the only things . . . I'm a very bad audience for a comedy.

Brian: Do you think there is a purpose to life, and, if you do, what do you think your purpose is?

Reed: Oh, gosh, that's a very difficult . . . that's awfully hard to answer. I guess my purpose is mainly to try to expose the things that I think are either good or bad or right or wrong about life and to try to influence other people into seeing it, when they might otherwise overlook the wrongs or the rights. And, hopefully, to be respected for my efforts in so doing.

Brian: Do you believe there is a life after death?

Reed: That I don't know. I'm not an atheist and I'm not an agnostic. But on the other hand I've grown so far away from the church since leaving home and living in New York that I really don't know. I haven't really thought about that in quite a while. I think we're here for a purpose. I don't think we're here accidentally, because otherwise we wouldn't have the intelligence that we have. I wouldn't really have any desire to continue through life with all of its pain and all of its disillusionment if I didn't think it was leading to something that's more important than what's going on right now. I guess I do believe there is a life after death.

Brian: Have any of the extrasensory things happened to you? Have you ever seen a ghost or been to a séance?

Reed: No, I never have, but I'm fascinated by it all.

Brian: Have you ever spoken to anyone you trusted who had a psychic experience?

Reed: I don't know if I trust actors, but a lot of actors insist, you know, that they . . . I mean I've met people who live in houses that are supposedly haunted, and they've "seen" people. And I've heard all of these experiences. But I'm very rational and realistic and I don't believe much of that. I'd kind of like to. I'd *love* to believe in witches and vampires and things. I often wish that they were around, you know. I'm fascinated by all of that.

Brian: Did Sandy Dennis ever interview you as she said she wanted to after her anger following your interview of her?

Reed: No, and I'm not sure she was really angry. I mean that has all been publicity, because I've seen her several times since and she's been more than charming.

Brian: It was your writing about her dirty feet and the cats' hairs in the glasses that was supposed to have offended her.

Reed: That's what I heard, yeh. And it may have. Sandy Dennis is a very strange girl, so it might have offended her one day and then she might have been not offended the next.

Brian: You have a reputation for being brutally frank and reporting whatever you witness during an interview, no matter how distasteful. If a subject, for example, was disgusting during an interview and didn't apologize, would you feel it fair to describe it as happening—if *The New York Times* would print it?

Reed: Yes, I would feel it was fair but I wouldn't do it, if I found it very offensive. I just wouldn't write about it. But I think anything is fair in an interview.

Brian: In that case, by omitting it, you'd be using your own taste?

Reed: I still am my own editor.

Brian: If you read another interview and that was done you wouldn't think it unjust?

Reed: I would think the interviewer was tasteless more than unjust.

Brian: What didn't you like about Candice Bergen's pieces about you? (Candice Bergen, actress daughter of Edgar Bergen, had interviewed Reed for *The Los Angeles Times*. It wasn't flattering.)

Reed: She came to my apartment before it was finished and all the workers were here and all the carpenters and all the painters. And she said: "And what is this going to be?" And I said: "This is going to be such and such." And she said: "What's going to be here?" And I said: "I'm going to have a tiger-skin rug here." And then she wrote the interview like the whole thing was me telling her this, taking everything out of context. And the whole thing sounded like: "And now I'm going to do this in lemon yellow, and this will be tiger-skin . . ." It just made me sound very pompous.

Brian: I think a lot of reporters remove the questions when they write up their interviews and at the very least it makes the subject sound more garrulous than he is.

Reed: Well, everyone does that and I've done it myself. You cannot just have a question and an answer. It doesn't make a very readable piece. But it was done in a very different kind of context. It was done to make me sound different than I really sound. I have run lots of quotes together to make an interesting paragraph but I don't think I've ever used people's quotes to make a point of my own, by giving them a different tone of voice for example.

Brian: Mr. Reed, you give the impression that you don't enjoy life, that you're an angry man, almost bitter. Is that true?

Reed: No, I don't think so. No, I enjoy life, I *suppose*. I guess I'm not enjoying it too much lately, because it's all work and no play.

Brian: Perhaps you give this impression because so many actors and actresses, after finishing a movie, say "It was marvelous. The director was wonderful. I've never enjoyed myself so much in my life." And after your first film, *Myra Breckinridge,* you said: "It stank!"

Reed: Well, that particular film really did. I wouldn't have said that if I hadn't felt it. I should never have agreed to do that film. I was very unhappy the whole time I was out there in California and I'm very bitter about the film, all of that is true. But I don't think I'm bitter about life. I'm rather bitter and unhappy and sad and disillusioned about man's inhumanity to man. I don't think people are nice anymore, at least in New York. I think maybe I should get out of New York for a while and see.

Brian: I imagine you're fairly liberal in politics.

Reed: Yes, very.

Brian: Have you ever tried to interview Garbo or J. D. Salinger?

Reed: No, those are two people that I would like very much to interview. I don't think Garbo would be very interesting but I think Salinger would. Garbo would just be a curiosity. I know a lot of people who know her and they say she's one of the dullest women in the world. Interesting only because she's mysterious, but that can be a bore after a while.

Brian: Do you believe that everyone has a price?

Reed: I don't think I could answer that because I really don't know.

Brian: Do you think you have a price?

Reed: I mean, for what? I have a price for a book, yes, but there are other things that I don't, that I wouldn't . . .

Brian: To work with the *Myra Breckinridge* director again, for example. Would you do it for a million dollars?

Reed: I would work with him for a million dollars [chuckles] if the property were right [chuckles]. I wouldn't do anything like *Myra Breckinridge* again for a million dollars.

Brian: No money would persuade you?

Reed: No.

Brian: Do you have any weakness or bad habits you confess to? Anything you dislike about yourself particularly?

Reed: Oh, there are physical things that I don't like. I keep pretending to give up smoking all the time and I don't. I'm probably basically a very insecure person. I don't know why, but I just am. I'm very shy and I'm always terrified of all these people when I go to interview them. I would probably be a better interviewer if I were not shy. I get so terrified that I end up having terrible headaches. Almost everytime I do an interview I come home with a splitting headache.

Brian: It's an ordeal?

Reed: It is really an ordeal. I have also a nervous habit. I bite the inside of my mouth a lot, which is very bad, and I'm always afraid of cancer—things like that, which I'm sure everybody has, you know.

Brian: Are you interested in drugs?

Reed: No, I'm not at all interested in drugs.

Brian: If you had a million dollars tax free, d'you know what you'd do?

Reed: I'd try to buy some peace . . . for myself . . . not especially for the world, I don't think. I think that everyone is obligated to make himself as happy and peaceful within the structure of a hostile society and therefore eliminate the hostile society. So I'd get away from everything and work on a novel. I have two novels outlined but I haven't really had any time to work on them.

Brian: D'you get much surprising mail?

Reed: I get a lot of marriage proposals, which is very odd. They've seen me in the movies and they've seen me on television and they've decided I'm a nice young man. And what a nice husband I would make for their niece and things like that. I get invitations to meet women's daughters and nieces all the time. And then I get a *tremendous* amount of requests for help. I get all kinds of letters from mothers whose children can't dance and they don't know David Merrick and they want me to introduce them and that sort of thing.

Brian: You ignore that mail?

Reed: I generally do. I try to answer nearly everything unless it's insulting. I mean I get kook letters. I have a kook file that I put everything in. Denise Minnelli, who's a friend of mine, keeps saying, "Save all of that because some day it'll make a wonderful book, just all of the nut mail that you receive." I don't know what kind of mail other writers get, but I think critics are most vulnerable because anybody who's in a position of expressing an opinion is vulnerable, because there are always people who disagree. I would imagine that editorial writers would get a lot of hate mail. I get mail from Barbra Streisand fans who want me to drop dead, you know, and things like that.

Brian: You're probably the only man who's starred in a movie who also has his number listed in the phone book. Is this because you're also a journalist?

Reed: Yes. I don't answer this phone very often. I have a service on this line. I also have a private unlisted number that nobody has. And I answer that because I know that [chuckles] it's somebody I want to talk to or they wouldn't have the number.

Brian: But I imagine a few people get through whom you don't want to talk to on your unlisted number.

Reed: Well, I've been pretty lucky; nobody really has yet. Get wrong numbers and things like that, you know. You have to be very careful who you give it out to. If you give it to press agents, for example, then they have files that people can find. I know people who are so insecure about their phone numbers that they have them changed constantly. Paul Newman has his number changed, I guess, about every six weeks. I have a string of phone numbers for Paul Newman and Joanne Woodward and everytime I call them the number has been disconnected and they can't give out the new number . . . and I have to end up writing them a letter or something and that happens all the time.

Brian: Your unfulfilled ambition is to write novels?

Reed: I would have said a year ago: "To be in a movie." Now I've done that.

Brian: And it was one of the unhappiest experiences of your life.

Reed: Yes, one of the worst things that ever happened to me. So now I want to write a novel.

Brian: Are you easily bored?

Reed: Yes.

Brian: Are you enjoying this?

Reed: Yeh. I mean, I . . . yes. Because you've got questions that have never been asked me before and they're fun. I love the challenge of being asked anything.

Brian: Have you any criticism so far of the way it's gone?

Reed: No, I think the questions are marvelous. They're much more imaginative than any of the things I ever asked anyone. I should be writing all these questions down.

Brian: Have you any superstitions that are unusual for an actor, or for anybody?

Reed: Let me think about that. I mean superstitions are kind of silly, I think, as a rule. But I'm very uptight about more than two people on a match. I really don't like to have a cigarette lit if two other people have used the same match. I have a lot of quirks and things but these aren't superstitions. I won't let anyone borrow a book or a record, for example. And I can't bear to see a glass set down on a tabletop and I can't bear to see anything set on a phonograph record, you know.

Brian: The book and the record are because you treasure them?

Reed: I guess because I treasure them and want them to last forever.

Brian: If you were landed on the moon with one companion, who would you take, of the people you've interviewed?

Reed: If I had one choice of all the people I've ever known it would be Tallulah Bankhead, for the simple reason that I never heard her say anything boring, as long as I knew her. But I think I'd rather have my record collection than a person. [Chuckles.]

Brian: Would you call any of the people you've interviewed near to genius or saintliness?

Reed: Uh, saintliness . . . I can't think of any that I've interviewed that I would consider a genius. I think that word's been overworked. But saintliness. Yes, there have been some. I think Jean Simmons comes very close to that. She's a very saintly person. And I think Melina Mercouri is a very saintly person.

Brian: Is this an impression you get from them, or from what they've done?

Reed: This is strictly from them as people. In the case of Melina Mercouri it's also very closely connected with some of the work she's done for other human beings. But they're totally different types, the two of them, so they're saintly on different levels and in their own way.

Brian: One very English and one very Greek.

Reed: Well, aside from that, in their temperaments and in their lives. Their approach to everything is different but in their own ways they're both really good human beings.

Brian: Have you ever been near exhaustion or nervous breakdown and contemplated psychoanalysis?

Reed: Almost every day of my life. [Chuckles.] I've ... in fact I'm contemplating it right now. I have never considered suicide and I would never do that. That doesn't interest me at all. There are too many things that I would miss, so even on a trivial level I can exist, simply waiting for the next thing to happen, so I would never want to give everything up. But I'm easily fatigued and I'm exhausted most of the time. I have very low energy levels, very low capacity for doing anything. And so that, I would say, leads me into severe depressions. But I'm also a very strong person in that I don't think I really need analysis because I know exactly what's wrong every time this happens, and I'm usually able to be my own analyst.

Brian: But you haven't got a cynical attitude towards psychoanalysis?

Reed: Oh no, not at all.

Brian: Is there any quality that specially attracts you in other people?

Reed: Compassion. The ability to overlook people's weaknesses and forgive is a very admirable trait.

Brian: Is there anything that repels you?

Reed: Deliberate cruelty of one human being to another. Especially if the other human being is defenseless.

I abhor boorishness and I abhor bullies and I abhor people taking advantage of other people. I mean I loathe anyone who would mug an old lady or hold anybody up. Or take unfair advantage of somebody.

Brian: If you could change one thing in the world, as if you were God, what would it be?

Reed: I would change the whole . . . oh gosh, that's a big question. What I would really do, is . . . is make everybody tolerant, I guess, of everybody else. I'd like to make sure that no child was ever born into the world unwanted, for one thing.

Brian: What's the most pleasant thing anyone's ever said to you?

Reed: I don't know, because the flattering, nice things are the things that you always tend to put back in your mind and you don't remember them, strangely enough. I've been flattered a lot as a writer and I'm embarrassed by flattery, so I tend to forget those things.

Brian: Have you had a shatteringly unkind comment?

Reed: [Chuckles.] Oh, I have those quite often. I just think that to exist as a person, as a writer, as an artist, as a creative person of any kind, it is *very* necessary to turn a great deal of the world off. You have to really tune out and be your own person and be responsible to yourself and for yourself. And I'm a strong believer in that: that every man is responsible for his own soul. And so I'm not too influenced by the opinions of other people, or what other people say or think about me. I mean, I've just had to toughen myself to a certain degree. The worst experience I ever had was I met Richard Harris at a Hollywood party at Jennifer Jones's house and he screamed and yelled and insulted me in front of a whole roomful of people and . . . er . . . for no reason. I mean, I'd never even met the man before, never written about him, never even reviewed him in a movie. And he was extremely insulting and for some strange reason it bothered me terribly because he was drunk and you don't punch Richard Harris in the nose because he's seven feet tall, you know, and loves to break people's houses up at four o'clock in the morning, and would have enjoyed nothing more than to bring the police in the middle of the night to the Selznick estate. So the only thing I knew how to do was just to say: "Goodnight. It was nice meeting you." [Chuckles.] Or something. Then I worried for days after it, because I thought I was a coward and everybody told me that I wasn't; that I behaved the only way that a gentleman could behave. And that, I guess, is the thing that I remember the most. That I've really kept with me for some odd reason.

Brian: You, in fact, walked right out?

Reed: So I walked out, yes.

Brian: Would you like to interview him?

Reed: No, never. The thing is, he never interested me at all. And I think one of the reasons that he was angry was because I really had been totally indifferent. I was a person there who had a reputation for being a power, if you will, as a critic, as a writer, as an entertainment observer, and I had paid very little attention to him. And in his neurotic need for attention he resented it and became abusive and now I'm even less interested [chuckles] than I was before.

Brian: In the Bette Davis interview I remember you said she mentioned Errol Flynn and then evaded the subject. In his autobiography, *My Wicked, Wicked Ways*, he said he almost hated her.

Reed: I don't think they got along very well, but she didn't go into a lot of detail. She just said: "Oh, the things I could tell you about him." Many actresses told me things and asked me not to print them and I have always respected their wishes. She told me many other things [chuckles] that she asked me not to print. She's terribly honest.

Brian: It's disappointing when people tell you the best things in an interview and then ask you not to print it.

Reed: Sometimes I argue with them. I say: "Oh, come on, that's so good." And sometimes they say, "Do you really think so?" and you can talk them into it.

Brian: Do you have to pay for writing what you believe to be the truth about people?

Reed: I was recently asked to do some liner notes for Columbia Records and the only album that I was interested in was the new Barbra Streisand album and they said, "Well, you're probably the only writer that she'd never allow to write them." So it backfires on you. I once wrote a very nasty review of a Nancy Sinatra television show and I have never since been able to see any of the clients that Frank Sinatra's press agent handles, because of the pressure from the Sinatra family.

Brian: Does this mean that you'll modify your opinions?

Reed: No, of course not. It just means that there are some people that I won't be able to write about. But there are hundreds of others that I can write about [chuckles] who are probably more interesting anyway. I only mention these things to show what happens when you aren't diplomatic. But I'd rather be true to myself, I'd rather be honest and let people know what happens, than hide these things for my own benefit. I suppose my reputation has been built on the interview and I don't know exactly why. I just started writing things that I wanted to write. It's very strange since the only C I ever made in journalism was in feature writing. I rated A's and B's in everything else, but in feature writing I rated a C because I tried to be different, and it was rejected.

Brian: I think Winston Churchill got bad marks for history when he was in school.

Reed: A woman at Mae West's press conference in New York raised her hand and said, "Miss West, what advice can you give for a child who is very bad at arithmetic?" And Mae West said [imitating her], "Don't worry about it, honey. I was always bad at arithmetic too but there was never a year in my life that I didn't make more money than Albert Einstein." Which may or may not have anything to do with what we're talking about, but I do think you have to be, I really think you have to be, true to yourself.

Brian: Mr. Reed, thank you very much indeed.

Reed: I hope I gave you something. I mean, I don't consider myself an intellectual, so I probably didn't give you as many interesting answers as some of the other people have . . .

Brian: I found it very interesting . . .

Reed: . . . but thank you very much for your interest.

Brian: . . . and good luck with your writing.

Reed: Okay. 'Bye.

Jack Thomas

PRESS SECRETARY FOR GOVERNOR LESTER MADDOX
OF GEORGIA

Brian: Are you familiar with Rex Reed's interview with Governor and Mrs. Maddox that first appeared in *Esquire*?

Thomas: That was an atrocious piece of writing. Governor Maddox was quite upset about it. I remember one criticism by a very close friend of the Governor. There was some comment in the article about Mrs. Maddox wearing Thom McAn shoes, implying that she was a very cheap dresser; and something about her hair, as though she hadn't been to the beauty parlor in months. Actually she had regular appointments, either once or twice a week, and her shoes were from a very expensive store here in town. She did wear good shoes. The gist of it is, this was a story written by a somewhat ignorant and biased Northern reporter about Georgia hillbillies, and I gathered from the story that he views all Southerners through this same tinge.

Brian: He is from the South, you know.

Thomas: He might have been from the South but he's a long way from it now.

Brian: His childhood was spent in the Texas area.

Thomas: Maybe until he was two or three or something, until he began to talk. But nevertheless, his bias showed through everywhere.

Brian: Yes, I wouldn't disagree with that.

Thomas: But Governor Maddox's attitude toward

things like this—for example, the play "Red, White and Maddox"—has been the less he says about it the sooner it will go away.

Brian: I know he has local newspapers taken off state property. Is it that he feels they distort or feels they're biased?

Thomas: Yes that's true in some instances. I've seen some rather blatant examples of plain biased reporting.

Brian: And they won't print retractions?

Thomas: It's the kind of thing it would be hard to retract. They rarely tell outright lies, but just implications here and there and putting things together that don't belong together, and taking things out of context and so forth.

Brian: Did Governor Maddox and his wife anticipate the Rex Reed interview might be a hatchet job?

Thomas: I'm sure the Governor never expected anyone to come in and paint a rosy picture, you know, that everything was great. But I think he had expected at least objective reporting.

Brian: Has he been interviewed on *The Today Show* or by Dick Cavett or David Frost?

Thomas: I don't think he has. He's had invitations to some of those but he hasn't accepted. He was on the *Joe Pyne Show* in California.

Brian: Well, that was one of the typically hatchet-job shows.

Thomas: Right, and that's what Joe Pyne attempted to do. [Chuckles.] And Maddox walked off the show.

Brian: Why did he accept that? Didn't he know that Pyne was a hatchet-man?

Thomas: He was apprised of it by me. I recommended that he not go. But we had all kinds of assurances from the producer and so forth that this would not be a hatchet job. And then, too, the Governor was of the opinion that Joe Pyne was a great American and a conservative.

Brian: Pyne gave that impression of being a conservative, I agree.

Thomas: But when he got out there Maddox noticed a couple of empty rows in front of the audience. And when Maddox came on stage they marched in about a dozen Black Panthers and put them in the front row.

Brian: And the Panthers questioned him, did they?

Thomas: They would have.

Brian: Did he walk out because of a specific insult?

Thomas: It just reached a point where . . . You know, it had been going downhill for several minutes and finally the Governor said, "I can always leave." And Pyne said, "If that's what you want to do, go ahead." The Governor said, "Goodbye, Joe," and put out his hand and Joe Pyne turned his head and wouldn't shake hands with him. What the Governor had objected to there was Joe Pyne wanted to keep talking about the old prison days in Georgia when the prisoners were in chains, and he asked him questions in such ways as to make it look like that was still the case, and that Maddox had something to do with it.

Brian: What newspapers were you with before you became the Governor's press secretary?

Thomas: I wasn't. I was working in a four-year Ph.D. program in psychology. And I stopped off with a master's degree and came with the Governor.

Brian: That's pretty good. I think psychology would be a great help. May I ask what you might take to be a naïve question? If the Governor's son had fought in Vietnam and his life had been saved by a GI who was a Negro: when they came back to the States would Governor Maddox, as the owner of a restaurant, refuse that Negro entrance—if he knew the man had saved his son's life?

Thomas: No. The Governor's attitude on race is rather difficult for most people to grasp. When he says, "I'm a segregationist, not a racist," it doesn't make much sense to most people. But he doesn't hate Negroes and he associates with them now, as he did back then. He regards them as human beings and had warm human feelings for them. But he simply does not want to get into situations where there will be intermarriage and where there will be an amalgamation of the races.

PART FOUR
Controversial Pair from the World's Greatest Paper

HARRISON SALISBURY
GAY TALESE

Harrison Salisbury

BORN IN MINNEAPOLIS, NOVEMBER 14, 1908

Name a forbidden place and Harrison Salisbury will try to get to it. Salisbury regards the Iron Curtain as something to be moved aside. He entered the previously forbidden Romania in 1957, then Bulgaria and Albania. He penetrated Mongolia in 1959 and reentered Russia—from which he had been barred for five years for what was considered to have been his unfriendly accounts of the place. But his biggest triumph—after eighteen months of beating his head against bamboo—was to reach Hanoi, North Vietnam, where he interviewed the enemy and got back home alive, only to face another enemy at home: fellow Americans who questioned his patriotism. In 1972 he became the first U.S. correspondent to visit North Korea and spent six weeks in China.

Salisbury was educated at the University of Minnesota. He started work on the Minneapolis Journal, then was with the United Press for about eighteen years winding up as foreign editor. He covered Al Capone's income tax-evasion trial in Chicago, and World War II from London, North Africa, and Moscow. In 1949 he returned to Moscow for The New York Times *and stayed five years. There Salisbury suffered the interviewer's nightmare: with few exceptions, from Joseph Stalin down, no one would talk to him. And what little information he could get was eviscerated by the censor.*

From Russia, Salisbury went to Birmingham, Alabama, and found it not so different. "Birmingham whites and blacks share a community of fear," he wrote. "Telephones are tapped, mail is intercepted and opened. The eavesdropper, the spy and the informer have become a fact of life."

Brooklyn, too, recalled Russia. "In some ways it was like a trip to Siberia," he said. His assignment was to write about teenage street gangs. Out of it came a book, The Shook-up Generation, *so full of meat that it was required reading for the New York police.*

Salisbury is a restless, driven dedicated man, who brings an almost religious attitude to his work. He gave up drinking and smoking to prepare himself psychologically and physically for his assignment in Moscow. He was still not smoking when I interviewed him. Tall, lean, white-haired, slightly stooped, he has a monkish air. Appropriately, the atmosphere of the tenth floor of The New York Times *where Salisbury has his office is that of a bright, comfortably furnished church. There's even a grandfather clock nearby with cheerful churchbell-like chimes.*

Brian: Interviewing Premier Pham Van Dong of North Vietnam, you mentioned scribbling down his answers to you. Had you rejected tape-recording?

Salisbury: I don't ordinarily use tape-recording—once in a while I do, in some special circumstance, but generally I prefer to take it down myself because, particularly when you're doing an interview where there is a translation involved, you have enough time to get the answers all down. . . .

Brian: It gives you a sort of breathing space to respond?

Salisbury: That's right.

Brian: Van Dong told you quite a lot off the record. Are you at liberty to mention any of that now?

Salisbury: No, I don't think so.

Brian: D'you feel it was very important?

Salisbury: Yes, some of it was extremely important.

Brian: Did any United States government officials interview you after your return from Hanoi?

Salisbury: Well, yes, I guess you might say that. I had several consultations with various people when I did return.

Brian: Did it go as high as the President?

Salisbury: Not quite that high.

Brian: The CIA?

Salisbury: No, I didn't talk to any CIA people.

Brian: What surprised me was that when Dean Rusk knew you were going to Hanoi—he was asked, "Have you any questions you want Salisbury to ask?" And Rusk answered: "No." Didn't that surprise you, too?

Salisbury: I think Dean figured that I would ask the right questions. I don't think that he felt that he had to put any to me.

Brian: After being told by the Catholics in Hanoi that they were free to worship, were you able to confirm this later through the Vatican?

Salisbury: I didn't go to the Vatican but I did talk *in extenso* with Monsignor Hussler (Secretary General of a German Catholic welfare organization), who was in Hanoi at the same time I was. And I consulted with him after I got out, and after he got out, on his findings. And his impression was, not that they were free to worship, but they were quite free or fairly free—freer than he had expected or I would have imagined.

Brian: Is this also true of Russia today?

Salisbury: I know the Russian situation perhaps better than I do the Vietnamese one, and my impression is that they're not as free in Russia as they are in North Vietnam.

Brian: In your novel, *The Northern Palmyra Affair* (Harper & Brothers, 1962), you wrote, ". . . so seldom was anyone what he appeared on the surface . . ." Was that true of Van Dong?

Salisbury: Perhaps less of him than of the people who were formed in that Russian crucible, because the Russian experience was so much one of internal terror and the paranoia that developed as a result of the executions:

so many people were killed by Stalin that people developed all these protective layers of personality which they used to protect themselves. Now Pham Van Dong comes from a much different sort of milieu. There was never that kind of internal terror in the Vietnamese party. He'd been in the leadership for a long, long time and Ho Chi Minh had established an entirely different atmosphere, sort of a collaborative one. So I would think that his personality comes through much more directly than that of one of the Russian Communist leaders.

Brian: But even in the best circumstances, with politicians of that caliber, d'you ever get much more than their guarded statements as a rule?

Salisbury: Well, it depends. And this depends a great deal on personality. You take a man like Khrushchev. He simply could not help revealing his personality and often revealing things that I'm sure he had no intention of revealing, simply because he was so expansive and he was carried away—as he was carried away into first-class diplomatic crises. But he certainly revealed a great deal of his personality. A man like Pham Van Dong is much more in control of himself.

Brian: Then you don't believe politicians can be typed?

Salisbury: No, I think they come in all sorts of shapes, sizes, and varieties.

Brian: Did you have any strong feeling about the kitchen debate between Krushchev and Nixon? Either who won or . . . ?

Salisbury: Yes, I happened to be sitting on the floor there jotting down notes in the same fashion, very furiously. I thought both of them comported themselves with a great deal of skill and ability. Each of them appeared as a champion of his own sort of ideology. And they stood toe to toe and argued very effectively on both sides, without losing their tempers.

Brian: Reading some of the material I got the impression that they were like two mothers-in-law praising their son or daughter as being much better . . .

Salisbury: [Chuckles.] Yes, that's a very good image. That's exactly the way they were.

Brian: Has your interviewing technique changed over the years?

Salisbury: Yes, I think so. In the early days it was much tighter and I had a series of very sharply defined questions and I was in a great hurry to put them across, bing, bing, bing. And as the years went on I've taken to a much more relaxed technique which I think is more effective, of letting the interview develop its own pace and establish a sort of a mood of interchange before bringing in the sharper questions.

Brian: D'you think that today's young journalists still use your young technique?

Salisbury: Some of them do and some don't. Again, I think it's a very individual thing. Lots of the very young ones do. They haven't had the experience to realize that this is self-defeating.

Brian: Was it *The New York Times* that heard you'd been arrested as a CIA spy and possibly tortured and killed?

Salisbury: [Laughs.] No. I don't know where that yarn came from. That was something that Talese has in *The Kingdom and the Power* . . . someone saying that there was a danger of that happening. And I tried to check that story of Gay's, after it was published, but the gentleman he got it from was unable to remember where he had heard it. So I think that's rather dubious.

Brian: Talese even mentioned your obituary had been updated.

Salisbury: Yes, but I couldn't find it. I looked all through [chuckles] the files to see if it was around. I could find nobody who admitted having ever written it.

Brian: Did you in fact feel it might happen?

Salisbury: Not as a real agent, no. But in the time of the so-called "doctors' plot" it seemed almost certain that *some* correspondent would be arrested to be a showpiece in the trial. And since there were only four of us in Russia at the time, we sort of [chuckles], we drew lots to see who we thought would be most likely to be arrested.

Brian: Who was it?

Salisbury: Well, I don't know. I'm just joking.

Brian: Had you any plans as to what you would have done if you had been arrested?

Salisbury: No, none at all. I did seriously think, in fact we all seriously thought, of getting the hell out of the country before it happened: but the story was too fascinating and we stayed on. Fortunately we weren't arrested.

Brian: D'you find any essential difference when you're face-to-face with a man you're interviewing in totalitarian and democratic countries?

Salisbury: Yes, usually the democratic man is much more at ease and, because of a similarity of attitudes, it's much easier to come to grips with questions. With the Communist leaders or totalitarian leaders, they're often very rigid in their minds and you have to angle around trying to find some key into some insight which they're trying to conceal from you.

Brian: And is it true that they could be executed if they gave you the wrong answers?

Salisbury: Sometimes this is true, yes.

Brian: As a novelist as well as a newspaperman, are you inclined to ask more personal questions to get a fuller picture of the man?

Salisbury: I try to get into the personal because it is a very good way of getting an insight. But I don't force it, because in some cases it's very embarrassing, as is true with some of these Communists who regard their personal life as sort of a closed book. But if they give me a little bit of an inkling, as they sometimes do, or if I am able to introduce the subject or something about my own situation, my own family, and then this opens up a little avenue I can move down, I'll dart down it as fast as I can.

Brian: Your persistence paid off magnificently with your unique trip to Hanoi, but the sixty letters you estimated you sent to Stalin in four years failed to get you one interview with him. Couldn't you have approached Stalin obliquely—possibly through other contacts?

Salisbury: No, I don't think so. At least if there was any other way of approaching him I don't know what it was. I know of no one who approached him in any other manner. Occasionally, if I happened to know of someone who was possibly going to see Stalin, I would put questions to them, to put in a word for me. But this happened very rarely, because actually he was seeing very few foreigners in that period of time.

Brian: He preferred to do the equivalent of answering Reston's questions impersonally, not face to face?

Salisbury: That's right.

Brian: If the Russians suspect the Jews of being Zionists or spies for the West, why don't they let them all leave Russia?

Salisbury: Because, after all, it's a very large number of people, perhaps something over three million: that's an extraordinarily valuable human resource just in terms of the contribution they make to their science, industry, and culture. And to their labor force. Also, were they to allow them to leave, with that number of people, they would automatically turn over to the West practically all the military secrets they have.

Brian: Oh, I see. But wouldn't it be true to say that only tens of thousands of Jews would want to leave Russia?

Salisbury: No, I don't think so. I estimated at one time—I don't know what the situation might be now—that if they were given freedom to leave, they would lose upwards of a million, maybe a million and a half people.

Brian: That's almost half of the total Jewish population in Russia. Did you talk with any Communist writers? I remember you gave a list to the chief of the Russian press department of people you would like to interview and you were told they were all out of town.

Salisbury: Oh, in the very early days I used to run into a very rare, occasional man at a reception or something of that kind. But it was extremely difficult to see any of them in that period.

Brian: Did the few you contacted ever state or imply that they envied the freedom of the artist in the democracies?

Salisbury: Not in that period of time. That would have been very dangerous to say. Nowadays, they say that, if they happen to believe it, fairly freely.

Brian: Did you ever hear the *Voice of America* broadcasts while you were in Communist countries and were they effective?

Salisbury: It depends on which period of time. You go back to the earliest period when they first began, I think I was in Russia at that time, '48 or '49. Then they were singularly ineffective because they were very hard-nosed, hard-line, argumentative, very strongly influenced by extreme *émigré* organizations who were extremely opposed to the regime, which was fair enough. But the Russians in Russia felt that it was very antagonistic and unsympathetic to them. Then, over a period of years it gradually improved until, say ten years ago, it was damn good. I don't know how it is now. I haven't heard it in recent times.

Brian: You had a very frustrating time with the Russian censors, particularly in the early days. Did you ever get to the point where you could ask if there were any ground rules?

Salisbury: We often asked the question. But since the only way you could ask it was by sending a note to the censor, and since he never responded to your note, you were left just as much up in the air as you were when you started.

Brian: It was really like Alice in Wonderland in those days.

Salisbury: Exactly.

Brian: But from Russia you wrote very frank letters to the executives at the *The New York Times* explaining your dilemma. Couldn't you have included news in those letters?

Salisbury: Well, in fact I sometimes did. That all came back through courier channels, not through the open mail, and I did sometimes send back news in that fashion.

Brian: Through diplomatic pouch?

Salisbury: We didn't use the pouch, but there were always travelers going out who could take things for us.

Brian: If the Russians had no enemies, if say the United States and China didn't worry them, d'you think it would become a freer society almost automatically?

Salisbury: No, I don't think so, because this is a very deeply ingrained sort of cultural, almost historical tradition. It might speed the evolution of their society, but it wouldn't happen overnight.

Brian: Is there anyone you wanted to interview very much, apart from Stalin, whom you never got to? Someone who intrigued you?

Salisbury: Yes, there'd be quite a few people in that category, certainly. I would very much like to have interviewed Akhmatova, the poetess (she's now dead). I wanted very much to go down and see Mikhail Sholokhov, the writer, even though he threatened to horsewhip me if he ever saw me.

Brian: Why was that?

Salisbury: I'd written a story which exposed some of the rewrites of his *And Quiet Flows the Don* because of censorship. But I would have loved to have talked to him. In recent years I would have liked very much to talk to Molotov. Impossible. And in more recent years I would have liked very much to see Mr. Khrushchev again. But it was impossible to see him.

Brian: Did you have any memorable interviews while you were in England during World War II—with Churchill, for example?

Salisbury: I saw Churchill several times but only with other newspapermen. He rarely gave interviews. He was not fond of newspapermen. Bernard Shaw didn't give many interviews either. He used to answer postcards. I remember sending him a postcard or two and getting a cryptic answer or two back.

Brian: I phoned his home once during the war and had a brief conversation.

Salisbury: One of our reporters just went down to that little house he had in Hertfordshire and walked in on him one day and got a hell of a good story.

Brian: That seems to be the secret with a lot of people.

Salisbury: That's right.

Brian: What would have happened if you'd done that in Russia?

Salisbury: I've done it in Russia but the difficulty is finding out where the man lives.

Brian: Was the Gay Talese account of you in *The Kingdom and the Power* accurate, generally speaking?

Salisbury: Oh, fairly so, yes.

Brian: Talese writes of your being nicknamed "Rasputin" and saying to someone who handed you a piece of paper: "When I drop a piece of paper on the floor that's where I want it to stay." Were you just kidding?

Salisbury: That was a joke. [Laughs.]

Brian: I'm glad you're laughing. Just before I came here I told this one question to my wife and she said, "Ask him that at the end of the interview."

Salisbury: [Laughs.] Marvelous!

Brian: I said to her, "I think he was kidding."

Salisbury: That's right.

Brian: Why wouldn't Talese have put it in his book, then, that you were kidding?

Salisbury: [Laughs.] It makes a better story. Gay was never one to spoil a good story.

Brian: You assented to that, eh?

Salisbury: Yep.

Brian: Did you feel when you were given the "garbage" story to do on your return from abroad that the editors were trying to pull you down a peg?

Salisbury: It could well have been that way, but since the editor was a rather pedestrian-minded man who didn't much differentiate between one assignment and another, I couldn't tell. [Chuckles.]

Brian: Did you then consciously set out to write a block-buster about garbage?

Salisbury: I did consciously decide to do that. I thought it would be fun to show what could be done with garbage.

Brian: Did you think Talese was fair to Clifton Daniel and Margaret Truman in his book?

Salisbury: No, no.

Brian: Was that just because he didn't like them?

Salisbury: I think that they're just different kinds of cats and they never did get along and it came out from the very beginning: they never could get on the same wave length.

Brian: What's generally the reaction of the others on *The Times* to the book?

Salisbury: I suppose it depends to some extent on how he treated people. But generally people were interested, sort of titillated to have a book about *The Times*, and the gossip is good, the stories are good, the reporting is pretty good.

Brian: Almost every sentence is interesting: I thought it was extremely well done.

Salisbury: Right.

Brian: Can you imagine such a book being written about one of the Russian newspapers?

Salisbury: No, but I wish it could be. Fascinating! Be a deadly story!

Brian: Would Gay Talese be welcome back to work for *The Times?*

Salisbury: Oh, I should think so. I'm sure he doesn't want to, but I don't think there'd be any feeling of that kind against him.

Brian: You don't think Daniel would give him a "garbage" story to cover?

Salisbury: Oh, he might. [Chuckles.] And Gay might do pretty well with it.

Brian: Is it true that you now have a dream assignment to travel and write as you wish?

Salisbury: Well, not at the moment. I'm editor of the Op Ed page (Opposite editorial columns) and that keeps me right here at the desk.

Brian: Can you express your purpose in life?

Salisbury: To do my best at illuminating the world in whatever areas I am competent to do that in.

Brian: Is there a quality you most like in people?

Salisbury: Yes, I think directness.

Brian: Apart from the opposite, is there one you most dislike?

Salisbury: Well, I guess there is a quality I dislike enormously in people. I dislike politicians that lie. Especially when they lie when they know that you know it, and you know they know.

Brian: Even when they lie "for the good of the country"?

Salisbury: [Quickly.] Yep.

Brian: You'd rather they didn't speak?

Salisbury: Exactly.

Brian: Have you ever been in a situation when you thought you were about to die?

Salisbury: Uh-huh. Yes.

Brian: Did you have any special feelings?

Salisbury: I was scared. [Laughs.]

Brian: [Laughs.]But you know the cliché about one's life flashing through the mind?

Salisbury: No, my life didn't flash by me. I was just frightened to death.

Brian: Is there any interviewer whom you specially admire?

Salisbury: Yes, there's one. Studs Terkel. I think he does the best job of interviewing of any man I've ever encountered. He's marvelous. He's interviewed me on two occasions and I've never seen anything like it for skill, for sensitivity, for having done all of his homework and knowing really more than I know about the things he was going to talk about.

Brian: Do you think America is the freest country in the world and has the freest communications system?

Salisbury: Yes, I suppose so. That is, the system is freest, but I don't know if the results that are given by that system are as effective as you sometimes get when you have to work a little bit harder at it. Maybe it moves too freely, so that things flow out without the gears turning over.

Brian: Are you completely free to say what you think of government officials, if you have facts to back up your views?

Salisbury: Oh yes, I think so.

Brian: What do you think of Rex Reed as an interviewer?

Salisbury: I think he's terribly amusing and quite naughty.

Brian: Edwin Newman?

Salisbury: He's more conventional.

Brian: Mike Wallace?

Salisbury: Mike, at one time, was the master of the tough-guy approach, which I don't happen to like. I think it creates false drama for television and I don't think it's necessarily revealing at all. When he dropped that I think he became extremely good.

Brian: David Frost?

Salisbury: Extremely good, very good on homework, very sensitive, very, very quick on the uptake. Has the wit to be able to forget that sheet of questions in front of him and pursue a topic when it evolves—which most of the people that run shows like David does have no ability to do at all.

Brian: When you and others got questions together to ask Khrushchev, did you bandy questions around and have a consensus as to what would be the effective ones?

Salisbury: Each of us put down about ten or fifteen questions. Then we got together and looked at what each had done and we consolidated them and perhaps seeing each others' questions suggested a few more.

Brian: Some people say that the interviews President Nixon gives are a waste of time because the interviewers never ask penetrating questions and they're too tame. D'you agree?

Salisbury: I don't entirely agree. This is a criticism I've heard periodically of presidents and their press conferences since the days of Roosevelt and it's always somewhat valid, because to some extent the President is in control of the situation and it's fairly rare—it depends on his own skill—he can control it almost entirely and once in a while a reporter may be able to penetrate and get through something which the President doesn't anticipate or doesn't really want to answer. But a clever President—a man can always command a press conference if he knows what he's doing. And it doesn't make any difference how damn clever the interviewers are, because you can always duck and twist, especially if you're President and have the authority of the office. So I believe in the President's press conferences and I don't really expect that much of them. I do think that perhaps television has made it easier for the President, in that reporters tend to be so eager to get on television that they get up, without regard to what the President has just said, and pop another question. Instead of as it would happen around the President's desk—if there was a crowd of men, they'd probably follow through.

Brian: D'you think that as much as can be discovered of a public figure should be revealed in his lifetime?

Salisbury: Well, I don't know. That's a terribly complex and philosophical question. It depends on the figure and what there is to discover. If you're thinking, for example, of Dag Hammarskjöld and his remarkable strain of mysticism or superstition or whatever the devil it was, which seems to have been concealed from the world during his lifetime and then exposed in a major fashion after his death, I would say that, well, it perhaps would have changed one's view of Hammarskjöld entirely to have known in what fashion he viewed himself. But since he kept it completely secret, he obviously didn't want it to be known publicly. Does it make any difference that we didn't know it? I just don't know that it makes any difference. On the other hand I can see where a public figure might be hiding something of enormous importance, which would give you a clue to why he makes his judgments in a certain way. So that it would serve a great purpose. Supposing it had never been revealed that Hugo Black had belonged to the Klan. Maybe Hugo Black would have been an entirely different man. Maybe it was the revelation of that which caused him to rethink his whole life and philosophy and make him determined to leave a record which would be a monument to a man without prejudice. So I don't see how one can be, you know, black and white on that question.

Brian: D'you feel possibly that *The New York Times*, by publishing the secret Pentagon study of the Vietnam

War (June 13, 14, and 15, 1971), has redeemed itself for not having published more about the Bay of Pigs operation in advance?

Salisbury: I don't think there's any question of redeeming. We published more than anyone else about the Bay of Pigs. It's not a question of redeeming yourself for something you have done or haven't done. I think you set the record straight everyday.

Gay Talese

BORN IN OCEAN CITY, NEW JERSEY, FEBRUARY 7, 1932

Gay Talese describes most journalists as "restless voyeurs who see the warts on the world . . ." He chose to write about the warts on his fellow journalists on The New York Times, *where he had been a skilled and embarassingly observant newsman for ten years. Then for over two years he interviewed* Times *newspapermen past and present, encouraging them to recall their feelings and thoughts as well as their words and actions in the domestic dramas that went on in the "fact factory." In the book that resulted,* The Kingdom and the Power, *here's a Talese-eye view of managing editor Clifton Daniel:*

"He's a most interesting-looking man but difficult to describe because the words that quickly catch him best, initially, seem entirely inappropriate for any man who is a man. But the impression persists. Clifton Daniel is almost lovely. . . . He actually became so enraged at one of the younger editors, Tom Wicker, the new bureau chief in Washington, that he pounded his fists on the desk several times, screaming and shouting, his soft chin trembling."

And of assistant managing editor Harrison Salisbury, Talese wrote: "The Washington bureau, not unexpectedly, was quick to condemn him, with one reporter nicknaming Salisbury 'Rasputin' and another explaining, 'Salisbury spent so many years watching who was standing next to Stalin that now he's standing next to Stalin.' The mere sight of Salisbury, to those who do not know him, conveys a sense of severity, a chilling aloofness. He has an angular face with a slightly drooping gray moustache over thin lips that rarely smile, and his small pale *blue eyes peer without expression through steel-rimmed glasses which, worn out of habit, do not appreciably improve his adequate eyesight."*

Talese went to work as a copy boy on The New York Times *in 1953, and left as an outstanding reporter. Besides* The Kingdom and the Power *he has written* Fame and Obscurity *and* The Overreachers.

When I first interviewed Talese he was completing a book about a Mafia family and through intense work was close to mental and physical exhaustion. Some months later I spoke with him again and he was a different man, relaxed and lighthearted. "Now I can speak somewhat more freely about my book," he said. "Before I was worried about the Justice Department. Until I finished the manuscript I was worried about subpoenas and having the manuscript taken from me. Now I'm not worried about that. It was not the great George Raft characters coming after me with dark limousines I was worried about. It was the nice, sweet men from the Justice Department. The title of the book,* Honor Thy Father, *is new journalism beyond what I did in* The Kingdom and the Power *and the interior monologue is much more part of the structure and of the writing style." He is currently (1973) working on a book about the sexual revolution in America.*

Talese has an immaculate, bright apartment on New York's East Side, with photographs on one wall of himself as a reporter at work. In one he and a New York policeman stand on either side of Frank Costello, a man who fascinated Talese. In another he is listening to Dr. Martin Luther King. Talese is a lean, pleasant-looking man, a neat dresser, with an air of being both kind and earnest.

Brian: Was it true that after you'd written your book about *The New York Times, The Kingdom and the Power*, Harrison Salisbury was the only one of the staff who would take you out to lunch?

Talese: Yes. Well . . . that would talk to me. Actually, he did take me out to lunch, that's true. Right away, yes.

Brian: I've interviewed him and he seems very pleasant.

Talese: Did he say anything about the book?

Brian: He seems to have enjoyed it very much.

Talese: The rest, their attitude is a rather benign reaction, somewhat condescending.

Brian: You had a pretty good review in *The Times Book Review.*

Talese: I guess it was a fairly good review. But the daily review was awful and I subsequently got a bad review of the collection that I have out now (*Fame and Obscurity*).

Brian: I asked Harrison Salisbury about the account in your *The Kingdom and the Power* of how he dropped a piece of paper on the floor and someone picked it up and, according to you, Salisbury said, "When I drop a piece of paper I mean it to stay there." And I said to Salisbury, "Why did you say that?" And Salisbury said, "I was joking." So I asked him, "Why didn't Talese write that you were joking?" And Salisbury said, "Gay wouldn't want to spoil a good story."

Talese: [Chuckles.] Oh shit!

Brian: Is this true?

Talese: No, of course it's not true. But it would be true from the way Salisbury would see it. Now all of us quite honestly, with the same sense of dedication to the facts and proper interpretation, can see things entirely differently. Salisbury is not known for his sense of humor, I assure you. And when he does anything, even drops a piece of paper on the floor and he makes the remark that he made—being a humorless man essentially, I don't think he would be inspired to humor on something like that. Of course, after the event when one has to interpret the trivial detail . . . I mean, I remember Salisbury talking to me about that and he said, "God, I remember doing that." Of course I didn't get that from him; I got it from a man who saw it and heard it right on the desk next to him.

Brian: But Salisbury does have a dry sense of humor.

Talese: When he's out of the office.

Brian: You think maybe he was irritated on that occasion in the office?

Talese: I knew Salisbury in various ways. I knew him in the office and he was not known for his humor in those days, 1962–63. He was the office hatchet man. Now that doesn't mean that after hours, in his own home or at a social gathering, he wasn't charming and capable of more than just a wry sense of humor. He could be rollicking. But that's the Salisbury outside the office. The Salisbury in the office is a dedicated, serious person and humor does not creep into his style readily.

Brian: I asked Salisbury if *The New York Times* would have you back after that book and he said: "I don't see why not, but I don't think Gay would want to come back."

Talese: I've never been asked, I'll tell you.

Brian: I said I thought you'd been cruel to Clifton Daniel, whom I don't know, incidentally, but it seemed a cruel portrait.

Talese: Yes.

Brian: And Salisbury said, "My feeling was that Gay and Daniel were never on the same wave length. Cats of a different color sort of thing."

Talese: Could well be. Incidentally, I think Salisbury may even be doing a book on *The New York Times* himself. I've heard this, not from him. Be interesting. You'd get an entirely different point of view from Salisbury, I think, than from me.

Brian: So you're convinced that he wasn't trying to be funny about the paper on the floor incident.

Talese: My source claimed that there wasn't any jest on Salisbury's face. It's just a matter of one referee seeing it one way and one the other. Salisbury is not a comedian. A most serious man, a most serious journalist. His personality around the office was that of sobriety and also his physical appearance, with those glasses, that moustache, and that piece of hair that always seems to be falling over his right eyelid [chuckles] gives the appearance of anything but humor.

Brian: You make him sound like a benevolent Hitler, or his older brother.

Talese: [Chuckles.] In 1961-2, when he first became an editor, a lot of people weren't sure whether "benevolent" belonged in that phrase of yours. He's not really that way: he gives the appearance you see. He's actually a man of charm and sincerity and very casual . . . away from the office. I've been to his home and he's a gracious person.

Brian: As an interviewer how would you resolve something like this? (Was Salisbury joking as he says he was, or serious as a witness says he was, about the fallen piece of paper?)

Talese: Let's say that Salisbury feels, as Dwight Macdonald apparently does, about journalism that I suggest is worthy journalism, something worth exploring. Let's say that Salisbury says: "Look at Talese. Here's an example of how parajournalism, new journalism or whatever, inclines to distort by being factually correct—but quite wrong." In this case the journalist, me, has to know a hell of a lot more about his character than even he reports. I knew Salisbury quite well before that anecdote came up. I knew my character. So that if the character behaves in a way that I think strange, or out of character, I would be alert to that. I don't think there's anything so tricky about the new journalism. In fact I'm not even sure it's new.

Brian: I spoke to Truman Capote who said: "I started the 'thought business' in *In Cold Blood*."

Talese: Interior monologue?

Brian: The writing down what people were thinking,

after first asking them what in fact they were thinking at the time.

Talese: Well, I wasn't influenced by Capote. I didn't even know who started it. I don't know if anyone started it.

Brian: Capote said that you saw his *In Cold Blood* in *The New Yorker* . . . before it went in *The New Yorker*.

Talese: He said that I, Gay Talese, saw it?

Brian: That's right.

Talese: Well, it's wrong.

Brian: Do you know him?

Talese: Yes, I know him because he's published by Random House and I've met him. (Talese's wife is an editor with Random House.) But I never knew him before *In Cold Blood*.

Brian: Capote wasn't making a big thing of it. He said it with a sort of chuckle. And he said you saw it before it went in *The New Yorker*. I presume he meant in proof form, galleys.

Talese: Oh no, of course not. I would have no access to *The New Yorker* magazine.

Brian: My feeling is that the mood and motive of people are so complicated, one's own mood and motive for example aren't always clear to oneself.

Talese: Did you read, sir, did you read the foreword that I wrote to *Fame and Obscurity?*

Brian: I did, yes.

Talese: All right. Well, the people that got me interested in pursuing this kind of journalism were two fiction writers, Irwin Shaw and John O'Hara. Now Tom Wolfe has given me credit for this. I'm not sure Wolfe is right. Maybe Mark Twain stole it from some fine English essayist in 1818. I have no idea. I don't care. I'm not going to say as Capote apparently did . . . It's absurd, because none of us knows what's going on outside of our little arena, which is our head.

Brian: Capote admits that he wasn't absolutely original: that Lillian Ross had done it before him. Not wanting to pursue this too far, but you remember I told you that Salisbury had said, "Gay wouldn't want to spoil a good story and I went along with it"?

Talese: He went along with it? He never knew I had that story. That's where Salisbury is wrong. And it's so easy to check him out on that. Salisbury read that story in *Esquire* magazine and it later appeared in the book. I didn't go to Salisbury and say: "Harrison, did you drop a piece of paper and say, 'When I drop a piece of paper on the floor that's where I want it to be'?" I knew the person who told me that story, a man who was sitting on the desk which Salisbury was in charge of, and I knew that person quite well, a person who did not tend to exaggerate things. But I didn't go to Harrison and say: "Harrison what about this anecdote here? Is it true or false?"

Brian: So you're basing his motives on what you know him generally to be like, and it wouldn't be anything exceptional to expect from him?

Talese: Oh, of course not. In fact I knew anecdotes that were much more what he would consider good stories that I'd be reluctant to see in print. Salisbury wishes to present himself as doing it as a joke and some very naïve journalist misunderstood his wit. So, in other words, it's Salisbury again pointing out wrongness in others. Yes, that's not one of Harrison's greatest qualities. [Chuckles.]

Brian: It was obvious that you didn't like Clifton Daniel or Margaret Truman. Did that in any way prevent you from interviewing them carefully?

Talese: Oh no, I interviewed them. And this kind of journalism, this very suspect form of journalism which may be very old or quite new, in any case legwork is what's involved. It's research. It's old-style reporting. It's getting to know your people very, very well. And there's a certain point at which most of the more traditional journalists would be ready to write, but a new journalist would have to spend a lot more time on research. It's a much more ambitious form.

Brian: How did Clifton Daniel or Margaret Truman respond to your portraits of them in the book?

Talese: I didn't get any response in writing. I have been in *The New York Times* since that book appeared and I got a friendly reception from Clifton Daniel. I don't suggest that he likes the book. I don't know what he thinks of the book, honestly.

Brian: How did James Reston react to your portrait of him?

Talese: Well, Reston is a man who has rarely been criticized. He's been so careful in his own writing, where, if he's not so aligned on the side of the angels, he is critical in such a general way either through soft humor or by taking a position that isn't so overwhelmingly negative; he manages the way, I guess, that Bob Hope as a comedian does, to be able to offend but not to lose his friends. Reston tends to be rather pontifical, serious, always presents himself in a way that he writes his column, that he's a man of concern, a man of serious concern, with a warm heart . . .

Brian: You feel this is a true picture?

Talese: I think it's true insofar as it goes. But Reston is also a very clever politician, in his own affairs as an editor on *The New York Times* and as a columnist representing *The New York Times* in Washington. Now Reston was quite offended by my portrait of Reston which by no means denigrated him as a first-rate journalist, but presented what he was in the office, and also was critical of him in pursuing the official line in Washington as he, for example, did on the Nixon motion with regard to that peace overture in Vietnam. Reston is pretty much the establishment columnist in this country. I'm sure if you said to him: "Do you consider yourself the establishment columnist?" you'd get a song and dance from him that he wasn't, you know. What is the point of this?

The point is that I interviewed people who weren't normally accustomed to being interviewed, people who, after the book appeared, were not accustomed to *reading* about themselves as an Arthur Miller would have been or Dean Rusk, for example, someone who was used to being bombed now and then . . .

Brian: It would make them uneasy.

Talese: And also very defensive about what's in print and quick to say, "I wasn't really being serious." Now if you went to Tennessee Williams, who has been bombarded regularly through his long career, he'd never be able to say, "I wasn't really being serious."

Brian: In a case like the Peter O'Toole interview, because you don't tape record, did you reconstruct your conversation when you got back?

Talese: I wrote what I remembered and wanted to use and when I left anything out I put dots. I don't string . . . you know, if I remembered four sentences out of nine I wouldn't string these sentences together even if they seemed cohesive. *The New Yorker* had a form of reporting where they would quote a person continuously sometimes for several pages. I never believed that. I always thought that was fake, in a way. Because they never gave you the impression that the person was interrupted: the person was talking, monologue, beautifully constructed monologue, and there was never a break, never a question from the interviewer. Undoubtedly there were questions from the interviewer. But the person being interviewed would go on and on and on, making wonderful transitions from one thought to the other. And I never knew how these interviewers got such marvelous long quotes.

Brian: They just eliminate their questions.

Talese: I don't do that.

Brian: Does Frank Sinatra interest you as a person or do you think he's a subject that people want to read about?

Talese: No, he interests me. There's no piece that I've done in that collection, *Fame and Obscurity*, that I didn't, myself, want to do. It would just be too hard for me to deal with people I don't want to.

Brian: I read somewhere that Sinatra behaved badly to people because of a sense of inferiority, through a lack of education.

Talese: Well, if you or I had to put up with what he has to put up with, I guess we'd be intolerant oftentimes. Sometimes, I imagine, he could be very, very nice. Very good for an interviewer. But I think one of the things he was worried about when I was out there in Hollywood was the Mafia connection. You see, he had been written about in the papers as having gangster friends. Well, I don't doubt that any performer, especially a nightclub singer, has gangster friends, because nightclubs aren't owned by George Plimpton's father, you know. Naturally if you're in the business of entertainment and for thirty years have been a singer, you're going to know some people that are going to be on the Attorney General's list of bad guys and sinners. Sure Sinatra knows gangsters. Hell, I know gangsters. A journalist knows gangsters. I know some gangsters I think a hell of a lot more noble than some of these priests that I know, too.

Brian: Did you say priests or police?

Talese: Both. You know, some of the men of the cloth and some of the FBI, presumably law-abiding cavaliers of our society, are pretty shady characters when you see them in their own element, too.

Brian: Is there anyone you particularly wanted to interview and you were never able to get?

Talese: One I wanted to get very much was a gangster named Frank Costello. In 1957 there was a famous case of Apalachin, New York. Then sixty-five alleged Mafioso leaders appeared in that little town, specifically in the backyard of a little home loaned by a man named Joseph Barbara, now dead. And I remember the tremendous splash made in newspapers in this country about that what they called "summit meeting" of underworld figures. But one of the major figures in 1957 was a man named Frank Costello. I was fascinated with Frank Costello. In my library I have a large picture dominating one side of the wall, of Frank Costello coming out of jail. He was one of the great bootleggers in American subculture and I wanted to write the history of bootlegging in this country during the twenties and thirties. And here was a man who was servicing the needs of a large market. One of the curious things about American law is that it prohibits whatever the human flesh craves: liquor in those days, maybe marijuana, prostitution, gambling, whatever. The law says we shall not do this, and human beings say we will do this, whether it's legal or not. I'm interested in the market and the demands for things the law disallows, and even though the law disallows these things the market demands them and there are always going to be middlemen who are going to be suppliers of these illegal demands. One of the great suppliers was Frank Costello. I wanted to write a book about him. He was a man who did not exercise, but what he did in lieu of exercise is steam bath. He used to go to the Biltmore Hotel steam room where he'd soak out with such people as Bernard Gimbel; the former heavyweight boxing champion, Gene Tunney; Hank Greenberg, a famous baseball player; Sidney Weinberg, a Wall Street financier; and a lot of other men who are members of the establishment in this country. And among them was this great supplier of illegal demands, Frank Costello. He was with them at four o'clock every afternoon at the Biltmore bath house. And I went down there and I spent several days trying to get an interview with Frank Costello, to try to make contact and convince him that he had a story he was going to carry to his grave and I wanted to do that book about him. I did make contact with him. I got pretty close to him. I talked to his lawyer, Edward

Bennett Williams. It would involve a lawyer, in the sense that Costello was wiretapped, there were bugs in his house, and they had men following him around. I was really interested in what he was like in the twenties when he used to have these steel-plated motorboats come shooting down from Canada filled with liquor and going into Detroit and the port of New York and Jersey, more likely Jersey. I wanted to know the logistics of bootlegging, that's what fascinated me. It would have been a hell of a story. And I got to him and he was interested a little bit. Actually, it failed. All my ambition and the trips I made to Washington didn't get me anywhere. His lawyer explained to me that Costello was worried about me writing a book about him because he didn't want to be deported. The law was kind of laying off Costello a little bit in the latter part of 1959, because they had other villains to worry about and Costello was then in his middle sixties and I think kind of out of the operation. And Costello didn't want to rock his own boat. He was worried about being sent back to Sicily or Italy.

Brian: Did you have any opinion about the Malcolm Cowley, Lillian Ross, and George Plimpton interviews with Hemingway? Did Hemingway interest you?

Talese: Sure he did. Absolutely. I remember A. E. Hotchner's book *Papa Hemingway* and, in some place, I believe it was there, Hemingway claimed he was kidding—doesn't that remind you of Salisbury's remark?—Hemingway was talking like a drunken Indian. D'you remember Lillian Ross's article? A lot of people were very offended at her making fun of the great man himself, but I don't think she would have faked it. I don't know Lillian Ross but I respect her work tremendously. But he might have been kidding. And she didn't indicate that. So Hemingway was probably saying as Salisbury was saying to you: "Don't you know I was really kidding?" Plimpton's interview was excellent for what it was, Hemingway sitting for a formal portrait. Lillian Ross was doing him in the act of a dance, she was getting in the movement. It was very effective. I don't remember the Cowley interview but I do remember the longer work by Hotchner, which I thought was very, very good. Probably the best book ever done on Hemingway.

Brian: Were you impressed with Rex Reed's piece on Lester Maddox?

Talese: Yes. I'm impressed with a lot of Rex Reed's pieces. He's done some marvelous pieces. One of the best I've ever read was on the actor James Earl Jones. Excellent. Wonderful reporting. Rex Reed is a first-rate reporter.

Brian: Do you think when people accuse Rex Reed of doing a hatchet job that he is in fact reporting accurately?

Talese: I think he has a way of "turning on" his subjects. I don't know how he does it, because I've never seen him work. He, for example, uses a lot of direct quotes. You notice how some people talk for paragraphs and paragraphs? But I believe Reed. I believe they did say those things. I believe if they didn't, word would quickly get around that Reed fakes quotes, and I don't think you could stay in this business if you fake quotes.

Brian: Have you consciously changed your interviewing technique?

Talese: I'm attempting now to report what goes on within people's minds and I'm not quoting them. I'm reporting thinking. And also reporting people changing. That's another thing I was never able to do before, but now I feel I want to and am capable of doing it. The way to do that is stay with your subject for a long time, years if you can, if you can afford it financially, to watch them move through situations that influence their life, report how they deal with these changing situations and how the situations change them. Reporting change. A very, very fascinating line of work. It reads like fiction. It's not fiction. What I do is describe what's happening to people. Now a lot of people who are writing novels are doing less than that and are claiming to do more. The value of this kind of reportage, the excitement, is that it's dramatic, because situations involving living people are very dramatic, revealing, pertinent. And yet to have that which seems like fiction, very dramatic situations that seem fictional, to be true—indeed to have occurred to people who are indeed alive—adds an element of fascination to the written word. And I think the reader would sense this fascination. It gives an art form to reporting: reporting has always been an art form, except that many reporters didn't want to indulge in it or work at it as an artist works at a craft. Is that clear?

Brian: Yes, it is. I know you're not trying to be different, but isn't that really what Capote did in *In Cold Blood* when he stayed several years with the murderers?

Talese: Sure. I mean, God, I think Capote's *In Cold Blood* was a magnificent work. An absolutely magnificent work. Capote is a magnificent reporter. Capote is one of the rare people who has great talent as a reporter and he writes like a son-of-a-bitch.

Brian: How exhaustively would you interview for a biography?

Talese: Well, what I've been doing since I finished *The New York Times* book—I went directly from one book into another—as you speak to me this month, I'm close to physical exhaustion. I've been close to that since the middle of the summer. I finished one book that took two and a half years, *The Kingdom and the Power*, in December of 1968. In January of 1969 I started the second book, practically going from one to the other. I went down to Key West to write the foreword for *The Kingdom and the Power*—I should have said the afterword, more properly. My wife and I were down there for a couple of weeks. Then I flew out from Miami to San Jose, California, where I had some people to interview in connection with what I've been doing this year and a half. It's a book about gangsters, a book about a particular family. I'm interested in the subject of organized crime in America. I had come to know quite intimately a family: by a family I don't mean in the sense that the Attorney General identifies family as comprising 400 machine-gun artists. I'm talking about a real family: father, mother, children, grandfathers, uncles, etc. I've come to know a family, a rather large family, back to three or four generations, who in one way or another are on the other side of the law. I've come to know them so well that I am now in a position with veracity to think as they think, which is a lawless way to think. I have about seven or eight hundred interviews. In the case of one person who is a major subject in my book, I have gone through every month of his life—he's thirty-eight years old—I've gone through every month of his conscious life through interviews, from his first year in school as a first-grader, right through high school, right through college, right through his first night in jail, right through his first crime, his first official crime, impressions that he has of his own misdemeanors, felonies, and those who exact judgment over him. I've really covered this man's life through interviews. The son is somewhat around my own age and I know this man very, very, very well: certainly know him better than his wife does. In many ways I could tell his wife things about him.

Brian: How did you persuade them to reveal themselves so fully?

Talese: When you're dealing with people who are considered lawless, if you can find people who have pride in themselves and who don't believe they're as bad as society is willing to believe they are, you can convince that person, as I think I have in two cases, that they have a certain amount of years left in their lifetime and that when they die their life as it is reported of them now, in newspapers and magazines, will be measured by what has been published about them, which, more often than not, has come off police blotters. It might be some

Sicilian numbers banker who has his whole history interpreted by some Irish cop in Brooklyn. I remember one case I said, "When you die some newspaperman will go into the morgue of his newspaper and get a file on you and in the file will be twenty or thirty clips ranging from the fact that you were picked up for running an illegal football parlor at CCNY in 1953 to the fact that you were accused of running a bootlegging concession here and there. And all your life, in the obituary itself, will consist of a series of sins. That which is reported about you," I said to the individual, "is a cop's version of your life. Surely your life is more than this? The other part of your life is how you see yourself. I'm interested in how you see yourself."

Brian: Was that enough for him to agree to talk?

Talese: This is not enough at all: timing and time were all important. . . . I'm interested, you see, in people who are really marching to a different drummer, who are out of step, who are living what is regarded as a lawless life. Why they do it, how they do it, and some of the problems of doing it. . . . I once wrote about the men who build bridges because they're not famous, because they're men who occasionally fall off and they don't leave much of a mark on their bridge. They don't leave their name plate; they don't leave a plaque hammered into the steel saying: "I, Sam O'Brien built this damn thing!" I'm interested in obscurity and I'm interested in defeat and I'm interested in what it's like to be disappointed and disillusioned. This is close to home with me.

Brian: When you say you're near to physical exhaustion, is that because you have a deadline to meet?

Talese: I do have a deadline but I can blow that. There's no one saying I have to make the next edition. Not anymore. It's just that I am so absorbed in this subject and these people, and writing of them, that I stay with them until I'm absolutely tired every night—I'm talking about the writing. I don't see them, obviously, I'm working now. And I don't sleep very well because I wake up a lot and I take sleeping pills just to get the machine turned off a little bit.

Brian: You wake up thinking about lines, or angles in the writing?

Talese: I wake up thinking about scenes. The whole book is scenes.

Brian: You must have chosen people with very good memories, because if you tried to take me over every month of my life, unless it was hypnosis, there'd be a lot of blanks.

Talese: In this case I had people with extraordinary memories. Do you know why?

Brian: They needed alibis?

Talese: Yes. They commit nothing to writing, you see. So they have developed memories, they are extraordinary. I've checked their accuracy. Peter Maas wrote a book called *The Valachi Papers,* and he told in that how accurate this man Valachi was. All these guys who are outside the law have remarkable memories. They don't put anything in writing.

Brian: Do you think any areas of a subject's life are sacrosanct or do you think, if the subject is willing . . . ?

Talese: If the subject is willing, there is no area sacrosanct. I myself, if I were the subject, if you were interviewing me and writing a book about my life as I am writing a book of other people's lives, be they editors of *The New York Times* or be they men who believe they own the waterfront, I would go as a portrait painter goes, not as a photographer. I'm interpretative. I try to get inside the character I'm writing about very deeply. And I believe some of the truths of these individuals are things that are going to be revelations to themselves, when they read about them, as much as they are to me when I discover them. I've gone into the personal lives, the private lives, of people that I've been writing about for the book now—their children, their marital relationships, their extramarital relationships—because they're all relevant to the understanding of the character.

Brian: If you were writing a book or an in-depth article about Truman Capote, would you ask him about his love life?

Talese: Most assuredly. And if he wouldn't tell me about it, I don't think I'd be doing it on Capote. For example, there's a very lovely Senator's wife that I know, and I'd be interested in writing about the Senator's wife and she could tell me what it's really like. And if she wouldn't, I wouldn't see any reason for doing it at all. I mean, I'd want to know all about her lovers, I'd want to know what she's feeling when she's with him in Washington. I'd like to do a story about the Senator's wife, but I wouldn't do it if I got some of this political pap that one would assume one would get. I'd ask Capote, sure, and I'm sure he'd ask me about mine. Indeed, Capote did pretty well with the people he wrote about.

Brian: He says his technique is to sometimes reverse the roles of interviewer and subject.

Talese: What I do is to reveal a good deal of myself, my own very personal life. I have no compunction about it at all. Sometimes I find that sharing experiences inspires a kind of confidence and gets them to reveal things about themselves that I don't think they would have done if the interviewer hadn't been honest about himself.

Brian: What was your reaction to *The New York Times* reviewer's comment that your piece on Joshua Logan was based on a cliché?

Talese: Look, anything *The New York Times* writes about my work, anymore, you can discount.

Brian: Is that, you think, because of your book about *The Times*?

Talese: Absolutely. I mean, I'm going to have to live for the rest of my life expecting little bombshells from that paper.

PART FIVE
Politics Right and Left

WILLIAM F. BUCKLEY, JR.
BENJAMIN DEMOTT

William F. Buckley, Jr.

BORN IN NEW YORK CITY, NOVEMBER 24, 1925

William F. Buckley, Jr., is a challenging interviewer who makes no pretense of being impartial. On his TV show Firing Line *he once invited three English liberals to turn the tables and interview him. In my opinion he emerged the winner—though in his encounter with a British Socialist, Richard Crossman, I think Buckley lost. Buckley can state his views in a sentence: "I have sought to revitalize the faiths of our fathers, because I believe that they knew more than we do about things that matter." He has interviewed Presidents and prize-fighters. His method is to invite men and women with strong opinions to defend their views and he acts as prosecutor or devil's advocate.*

Son of an oil millionaire, Buckley was born into a conservative and Catholic home, one of ten children. After graduating from Yale in 1950 his book God and Man at Yale *was published. He wanted more of God. Of his coauthored book* McCarthy and His Enemies *of 1954, Buckley wrote: "Our ambition was to set down the facts upon which a responsible judgment can be made of the issues Joseph McCarthy raised, through the years that made him prominent." Buckley tried and failed to become Mayor of New York City and wrote a book about it in 1966. He was appointed by President Nixon as one of the five members of the board of advisers to the United States Information Agency. It is partly in that capacity that he traveled to such places as Russia, South America, and Northern Ireland.*

He is founder and editor (since 1955) of the National Review, a conservative magazine, and he writes a twice-weekly column of political comment that is syndicated in 315 newspapers. Buckley's most spectacular appearance on television was with his enemy (the feeling is mutual) Gore Vidal. During their televised comments on the Democratic convention of 1968, Vidal called Buckley a "pro-crypto Nazi," and Buckley said: "Now listen, you queer. Stop calling me a crypto Nazi or I'll sock you in your goddam face." After that they both used the pages of Esquire magazine to continue the fight. As a result Buckley sued Vidal for $500,000 in libel damages, and Esquire for $1 million; Vidal countersued for $4,500,000. The cases were settled out of court in August 1972 when Esquire agreed to pay Buckley's legal expenses of $115,000 and Vidal's counter-claims against Buckley were dismissed.

I first contacted Buckley through his secretary. She said that after being exhaustively interviewed by Playboy, Buckley was "interviewed out." He was also almost constantly on the move. And when he wasn't, he liked to relax by painting or playing Bach. But he found time. In fact I interviewed him twice.

Brian: Would it be fair to say that you have natural sympathy for Irish Catholics?

Buckley: I suppose so. I would have sympathy, I hope, for anybody who's been persecuted. And there's no question about their *historical* persecution. But there's no question in my mind that some of the solutions being called for by such as Bernadette Devlin are both out of this world and mischievous, which is a bad combination.

Brian: When you went to Northern Ireland, where there's conflict between the Catholics and Protestants, you could be reasonably unbiased?

Buckley: I think I proved I was, because in the wrapup column I published, people might accuse me of being too pro the Protestant side.

Brian: There's a quote attributed to Bernadette Devlin:

"There's a lot of religion in Ireland but not much Christianity." D'you feel that's reasonable?

Buckley: I don't think I know Ireland well enough. I would say that this would be true everywhere.

Brian: Everywhere where there is Christianity, ostensibly?

Buckley: Yes. Sure.

Brian: Did you see any unique solution to the problem?

Buckley: Yes, I proposed one, which was the abolition of the Stormont. Because it seems to me that the Paisleyites and, to a slightly lesser extent, the Devlinites have a leverage on affairs that is exaggerated because of the existence of the local parliament. If that were to be abolished—after all there's no counterpart of it in Wales or in Scotland—you have, I think, a situation in which the influence of the incendiary elements would be greatly diffused since it would have to be exercised through Westminster. And Westminster would simply get bored, you know, when Ian Paisley gets up and talks about popery. Therefore, you might then have ten or fifteen or twenty years of stability, during which people would gradually recognize that the other side was not bent on genocidal warfare against the minority. And then with their experience in a little practical pluralism, they might more logically decide, at a more convenient historical juncture, whether the next step would be union with South Ireland or genuine integration with U.K.

Brian: You think Westminster would be reasonably fair, compared to Stormont?

Buckley: I don't see that there'd be anything in it for them to be unfair. What they would in effect do is simply guarantee, or try to guarantee, civil liberties. As you probably know, there's a lot of unemployment over there. This is one of the reasons for the tension, because some of the people who get the choice living quarters and so on do so by political leverage. So that, if that political leverage is lost—for example, if Londonderry were governed by the majority—a lot of people who now occupy sinecures would be booted out and Catholics would replace them. This is one of the reasons for that tension. Meanwhile, of course, that stability would encourage more business, I think, to go over there and do something about the unemployment.

Brian: Not long before your visit to Ireland, you were in Russia. Why did they let you in, knowing you're so anti-Soviet, so anti-Communist?

Buckley: Because it was the line of least resistance. I had a diplomatic passport and although they had the right to refuse me entrance, to have done so would have probably cost them more adverse publicity than they got from my having traveled there.

Brian: How did you get your very anti-Soviet reports through?

Buckley: Ahh. [Laughs.]

Brian: Diplomatic pouch?

Buckley: As a matter of fact, yes.

Brian: Was there anything you liked about Russia?

Buckley: The caviar.

Brian: The people?

Buckley: Sure.

Brian: But nothing about the officials?

Buckley: I couldn't find a single redeeming quality in the officials.

Brian: You didn't change your mind about anything after going there?

Buckley: Before going, although I've read a certain amount, I guess I've read a great deal about the Soviet Union, I was not able to predict how *palpable* the totalitarian atmospheric pressure is. It really is that. And that I found *unbelievably* depressing.

Brian: Were you fairly free to speak with people or was there a list of those you could meet?

Buckley: As you probably know, anybody who's over there on a diplomatic passport has to have permission to do things which are granted routinely to tourists. So that, for example, simply to go to Nagorsk I had to get permission and apply for it forty-eight hours ahead of time.

Brian: Did you try to contact the underground?

Buckley: I didn't, in fact, try to get in touch with the underground. I was asked not to by the American security people. So I didn't.

Brian: Is there one political opponent that you found most persuasive in the years you've done your TV interview show?

Buckley: Most persuasive? As distinguished from most skillful?

Brian: One that you thought gave a very good account of his beliefs, to the extent that you found yourself very evenly matched, maybe even on the defensive.

Buckley: James Foreman was *extremely* convincing on the necessity of Federal intervention on the matter of equal restaurant facilities. Whether he would have been as persuasive, let us say, if I had been arguing with him on Vietnam policy, I don't know. But the combination of the subject and the man was very formidable, I remember, in that particular connection.

Brian: Although you wouldn't have opposed him on restaurants, would you? Did you?

Buckley: I oppose anybody on the basis of the principle of subsidiarity. It has to be shown that there is a reason to override the presumption *against* that becoming a state activity.

Brian: D'you feel that you were ever outmatched?

Buckley: I remember I had a debate with Senator Gore on the Tennessee Valley Authority and at the intermission for the commercial, he leaned over to me and said: "You know something, Mr. Buckley, I know more about TVA than you do." [Laughs.] Of course he'd been practicing it for twenty-five years. And in that sense, sure. Because, after all, as you probably know, the guest chooses in almost every case what it is he wants to talk about. And he normally chooses something which is his lifelong specialty. And, therefore, no matter how much time you give to reading up on the contrary argument, often you simply are at a disadvantage.

Brian: Were you honestly quoted when you said Bobby Kennedy refused to appear on *Firing Line* opposite you because, "Why does boloney reject the grinder?"

Buckley: Yes, I guess so, yes.

Brian: Did you think he was scared, really?

Buckley: It wasn't so much a matter of fear, in a sense of . . . I'm not suggesting that *machismo* was involved. What was involved, obviously, was that he saw nothing in it for him. If he was humiliated, that would hurt him. If he won, it wouldn't mean that he would get any more votes than he was going to get anyway. So I guess he just figured that there was nothing in it for him. And the Kennedys and a lot of politicians are very cunning about matters like that. They're perfectly prepared to subdue their natural combative instincts when they can be proved to have no instrumental purpose.

Brian: In an interview, you listed Gore Vidal as the one person you wouldn't want to appear opposite. And also somewhere else you'd called him "my enemy." Do you feel the same thing about Vidal that Robert Kennedy might have felt about you—that there'd be nothing in it? That the thing might be unpleasant . . . ?

Buckley: I don't think so. Because I don't think Kennedy ever doubted my honesty. At least, if he did, he never said that to anybody or me. And occasionally we'd exchange a little note or two. So I don't think there was any personal animosity there that I know of. Of course, we were hard political antagonists.

Brian: D'you think it's a mistake to try to assess contemporary history or the men in control before most of the facts have been obtained? This is specifically in regard to Prime Minister Neville Chamberlain, for example, and the Munich Agreement, as epitomizing appeasement.

Buckley: I think it's a mistake to assume that history has spoken finally on a subject like that. Another example, of course, would be Lindbergh, who was widely condemned in this country for having accepted the Iron Cross from Hitler in 1937. It wasn't until 1954 or 1955 that it was revealed he was under a Presidential request to do so, in effect for Intelligence reasons. On the other hand, it's simply, as a *human* situation, impossible to wait. In the first place you don't know when history's going to come in with the incremental datum and, in the second place, one has to make contingent judgments simply as a matter of necessity. For example, you have to know who to vote for.

Brian: A recent biography of Lord Dowding, head of R.A.F. fighter command during the Battle of Britain, maintains that Dowding and the British government pressured Chamberlain into the Munich Agreement, because they were poorly armed and desperately needed time to arm. So that, in fact, a new view of Chamberlain might be that he was the savior of the free world, rather than an appeaser.

Buckley: Well, as you know, there has been a very sympathetic biography of Chamberlain written saying that. However, as a matter of fact, it happens to have been a very early experience of mine. I heard him utter those words at that airport. He did say: "I bring you peace in our time."

Brian: Over the radio or in person, you heard it?

Buckley: In person. I was on my way to school. I think that he overacted his optimism, if indeed it's true that it was synthetic.

Brian: How do you respond to Arthur Schlesinger's quote: "In the last half century the only freedoms destroyed by increase of national authority have been the freedom to hire little girls to work ten-hour days in mills and sweatshops and the freedom to market fraudulent securities and the freedom to deny equal opportunity to people of other color." (In a *Playboy* interview.)

Buckley: [Laughs.] I think it's as silly as to say that freedom is unrelated to what you earn. It seems to me plain that the principal exercise of human freedom anywhere is by the free expenditure of one's own coffers, and when you have a situation in which 33 percent of the Gross National Product is preempted by the government, it seems to me that this is the plainest and most generic indictment of a government. There are other catalogues that I could go into but I think that's the most general one.

Brian: You think taxation is the most dramatic?

Buckley: Oh, sure. I guess everybody would agree that if they confiscated 100 percent, then there would be zero freedom. So therefore is it fair to say that en route from zero to 100 percent, freedoms are diminishing?

Brian: Are you able to reconcile the conservative goal of small decentralized government and the huge bureaucracy regarded as necessary to combat Communist aggression, actual or potential?

Buckley: Yes, sure. Because I do believe that *"salus publica lex est"* or whatever it is. For ontological reasons you cannot have fifty separate navies or fifty separate foreign policies. And under the circumstances it does become necessary for the single unit to *attend* to the business of the state, properly defined. The problem is always, of course, what James Madison called the government's tendency to turn every national contingency into an excuse for aggrandizing power in the state. And this was the great central thrust of the New Deal and one which is now being belatedly rejected by some of its erstwhile most enthusiastic advocates. For instance, executive supremacy is for the first time no longer the principal enthusiasm of such as Schlesinger, although they were *baptised* in it in the thirties and forties and fifties.

Brian: Could you make conservatism appeal to an untalented, possibly sick, poorly educated man, who had little money and very little prospect of making money?

Buckley: Oh, I think, obviously, yes. There has never been any study that shows that conservatism in America is primarily the enthusiasm of wealthy people. I give you, as an example, that Barry Goldwater had very little trouble financing his campaign, but it was all in dollar bills and five-dollar bills. I don't think there's any question about that. Because conservatism at certain levels appeals to values, to patriotism, to religion, to tradition and that is not, in America at least, by any means the monopoly of the best educated.

Brian: In the *Unmaking of the Mayor* you say: "Politicians can look you straight in the face and lie." And you mention F.D.R., Nixon, and Schlesinger. Would you lie for a good cause?

Buckley: I would lie to the extent that it was inescapably a part of my duty. For instance, if I were a diplomat and let's say the prime minister of this particular country said to me: "I happen to know that Nixon has the lowest opinion of me personally"—and I knew that that was the case—I would find it perfectly acceptable to say, "No, that isn't true."

Brian: Or "I don't know."

Buckley: No [laughs], if I didn't know, that would in effect confirm that it was true.

Brian: Have you ever lied in that respect?

Buckley: Yes.

Brian: What do you mean when you say that temperamentally you aren't a conservative?

Buckley: Conservatives are thought of as being, among other things, very prudent and very reflective before they act. I'm not all that prudent. I sometimes act impetuously.

Brian: Which might lead to this question. Do you regret your proposal for rehabilitation camps for welfare recipients?

Buckley: No. Hell, no. It's one of the best things I proposed and incidentally I was told shortly after by one of Lindsay's speech writers that they thought in their camp, even while they were denouncing it, that it was one of the most interesting suggestions that had been made.

Brian: How d'you reconcile it, though, with your belief in the freedom of the individual?

Buckley: I never said that people should be *conscripted* to go out there. In the first place I talked about experimental units and much the same thing has since been proposed, using slightly different language. But if you've got, let's say, a block, whether in Harlem or on the East Side or whatever, where there are known addicts, known mothers who neglect their children completely, the children are becoming addicts and troublemakers and so on and so forth, my point is that genuine rehabilitation is much easier done *outside* the context of the city than inside it. And you can't force, in most cases, these people to move—sometimes you can because there are, of course, laws in the book that authorize one to take children away from delinquent mothers and that sort of thing.

Brian: The stress would be on rehabilitation.

Buckley: Exactly, yes.

Brian: In *Up from Liberalism* you criticized Eleanor Roosevelt for muddled thinking, for saying she wouldn't shake hands with mass-murderer Hitler, but that she had shaken hands with Vishinsky, who you point out was responsible for mass murders too. How would you solve her dilemma, if you were working with Vishinsky at the United Nations?

Buckley: I would have shaken hands with him, but I would not then have proceeded to speak generally on the subject in the way that she did. I would simply have said that my diplomatic duties require me to engage in certain amenities. I have to admit that I would have done so with a certain amount of internal misgivings.

Brian: Did you in fact shake hands with the Russian officials on your trip?

Buckley: Oh, hell, yes.

Brian: With the same misgivings?

Buckley: I wrote about that as a problem that I faced, because actually it was the first time, and I wrote it in a little piece I did for *The New York Times*. With fewer misgivings than I would have in the case of Vishinsky for the very simple reason that the kind of people I shook hands with were professional bureaucrats. Now that doesn't excuse them any more than Adolf Eichmann, since he could have been called a professional bureaucrat. But I recognize that this is what one does now, and it would have been rather preposterous of me to go to the Soviet Union and refuse to shake hands.

Brian: On a recent *Firing Line* one of your guests mentioned several hundred children starving in the United States and the possibility of military men being able to help feed them. Were you able to do anything about it?

Buckley: It was something which has always annoyed me when it comes up, because in the first place the statistics are pretty damned elusive. And on one occasion, when I first heard this charge made on my own program, about people starving in New York City, I wrote a letter to Mitchell Ginsberg and a letter to John Lindsay. And I said: "Goddamn it, if people were starving in New York City, they oughtn't to be allowed to. Starvation shouldn't be permitted where there's an ounce of residue." And they both wrote back and said this simply wasn't the case. Since then I've come out for totally free food. The trouble with this business of people starving, like narcolepsy, it's a deduction. People simply deduce the fact of it. And then they simply go ahead and proceed on the assumption that the *cause* of that starvation was the unavailability of food, which may in fact have been and undoubtedly was and by definition is the proximate biological cause. But what the antecedent cause was is of course the social problem. If it's penury, which they go on to suggest, then the answer is obvious. But when it isn't penury, which is more often the case in the opinion of Mitchell Ginsberg, who's paid to know these things, and John Lindsay, then it's something else. It's addiction, neglect, whatever. And that becomes a much more difficult problem than seeing to it that the "Army feeds" the people who are starving.

Brian: So if he'd given you specific or accurate information you would have acted on that? But not on a general charge?

Buckley: I would have doubted his capacity to give me that specific information because people in the United States aren't waiting for me to act on starvation. There are twenty-five thousand ministers of the Gospel in New York City and if you assume that half of them are Elmer Gantry, that still leaves half who would see to it that somebody not starve if they knew where that incipient starvation was.

Brian: I feel that your opponents often say that you're

not interested in this sort of thing, so they try to catch you out.

Buckley: That's right. And I refuse to go into a Jack Paar kind of lachrymose exhibition in order to insist that I belong in the roster of the humanitarians, which is why I sometimes give the impression of being indifferent but I would rather give that impression than be completely sycophantic.

Brian: But you're not indifferent, there's no question about that, are you?

Buckley: [Laughs.] Well, if I were I wouldn't tell you.

Brian: Edgar Smith, the condemned murderer (since freed), regards you as his best friend. Did you share the name of the suspect he gave you with the man still investigating for him?

Buckley: Yes.

Brian: Does this man think it's a good lead?

Buckley: Of course he knows all about the possibility. It happens that he has another thesis. He thinks that the killer was somebody else. I think that he's dead wrong.

Brian: The only important thing I felt about it was Smith's loss of memory, when he describes himself as a cool man—why he should have a memory loss for that episode? That was the one puzzling thing to me.

Buckley: Yes, I think it was puzzling, extremely puzzling. Now, whether or not he has acquired his coolness is another question. I have the feeling that he has. Because he was a volatile young man and sort of given to total spontaneity. In the course of his travail he has become a man of absolutely total self-control.

Brian: Do you recall the Mike Wallace interview?

Buckley: He interviewed me half a dozen times.

Brian: Did you find him reasonably fair?

Buckley: Sure. I'll tell you, what he's most fair at doing is recognizing if in fact you have answered, satisfactorily, a reservation that he had. Some interviewers, if you answer them satisfactorily, refuse to admit that it's a satisfactory answer, in the sense that a lawyer will refuse to believe that his adversary has actually made the point. And Mike Wallace, I think, is awfully good on that.

Brian: Do you regret having said colored people are ready to form governments when they stop eating one another?

Buckley: I regret that it's quoted, and the reason I regret that it's quoted is because it's terribly unfunny unless it's done in the light of an immediate situation. It happened that that morning there was a report of cannibalism in *The New York Times*. So if I thought it was going to be quoted for ten years I wouldn't have said it.

Brian: Is there a quality in people that most appeals to you?

Buckley: Yes, spontaneity.

Brian: And repels you?

Buckley: Um, I don't like much people who are totally self-concerned. They're rather easy to spot.

Brian: Can you think of any?

Buckley: Did you ever read that funny little book by Galbraith called *The McLandress Dimension?*

Brian: No, I didn't.

Buckley: It can be summed up in a sentence. The length of time that people can go without turning the conversation to themselves. I think the McLandress interval would be very, very short, for instance, for somebody like Harry Truman, say in the fifties. He has other qualities. But that certainly wasn't one of them. He became a real megalomaniac.

Brian: This is like the actress who says: "Now let's talk about you. What do you think of me?"

Buckley: [Laughs.] Exactly, yes.

Brian: Here's an offbeat question, Mr. Buckley. Would you love your brother if he were a Communist?

Buckley: In the formal sense, I would, yes. In the theological sense.

Brian: Did you ever have an unexpectedly good interview, which you had expected to be routine?

Buckley: Yes. With George Reedy. And, you know, he had a reputation for being a sort of mousey little bureaucrat. He's really written a most extraordinary book, that's *full* of personality, vivid, exquisitely written. And the guy is just a first-rate human being. So I was terribly pleased by that. He was the press secretary for L.B.J.

Brian: Did you have a most disappointing interview?

Buckley: I'll mention it to you, but not for publication. Absolute disaster with _____. And there was no reason for it to have been because he's an incredibly bright guy.

Brian: Are you continually adding to your vocabulary with what some regard as esoteric words?

Buckley: Not consciously, no. I probably know fewer words every day than I knew a week earlier simply because one's memory tends to fail.

Brian: I remember the Jack Paar attack on you, as it were, for using more than one-syllable words. Your answer was that these words are necessary for politics, etc., and I wondered if you had learned them in your young days or whether you were so interested in words that every week you had a new one.

Buckley: It's commonly supposed that I have an enormous vocabulary. In fact it's not true. The difference is very simply that I habitually use what vocabulary I have more than a lot of people.

Brian: Half in jest, when you were interviewing David Frost, you proposed a question one might put to the Archbishop of Canterbury: "Is it all right to fornicate?" D'you think anything should be discussed among adults? Any topic?

Buckley: Provided the purpose is serious. We faced that at *National Review* a few months ago when we ran a piece on Chicago and it had a couple of "fuckings" in it. And then there was the usual wave of mail saying, "This is a family magazine," and so on and so forth. So I wrote a little thing and I said that in certain situations in my judgment it was impossible to proceed without being pretty explicit but that this was not to be mistaken by people who like the *National Review* as a license. Then I said, "Our policy is . . ." and I used a little Franglais for the fun of it, which roughly translated means "no fucking around."

Brian: Have you ever been shocked by people you interviewed?

Buckley: No. [Laughs.] I was constrained to tell Eldridge Cleaver before we began our program, that by sheer coincidence the cost of editing out a four-letter word was exactly equal to his fee. [Laughs.]

Brian: And he would have to foot the bill?

Buckley: I didn't say that. He drew the obvious conclusions. And he was saving money to lam the country . . . There was one "shit" but that was all. We didn't pull it out, but we recorded in the little thing that accompanies tape where actually it occurred, and then individual station managers made the decision.

Brian: Do you believe you have a purpose in life?

Buckley: Sure. To save my soul.

Brian: This is the purpose of every Catholic, isn't it?

Buckley: Yes.

Brian: Do you have anything other than that? Anything specific?

Buckley: You mean temporal?

Brian: Yes.

Buckley: Sure. To try to exercise one's talent. That talent which is death to hide. Remember? Milton.

Brian: Is that *Paradise Lost?*

Buckley: No, "On His Blindness." "When I consider how my light is spent, e're half my days in this dark world . . ." etc.

Brian: Have you much left unfulfilled? You've written seven books. And given, I think you said, one hundred thousand speeches.

Buckley: One hundred million. [Laughs.]

Brian: Would you like to write a novel, for example? Or a play?

Buckley: My guess is that I'll probably be writing books as long as I live. Though not as many as say Arnold Lunn; he's on his fifty-sixth. But if you mean is there a *category* of things I'd like to do, the answer is not that I know of at this point, but I'm sure that something will suggest itself, whether it's a novel or whatever.

Brian: Do you see Hell as a place?

Buckley: No, it's a condition.

Brian: I mention that because you quoted Toledano writing of Hell with a capital "h" because he said it was a place "just like Scarsdale" and I wondered if you agreed with him.

Buckley: [Laughs.] Well, what he was using was a rhetorical device, *reductio ad absurdum.* But "It's a place like Scarsdale, New York," is a metaphor, really,

Brian: Do you see the devil as an entity?

Buckley: As an entity, yes, sure.

Brian: What do you mean by "entity"?

Buckley: It is a force, and, as a force, using a formal philosophical vocabulary, it's an entity.

Brian: But, in fact, it wasn't embodied in man, as you believe God was in Christ?

Buckley: I don't deny that it could happen. I just don't know.

Brian: Apart from being a language purist and a conservative, how else are you like your father?

Buckley: I'm decisive. I'm very fond of my family, but that's hardly a unique quality.

Brian: But was he specially?

Buckley: Yes.

Brian: And your mother? Have you any similar traits?

Buckley: Since she's absolutely perfect, anything I said would be self-serving. [Laughs.]

Brian: Does your son share your political views?

Buckley: He has no political views.

Before interviewing Buckley again I spoke with Arthur Schlesinger, Jr.

Brian: I told Arthur Schlesinger that you thought increased taxation was very constricting of freedom. He said: "I don't think his freedom had been notably impaired." And he added: "I agree with Justice Holmes that taxes are the price we pay for civilization."

Buckley: Well, of course, in the first place, he didn't say that. As a historian, Schlesinger should proceed more carefully. What Holmes said was: "I don't mind paying taxes. That's what I pay for civilization." I consider that to be [laughs] brilliantly qualified, as to serve his ... as an example of mass man. I'm much closer to Emerson, who said to the tax collector: "Don't come near me or I'll slit your throat."

Brian: Mr. Buckley, can you recall an era in which capitalism or the free enterprise system was least restricted and closest to your ideal, in any country?

Buckley: Well, closer, not closest. Sure. I think an awful lot of regulations on the books now are not only unnecessary but deleterious. An excellent example would be an attempt to regulate the railroads which has failed miserably. And I would like to see the whole ICC repealed, abolished. The lousy agricultural surplus mystification seems to be uncalled for and unnecessary. There's a great deal, in my judgment, of unnecessary regulation. Try, for instance, to build a house, or, hell, an outhouse, as far as that goes—and see the number of people that you have to go and get building permits from and the number of different specifications you have to meet to get an idea of the ways of bureaucracy.

Brian: But do you think, for example, that the Victorian era was better than today?

Buckley: I don't know the laws in your country during the Victorian era well enough to know. I simply contend that the amount of paper work required to do things in America is monstrously great. And without saying that era "X" would have been better, because unquestionably in the course of years there have been laws passed that were beneficient and wise. If I narrowed the field to the economic situation, I would say that much of that which was intended by the government to accomplish has not only not been accomplished by such legislation, but something like the opposite of it has been accomplished. Minimum wage is an excellent example.

Brian: You mentioned it was on behalf of the U.S.I.A. that you went to Russia on a diplomatic passport. And that the only tough questions you asked were at the Institute. Did you record any of them in your column?

Buckley: The questions were pretty much boiler plate, if you know what I mean. Standard fare.

Brian: Did you ask the typical thing? "Why don't you let people leave Russia freely?"

Buckley: Oh, no. I didn't, no.

Brian: Would you call that "simplistic"?

Buckley: Those are, of course, the real questions, those are the great questions, the great themes. But in a case like that one more or less accepts the rubric and things get to be a little bit Aesopian and there's not a hell of a lot of point in going to the U.S.I.A. Institute and saying, you know, "Lead me to Isaac Babel."

Brian: None of the answers floored you? They were what you expected, were they?

Buckley: Pretty much. The one thing that I found them very, very nervous about was Henry Ford's visit. They *desperately* wanted the truck plant and they treated Henry Ford with greater hospitality than has been shown since Marco Polo arrived in China. And they kept saying to me that domestic American opposition was really rather silly, since it was easy enough for them merely to beckon to the automobile builders of a European state, and they'd get what they wanted. Gradually it dawned on me that in fact this wasn't so. That it was Ford or nobody. And about a week later Ford made his decision not to go. But they hectored me at some length about domestic American opposition to doing something which a) could easily be done by somebody else, and b) would greatly help on the matter of our balance of payments. That's the one sort of totally unusual thing. For the rest, they all sounded like American liberals, you know. Peace-loving and anti-escalation . . .

Brian: Humanitarians . . .

Buckley: Yes. But after all, if you picked up the *Daily Worker*, it isn't that different.

Brian: Do you find Tito's brand of Communism more acceptable than the U.S.S.R. or Red Chinese?

Buckley: Hell, yes. The only thing wrong with Tito's government, at this point, is nomenclature. He's headed right smack in the right direction. He's heading towards decentralization, economic and political. One of these days there's going to be a little formal freedom there, but there is certainly much more than there was and everybody's extremely enthusiastic about it. I had a long talk with the editor of the official Communist paper there, at the end of which I told him he might as well be the editor of *National Review*. But they insist on calling it Socialism, so who cares.

Brian: You don't mind that?

Buckley: I don't care what they call it, as long as the people have a little freedom.

Brian: I don't know if the idea appeals to you, but if Jesus Christ returned to earth, would you have any question for him?

Buckley: [Chuckles.] Yes, how was I doing on the matter of my immortal soul?

Brian: There are things some people question, like why

did he blast—was it the fig tree—do you remember? Do any of those slight peculiarities intrigue you or not?

Buckley: You mean the enigmas? Yes. But that would make for a long session.

Brian: Do you think he wouldn't spare a long session for you?

Buckley: The Christian faith is based on the compatibility of certain mysteries with its essential message. And there are certain questions I wouldn't ask Christ, even as there are certain questions I wouldn't ask Shakespeare.

Brian: Do you think Christ would be an enthusiastic conservative?

Buckley: Certainly on obvious matters.

Brian: What d'you think of his advice to the rich young man asking how he could be a Christian, and Christ said "Give all you have to the poor and follow me"?

Buckley: Well, this is the way to sainthood. In fact an oath of poverty is incorporated into the oath that many religious orders minister, though not all, by the way.

Brian: Have you ever met anyone you would consider a saint or saintly?

Buckley: Yes, but most of them are people you wouldn't know. But I would consider Whittaker Chambers saintly.

Brian: How would you answer somebody who shares your distaste for a political and philosophical system which is inflexible, yet says most Catholic-oriented views are inflexible too?

Buckley: [Chuckles.] Oh well, I guess I would say, *"Quod licet Jovi non licet bovi"*—you know that one?

Brian: No. Could you translate?

Buckley: "That which is permitted to Jove is not permitted to a cow."

Brian: That's a great quote. Do you agree with Freud

that "a man's intellect, no matter how enormous, is circumscribed by his emotions"?

Buckley: That seems to make sense.

Brian: Who declined to appear on *Firing Line*?

Buckley: Fulbright has steadily declined, and Lindbergh.

Brian: Did you see the Susskind interview of Khrushchev?

Buckley: I didn't, but I read it.

Brian: Were you impressed?

Buckley: [Laughs.] By what, Susskind?

Brian: By the exchange?

Buckley: There wasn't anything particularly unexpected there. What amused me most was that six months earlier Susskind had said to me, in the middle of his program, "You sound as though you don't believe in cultural exchanges with the Soviet Union." I said: "I don't." And he said with his characteristic gesture of throwing up his arms into the air: "Why not?" And I said: "Because we have no common vocabulary." And at the end of the Khrushchev interview [laughs] I found Susskind with his arms up in the air saying: "We have no common vocabulary."

Brian: Would you like to have tackled Khrushchev?

Buckley: No. A waste of time.

Brian: How do you reconcile the belief that Communist Gus Hall shouldn't be allowed to speak at Yale? Don't the students have the freedom to attend or not attend?

Buckley: Yes. You see, I make the distinction that the students have the right to invite him, but that they shouldn't exercise that right. And that it's a sign of immaturity if they do. I find it worse than immaturity.

Brian: Even if they're young men who haven't heard the arguments?

Buckley: If they haven't heard the arguments they're not smart enough to matriculate at Yale.

Brian: Did interviewing Truman Capote influence your views on capital punishment in any way?

Buckley: He's against it on the grounds that it cannot possibly serve as a deterrent practiced as desultorily as it is. I think he's possibly right.

Brian: Did your attempt to be mayor of New York disillusion you in people and the press?

Buckley: I saw a great deal of distortion, an incredible amount of distortion in which an awful lot of people conspired, for instance the whole business about "concentration camps," and I thought it pretty ugly. But then I came to certain conclusions: which is that what matters is the existential communication rather than formal communication.

Brian: Of the critical articles that are written about you and possibly the things you have heard about yourself on television or radio, how essentially do you find them to be distortions of what you consider to be the real William Buckley, Jr.?

Buckley: This is too encyclopedic to even begin ... Well, for instance, I saw a lead article in *Saturday Review* about me by Benjamin DeMott, who's supposed to be a great big responsible literary tycoon at Amherst. He started right off by mentioning apartheid as one of my "pet causes." And then he quoted a passage from a book of quotations of mine, in which, if you'll read it closely, what I said was that I trust the *bona fides* of people who are in charge of administering apartheid in South Africa—which was true, when I wrote that in 1962. The balance of the article, which is 8,000 words long, went on to condemn apartheid. And I've never mentioned apartheid since, and now this all of a sudden graduates into one of my "pet causes" in one of the leading literary journals of America. Another example which is a sort of *locus classicus* is a review given a book of letters by Whittaker Chambers addressed to me, and published in *New York* magazine. And the remarkable thing about it was the review was done before the book had left the warehouse. [Laughs.]

Brian: Couldn't he have had an advance copy or proofs?

Buckley: No. There were none, because there was a very tight legal shroud of secrecy. Even I didn't have an advance copy.

Brian: How do you think he did it?

Buckley: He just simply assumed that the book was lousy.

Brian: Is it because people act emotionally toward others rather than try and examine intellectually or rationally what they're saying?

Buckley: It's in part that, in part sloth, in part ideological rigidity.

Brian: It's a bit like the occasion when Gore Vidal said you'd used a double negative and you said it was litotes.

Buckley: Exactly, yes. You can make double negatives sound invidious, when, of course, it's a perfectly legitimate rhetorical qualifier.

Brian: Is there one particular misquotation that most enraged you?

Buckley: There's one that I sued Vidal about.

Brian: Is that the one he wrote in *Esquire* or said on TV?

Buckley: Both.

Benjamin DeMott

BORN IN ROCKVILLE CENTER, N.Y., JUNE 2, 1924

Professor of English at Amherst College, Massachusetts, Benjamin DeMott is also a novelist and social and literary critic. He advocates the liberal approach as Buckley advocates the conservative. It was DeMott's review in The Saturday Review *of a half-dozen books by Buckley that angered Buckley. So I called DeMott.*

Brian: I asked William Buckley, Jr., if he considered that things he said were often distorted or misrepresented in the press. And Buckley said: "I saw a lead article in *The Saturday Review* about me by Benjamin DeMott. . . . He started right off by mentioning apartheid as one of my 'pet causes.' And then he quoted a passage from a book of quotations of mine, in which, if you'll read it closely, what I said was that I trust the *bona fides* of people who are in charge of administering apartheid in South Africa—which was true, when I wrote that in 1962. The balance of the article, which is 8,000 words long, went on to condemn apartheid. . . . and now this all of a sudden graduates into one of my 'pet causes' in one of the leading literary journals . . ." Do you think Buckley's point is fair?

DeMott: No I don't, obviously. It's very simple. One of the subjects taken up in the book of quotations was apartheid. The only words said about the subject in that book are favorable to the sponsors of apartheid. If

Buckley didn't approve that way of representing his views, he should have forced the editors to include something against those sponsors. As things stand, he's claiming I misrepresented him when in fact the only guilty one is himself. First he allowed or, for all I know, encouraged an anthologist to falsify an article of his. Then he attacks somebody for accepting the falsification as truth. A classic case of having it both ways. Very Buckleyan, in my opinion.

Brian: Yes. But where Buckley said "if you read it closely," etc. Was that in the book?

DeMott: Absolutely not, and the point is that if you look in the quotations in what is called *Chairman Bill*—I believe that's the title of it—if you look at the remarks about apartheid here that are quoted in that book, there is no suggestion that there would be any 7,000 words surrounding them or qualifying them in any way whatever. I simply quoted what he had to say. He was saying that people who sponsor this policy are, in essence, good people, responsible, decent, clear-headed people with a vision of their own about how peace can be restored to South African society. And so far as he was concerned, he felt that it was important for us to see that they were essentially responsible people. Well now, I don't care whether he surrounds it with 40,000 words, I do not myself consider that any South African who adopts the policy of apartheid, who espouses it, recommends it, or administers it, *could* be described as a responsible, moral, decent human being. I think what he's trying to say in his piece, in the other 7,000 words, may be that these people pay their bills. I have no doubt that they pay their bills, but I don't think that the bill-paying or the fact that they don't beat their own servants (I think that might also be in the equation, too), that they don't beat their own servants, that they don't really look forward to a society in which beatings are necessary and so on and so on—I don't think any of that changes the fact that the quotation that I saw, and that was all I had to judge from—was in defense of the sponsors of the policy.

Brian: Did you in fact say "pet cause"?

DeMott: I did indeed say "pet cause" and I'll stand by the phrase on this ground, that the apartheid cause is morally offensive, and the idea of speaking for it, speaking in defense of the people who sponsor that cause, in any terms, seems to me to deserve condemnation. It may be that someone will say: "He only did it once." If someone says to me: "Look, Gerald L. K. Smith only spoke once in recommendation of Buchenwald. He didn't do it two or three or a dozen times. Why don't we let him off?" As far as I'm concerned, I stand on my piece. I do let him off in a sense. I let him off in the sense that I try to suggest that, while Buckley would say a thing like this about the South Africans, on one occasion, he does on another occasion object to people's obliviousness about the Biafran slaughter. I tried to be as fair to him; indeed, in my opinion I'm fairer to him than the man actually deserves. But he wants to call me on the validity of the phrase "pet cause" and I want to come back and say, "Only once with things of this sort, when there are beatings and murders involved, you only have to speak up once for the people who do that, in my opinion, to qualify as a person who has made their cause yours."

Brian: Have you met Buckley?

DeMott: Never seen him in my life.

Brian: Have you seen him on his TV interview show *Firing Line*?

DeMott: Not really, no.

Brian: Have you read a fair amount of him?

DeMott: I've read all the books. That was the job.

Brian: You read all the quotations of his, you mean?

DeMott: No, no. There is quite a stack of books.

Brian: I wonder if you'd agree with me: he strikes me as being a brilliant man who confuses issues, almost because of his brilliance. He seems to go more into the legal or rhetorical aspect of a thing than the moral issue.

DeMott: Yes. I think that another way of putting it, so far as I'm concerned, is that he has a very abstract mind and that the moment-to-moment quality of the lived life of the people who are badly treated under the terms of the civilization and the general culture is something that does not come across to him with much force and vigor. He has lived an extremely privileged life all his years, and now and then he is carted out under the auspices of one or another urban council to meet some bright black leaders and so on. He has cards of entry into conversation with the best of them, of the blacks, the people who manage to make their way into positions of significance, and so on. And for them, I think he has an unfeigned respect. But the point is that in his sense of things, what it's like to be a black man in West Point, Mississippi, what the daily life of the black man who lives in a Delta County in the Deep South is, what that comes to, is something he won't speculate about, won't try to imagine, won't care about. He will deal with that in a purely abstract way. Well, that is the life of the Southern black, and he has a label for it, and the label he has for it is one that makes it possible for him to escape thinking about what it would be like, as I say, getting up in the morning and going to bed at night, in that situation. What he has instead is a very strong moment-to-moment feeling for the life of people that he describes as sentimental Northern liberals of my kind. He knows what we feel like. He knows that there's a certain amount of self-righteousness in us. He is very concerned about imagining the texture of my life and the life of people like me, and what we feel like and how we congratulate ourselves and how we think that we are the only decent ones on earth and so on. He works very hard at imagining that. But he's goddamned if he'll pay that kind of attention and that kind of care to the life of the much more numerous people who are getting the dirty end of the stick. And that is what I mean by saying he's a very abstract man. You can say he's brilliant. I think to a certain degree brilliance depends upon that capacity, brilliance in political terms at least, depends upon an ability to empty out issues of their human content, and I think that's what he does.

Brian: Are you familiar with the piece written about Ernest Hemingway by Lillian Ross and also the George Plimpton interview?

DeMott: Yes. I think that in a way the Ross piece represented a kind of withdrawal of sympathy from the man. It's not the only time there's been that kind of withdrawal. I don't know whether you know the Leslie Fiedler piece about going to visit Hemingway in Montana just a few months before he committed suicide. There was the same kind of feeling there, a sort of, "How could this man, who was the great type of American letters, have a *Reader's Digest* on top of the television set?" In a way, the interviewer—it doesn't matter who he is, whether it's Rex Reed or Lillian Ross—is often a person who, in order to do his job and make interesting copy, can only do it by withdrawing his sympathy and his concern from the object of the interview, presenting the gestures and the talk in a flattish way that in effect says that at some point at some time on earth, there are deeds done and talk made without anybody present, without anybody feeling his way into the other person's mind. And I don't think that's the way it ever goes in life. There's always somebody there listening, if the person's talking, and that person's always being invited into some kind of relationship with the person talking. The interviewer's style, the one that's been fashionable for years, is one that pretends that there is no invitation, and there is no invitation to hear anything more than the words being said.

Brian: Do you know Studs Terkel's work?

DeMott: I think he's about as good as they come, maybe a little better.

Brian: Harrison Salisbury thinks Terkel has made interviewing a work of art.

DeMott: From what I know of Terkel he's the best of them. He knows that there's something more than standing back and perceiving it as though you were a basketball coach.

Brian: Although when a Terkel interview is printed it appears to be where the interviewer is least involved. In fact there must be a lot of sympathy and empathy involved, is that what you mean?

DeMott: That's it. He's not there, but my feeling is he lets the person or the subject spell himself out in adequate lengths, so that you feel that the person speaking is not being done in, or if he is being done in, he's hanged himself, and that somebody who would be listening would be sorry for him.

Brian: It's only slanted if the subject himself is slanted.

DeMott: Yes.

Brian: I spoke with Lillian Ross and she said she was very fond of Hemingway and admired him and that it wasn't meant to be a brutal piece. But it apparently shook a lot of his friends. I spoke with Arthur Schlesinger and he thought it pictured a man who had almost lost his gift and was cracking up.

DeMott: Yes. Nevertheless it is a piece of writing and if the person there is someone who is cracking up and has lost his gift and so on, for him then to be represented merely as a fool and not as a person who had any quasitragic dimension . . . well, it's wrong, what came out. I don't care what the *intention* was. We all know about intention. Nobody means to do anybody in and so on, but here it comes forth in this way.

Brian: Do you feel, as one psychological investigator of the subject of interviewing does, that the ideal interviewer is the man or woman's peer? The ideal interviewer of deGaulle, shall we say, would have been Winston Churchill.

DeMott: That's a way of putting it. Imagining it that way, presupposes, doesn't it, that peers would be willing to turn themselves into interviewers, and no peer would. I mean, being a peer, being the equal of a great man means, I think, among other things, knowing that interviewers are likely to be small men. They are people whose fundamental interest is not in clarification of issues, not in the making of an understanding of ordinary human beings, but rather that of doing a piece. I remember I was in Washington when the hearings were going on in the Mayflower: the platform committee hearings for the Democratic party and Senator Eugene McCarthy came in, not to give testimony—this was during the McCarthy primaries and he just happened to drop by. Those hearings came up and he spoke briefly to a CBS correspondent and it was a very good interview; lasted about three or four minutes. It was six o'clock or something like that. That night I watched for that interview with interest in my hotel bedroom. I was staying at the hotel. And it wasn't there and it was the night the great story of the Hungarian uprising came on television. I went downstairs into the bar and I saw the interviewer. I said, "You got blocked off" and his response was one of absolute fury that there could be such a world in which a marvelous piece of interviewing in his fine bit of tape could get bumped from the evening newscast, because of an event of the kind of significance the one in question had. Something about that experience showed me more clearly than I had seen before that people who do this kind of work don't really have much sense of themselves as other than performers. It's different being an interviewer than being a teacher or a writer, at least in my opinion. I think it's a lower form of intellectual inquiry.

Brian: Don't you think it has the possibilities, though, of the Socrates-Plato aspect?

DeMott: [Chuckles.] Well, yes. But where is he?

Brian: Where are they today!

DeMott: Yes, if you want to call Socrates an interviewer, sure, but I think the step between that and what we're talking about here ... I don't see Socrates [chuckles] and Rex Reed on a par.

Brian: It's funny you should say that, because when I interviewed Rex Reed he told me that he did very poorly in feature writings when he was studying journalism at school. And I said to him, "Well, Churchill did very poorly at history in his school." And my wife was astounded that I would compare the two. But it was just something that came to my mind. But don't you think highly of Plimpton and his *Paris Review* in which writers are interviewed?

DeMott: There are some good interviews in *The Paris Review* but some of those interviews are terrible. Some of them are very responsive and draw forth in a sympathetic and caring way what the man truly has in his head, but I don't think myself that ... if someone said, "All *The Paris Review* interviews are swell stuff and the thing itself shows the possibilities of the form," I'd have to say, "No, I don't see that at all. I think some are awfully done and some are not."

Brian: Do you recall Lillian Hellman's? That was great, I thought.

DeMott: I wish I could remember it better.

Brian: Do you think David Frost is also the kind of interviewer who makes it entertainment, rather than an attempt to find the truth about people?

DeMott: I'm not sure whether there isn't, in his way of doing it, a kind of routinized cordiality and somewhat overplayed interest in the person. In order to have a good interview you have to have a person with a mind as good or as bad as the person being interviewed. It's like a novelist trying to interpret a character who lived in real life. If you haven't got a mind good enough to penetrate the mind that you're dealing with, what can you possibly come up with? The whole question is what kind of interpretive intelligence has the interviewer got? Is he really as comprehensive and penetrating as the mind he's dealing with? If you've got an interviewer smarter than the person he's talking with, well then—smarter, or more sympathetic, or more comprehensive in his understanding of life—what can issue is a piece of work that doesn't do dirt on a person but simply shows us what all of us intermittently are. But I admit I don't think that very often happens.

PART SIX
Circling the Kennedys in Search of the Myth Makers, or, How Interviews Set the Record Straight

WALT ROSTOW
HUGH SIDEY   GEORGE REEDY
THE LASKY-LONGWORTH AFFAIR
ARTHUR SCHLESINGER, JR.

Walt Rostow

BORN IN NEW YORK CITY, OCTOBER 7, 1916

Walt Whitman Rostow was one of President Kennedy's most influential advisers—while on leave of absence from his job as an M.I.T. professor of economic history. Rostow became chairman of the State Department policy planning council (1961–1966) and from 1966—1969 was special assistant to President Johnson. He is now (1973) professor of economics and history at the University of Texas, Austin, Texas.

Rostow: I'll tell you what my problem is. I get about three requests every two weeks of people to interview me. I'm a hard-working teacher and writer. And I've had to lay down a flat rule that no matter how interesting the enterprise, and this sounds a most engaging enterprise, I've got to have a flat "no" or I'll just go down for the third time. So I'm afraid my answer's no. It doesn't help you, but I just wanted you to understand why. So forgive me and good luck with your work.
Brian: Might I possibly ask you merely one question?
Rostow: [Chuckles.] You can always ask me a question. I don't know whether I'll answer it.
Brian: This is half of the one question. Did you read Jack Newfield's memoir of Robert Kennedy? (*Robert Kennedy: A Memoir.*)
Rostow: No.
Brian: Well, he mentions you, and he says that in *Time* magazine and *Newsweek* a meeting was reported at

which you were present with President Johnson and Robert Kennedy, and Newfield says: "*Time* Magazine reported that the confrontation was so bitter that Kennedy called the President a 'sonofabitch' at one point." (Victor Lasky reports the same incident in *Robert Kennedy: The Myth and the Man*.)

Rostow: That's not true. That's off the record but it's not true. You can just take it that I was there and nothing of that kind was said.

Brian: Kennedy himself insisted it wasn't true.

Rostow: It was not true. It was not true at all. And it was, I don't know by what process exactly, grossly distorted in its public projection.

Brian: There were three of you present, then?

Rostow: I think Katzenbach was also present.

Brian: That's right, Katzenbach, the President, yourself, and Robert Kennedy.

Rostow: That's right.

Brian: Do you know the recent biographer of Huey Long, T. Harry Williams?

Rostow: No.

Brian: Because in an interview he gave (to Peggy Ann Brock in *Writer's Digest*, September 1970), Williams says: "Another advantage in oral history is that in many areas of life, and this is particularly true in politics, even before the age of the telephone, the full inside story isn't written down. People just don't write these things down, but they'll tell you. They don't mind talking but it would never occur to them to put it on paper themselves."

Rostow: Uh-huh.

Brian: May I then just say: "It wasn't true." Just that?

Rostow: Yes, you may say that, as it addresses to that simple point.

Brian: Thank you very much.

Hugh Sidey

BORN IN GREENFIELD, IOWA, SEPTEMBER 3, 1927

Sidey has been correspondent for Time *and* Life *magazines since 1958 as their man in Washington. He began his reporting career on* The Adair County Free Press, *Iowa, in 1950, after graduating from Iowa State University. His biography of* Kennedy, John F. Kennedy, President *was published in 1963.*

Brian: In your biography of President Kennedy and in your interviews with him, did he request that you leave quite a bit out?
Sidey: No. I met Kennedy very early, working in the Senate, and covered him quite intensively over those years. And we got so familiar with each other's kind of tacit signals about what was on or off the record, what could be said and what couldn't, that there was never any instruction at all. Even when he became President he talked to me quite openly and left it up to my judgment.
Brian: Arthur Schlesinger, Jr., said he was criticized for reporting President Kennedy's unflattering view of the State Department in his Kennedy biography, *A Thousand Days*. And he told me that you reported the same Kennedy comment in your biography.
Sidey: I always accused Arthur of stealing that. In fact, he credited me with that quote in his book—that Kennedy said: "The State Department is a bowl of jelly." My book came out in the fall of 1963 just before he was killed and I had had all these conversations with him: some of the stuff I'd left off the record and some on, but I put all

in the book that I wanted to. There was only one thing that bothered me and I came to him about that. One night in the office I asked him whether he was going to run again and he said yes, of course he was going to run. And I had originally ended my book with that quote. It was the only one I had any doubts about, so I took it to him. And he said: "No, you'd better take that out, because I want to make that announcement." That was the only thing he took out—that one sentence. So I finally ended the book with Kennedy saying: "What do you think?"

Brian: Did you find him a very frank and open man, despite being a politician?

Sidey: Yes, very much so. That was perhaps his most engaging quality. Kennedy talked quite openly, quite candidly, and quite honestly.

Brian: Were you amused by Paul Fay's description of you in his book about Kennedy, *The Pleasure of His Company?* (Fay and Kennedy served together as PT boat officers in training and in action. In 1961 Fay was appointed Under Secretary of the Navy and served until 1965.)

Sidey: Oh yes, it was quite right, it was quite honest.

Brian: Fay described how President Kennedy arranged the chairs so that you, as his interviewer, couldn't look at him and Fay at the same time.

Sidey: That's right, and they signaled back and forth. (As a joke Fay signaled to J.F.K. when Sidey's questions appeared dangerous.)

Brian: Were you aware that Fay and Kennedy were signaling?

Sidey: Oh, I tell you, we were playing games there. We always did. It was always great sport. And I wasn't aware that he and Fay had any signals rigged up, but between them there were chuckles and that sort of thing. That was part of the game: it was a little more elaborate than I had understood.

Brian: Were you trying to find out if his father, Joseph Kennedy, was influencing the President a great deal?

Sidey: Oh, sure. This was the big factor. As a matter of fact I was interviewing the President for a cover on *Time* magazine and that cover story was about the family. We had all the family members on the cover portrait. We had old Joe with his hand on John Kennedy's shoulder, and there was a picture on the wall of old Honey Fitz. It was kind of a fun picture, you know. So it was about the family, and of course a part of it was on the patriarch. And one of my commissions was to find out the extent of Joe's influence. That was impossible, of course, to find out from the Kennedys. But it was fascinating to find out the President's reactions to these questions. And how he vehemently denied his father's influence. And also his opinions of his father's political expertise, which weren't very high.

Brian: In fact his father didn't influence him very much.

Sidey: The old man, I think, furnished dough and gave him a lot of advice which he ignored.

Brian: How did you react to the line in Fay's book: "When the cover story came out Jack was generally pleased but he did make a mild accusation that the magazine had attempted some character distortion?

Sidey: We fought that battle continuously with Kennedy. He was never pleased totally. And that was just part of it. We just fought back and forth. There was one time after he read my book he froze me out of the White House, instructed everybody not to talk to me, or anybody from *Time* magazine. That lasted for two weeks.

Brian: Did you ever get to the bottom of the "L.B.J. driving fast while drinking" story?

Sidey: Well, I thought so.

Brian: I spoke to George Reedy, L.B.J.'s Press Secretary, about it. And I said: "Why was President Johnson so upset by the report? Was it untrue?" And Reedy said: "The media didn't get it in the right context, didn't put the right construction on it." And I said to Reedy: "Could you tell me what happened?" And he said: "It would take an hour."

Sidey: I think that's typical of George's loyalty. But I think our story was right on the head. I wasn't there. I was off that weekend, but I reconstructed it and went back over it, and this came straight from people who were there and I talked with them all. And I think we were right on the nose. This was Johnson showing off.

Brian: What d'you think an hour of Reedy's explanation would be?

Sidey: He would probably say how L.B.J. reacted to the open spaces and when he said certain things he didn't really mean them. Those friends of Johnson, you know, rationalized his movements and they were right in some instances. But the fact of the matter is, I think the *Time* story which caused all the trouble was right on the button.

Brian: Do you remember the occasion when Robert Kennedy was involved in possible peace overtures from Vietnam and had a meeting with L.B.J. and was purported—according to *Time* magazine—to have called Johnson a son-of-a-bitch?

Sidey: Well now, that was our doing and I think we were wrong. In fact I was involved in that. That story came out of the White House. The whole thing was confused. It got to be a very heated meeting, which was arranged by Nicholas Katzenbach. And the rumors were just incredible about who'd said what. Johnson accused Bobby of causing Vietnam casualties. The story that I got out of the White House was that the exchange got so bitter that Bobby called the President an s.o.b. (and Sidey printed this in *Time*). And Bob denied it. And I talked with him at length on it. And I ultimately came to believe that he was probably right, that he had too much respect for the President. But in the course of trying to figure out what had been said, Lyndon Johnson's own account of what had been said would tend to be distorted . . .

Brian: Is that right?

Sidey: Oh yes. His own accounts of what happened under certain conditions were very much colored by his own remarkable personality.

Brian: Was it true that Johnson often tape-recorded these sessions?

Sidey: We don't know. I assume so. Either they were tape-recorded or immediately afterwards he dictated his account to some secretary. We do know for a fact that some telephone conversations were recorded.

Brian: I spoke with Walt Rostow recently and he agreed to answer that one question about Robert Kennedy. And Rostow was one of the four at the stormy meeting. And he denied it flatly and said that the mood of the meeting was grossly distorted in the press.

Sidey: I would question whether the mood was distorted because I talked to Robert Kennedy myself shortly after that and he said it was a tough meeting. He was very shaken up by it. And when they walked out into the hall Katzenbach whistled under his breath and said, "Boy, I'm sorry about that!" Johnson had really lit into Kennedy, you know, accusing him of causing deaths, casualties in Vietnam, of meddling there and so forth, and had been really tough on him. But it is possible of course that Bob Kennedy could exaggerate. Again, Bob Kennedy wasn't that used to Lyndon Johnson. Lyndon Johnson was very frequently just mean. And anybody who first came up against him was horrified. Those who'd lived around him understood that beneath that meanness were a lot of other emotions, a lot of other feelings, and it wasn't quite what it seemed sometimes on the surface.

Brian: But at the time of the stormy meeting it wouldn't have been possible to get Katzenbach, Rostow, or Robert Kennedy to give you the true version?

Sidey: We couldn't. We went to everybody on that. We printed in *Time* that Bob had called him an s.o.b. and of course that broke everything up. Then Bob denied it and called me. And Lyndon Johnson and George Christian (press secretary) denied it. And then they wouldn't give the true account. Because the true account was obviously not very flattering.

Brian: It wasn't much better, in fact?

Sidey: That's right: that's the point.

Brian: Victor Lasky in his biography of Robert Kennedy, *The Myth and the Man,* said that Bobby snarled at Mrs. Alice Roosevelt Longworth, "What arrangements have you made for your funeral?" when the old lady had just recovered from an illness. And a *New York Times* reviewer of the book said that the things Lasky had said about Robert Kennedy in the book, including this quote, were "obscene." Lasky, in his reply, said that although in fact it wasn't his source, the Longworth quote was also in a *New York Times* interview Mrs. Longworth had given to Henry Brandon. In fact the interview with Brandon had Mrs. Longworth saying that Bobby's remark was all in fun, that she had deliberately driven Bobby into saying it, and that she was delighted with his response. And I spoke with her a few nights ago and she said she was unhappy that Lasky had distorted the account, by omission, in his book.

Sidey: I didn't even bother to read the Bobby Kennedy book but my book came out about the time that his book on J.F.K. came out, *The Man and the Myth,* and he did no original reporting, he talked to no one in the White House. He went to the morgue and took clips, many of mine from *Time* magazine, and he distorted events and took things out of context all the way through. That I know about the John F. Kennedy book. He's rather a facile writer. He just sat down and collected all the stuff and constructed the story he wanted to.

Brian: Was J.F.K. alive when the Lasky biography came out?

Sidey: Oh yes. As a matter of fact there was a rather amusing incident. I don't think it's been reported anyplace. Kennedy talked to me about it. He said, "How are you coming? How are your sales?" I said, "We're doing all right, but Lasky may have the edge." He said, "I've read Lasky's book. I understand. I'd want to read it if I were somebody else." I said, "That's amazing!"

Brian: He was amused by Lasky's book, not shocked?

Sidey: Oh no, no. This was again part of his charm. Most politicians would say: "I never read it." But he said, "I read the whole thing and found it fascinating." [Chuckles.]

Brian: The big question is the Bay of Pigs and press freedom. Do you think *The New York Times* and other publications should have revealed the planned invasion?

Sidey: I think so. I didn't think so at the time. But now I think that whenever we begin to temporize—except in cases where national security is *really* at stake, like the Cuban missile crisis—when we begin to pull our punches, it's wrong.

Brian: But if the press had revealed that the Bay of Pigs invasion was imminent and they'd gone ahead with it, and it was the fiasco in fact it turned out to be, then the press would have been blamed for the defeat.

Sidey: Well, that's the normal thing. We get blamed for all that anyway. It doesn't bother me. It's more or less "kill the messenger." I think press revelation would have altered the thing. I think there would have been many more discussions and it might have been thought out. Kennedy might have had second thoughts. As I look back, it probably would have been a healthy thing.

Brian: You know *Time* magazine gets a tremendous amount of criticism for inaccuracy . . .

Sidey: You think so?

Brian: I'll give you one instance. I've an acquaintance who's something of an expert on oil in Kuwait. *Time* contacted him and he gave them a lot of detailed information. Quite some time later the feature on oil came out and they hadn't used one of the things he'd told them. And he said what they had used was inaccurate.

Sidey: I've always felt that factually we're probably more accurate than any other publication because we spend so much effort to get correct facts. But people object to our point of view. Our point is that we're not *The New York Times* and our original declaration was that "we say it like we see it" and in the course of that we naturally use facts that support our viewpoint, and ignore others. We don't present both sides of it. Sorensen has a long critique of *Time* in his account of Kennedy, and the fact of the matter is there are several factual errors in that—that I can see. I think it's nonsense, most of it. Sorensen's main argument is that we don't present the news like *The New York Times.* Of course we don't. We made up our mind and we said: "We make our judgment." And I suspect that a lot of the accusations for being inaccurate are simply pique at us for not agreeing with the subject or for taking another viewpoint. You know how we do it. We're snotty about it frequently and this drives them up the wall.

Brian: You think in the case I cited there might not have been time to use his material?

Sidey: No. To begin with your friend may be absolutely right, that this was a case which we screwed up. We do that. But to suggest that *The New York Times* doesn't, or *Newsweek* doesn't, or *U.S. News* doesn't, is nonsense. We all do it, you know that. It's a comedy of errors. Agnew's right about a lot of it. It's human endeavor, the struggle to get the best. But my suspicion is that we're not a bit more inaccurate than anybody else.

Brian: Do you have a theory of interviewing?

Sidey: I have one theory. I listen. I ask questions and I listen. We have so many people around this city, it just staggers me. I've gone to these breakfasts, you know, where various correspondents meet and at dinners and lunches. And I'm constantly overwhelmed at the number of first-rate reporters who spend the time *telling* the source what they think. As a matter of fact one of the jokes: I went to one of the restaurants in town one day and Joe Alsop was in a booth with a source. And the joke at the end of our lunch was—the source never opened his mouth. Alsop simply talked to him all the time. I have no theory other than I have short, rather blunt, open, simple questions, and I encourage, in a very low-key way, the source to talk. Another kind of secondary theory is not to be afraid to ask about inconsequential things. I have discovered that I have wasted more hours by asking people about the great, sweeping questions of policy, which they are both unable to articulate at certain times because they're not built that way, or they can't because of security. And I've noticed in public press conferences and private press conferences, that reporters sometimes waste the whole time going back and back and back to try and get Dean Rusk to say that Vietnam was going to collapse, or to try and get someone else to say something that any fool could tell you he wasn't going to say. I have certainly tried some of these questions, but immediately upon sensing that the guy wasn't going to talk about them, it's never been below me to ask when he got up, how he felt, how he treated his kids, what books did he read, what movies had he seen. And I must say in my years in journalism these insights into personality prove invaluable.

Brian: Did you think Robert Kennedy's critics, tagging him as ruthless, at least in his early days, were justified?

Sidey: Oh sure, yes. Again there was that part to him.

He was many people. But you have to describe the conditions: there was always a reason.

Brian: Do you agree that he grew out of that?

Sidey: Yes, I think he learned a great deal after his brother's death, through that experience and the campaign. He said it himself. He discovered that not everyone was born with 400 million dollars, not everybody has seventeen servants. He had a kind of guilt complex about it. He was a step ahead of these beautiful liberals who discuss all these issues and then go back to their estates on the Potomac with the servants and parties, and live their marvelous lives—and don't think a thing about it. Bob Kennedy did all that but he was bothered about it.

Brian: Is there any chance that you could get on the same terms with Ted Kennedy as you were with President Kennedy?

Sidey: No, I don't think so. I don't know Ted Kennedy that well and he's not close to anybody. There are defense mechanisms there. I don't think he's the same man that John Kennedy was or Bob Kennedy was. I think John Kennedy's great strength was confidence, intellectually, socially, and personally. He wasn't afraid of any situation I know of. I think Ted Kennedy has walled himself away.

Brian: You think this is normal, or that Chappaquiddick has emphasized it?

Sidey: I think Chappaquiddick is possibly the proof of it. I think there's a lot of ability there. But in trying to describe what makes a leader like John Kennedy—well, people write books about that. The fact of the matter was there was this tempered self-confidence, this kind of dignity and understanding. He'd seen a lot of the world and knew a lot of the people. He wasn't afraid of it. On the other hand, by the same token, there was a certain modesty. He realized he wasn't going to solve it all.

George Reedy

BORN IN EAST CHICAGO, INDIANA, AUGUST 5, 1917

President Johnson's Press Secretary. Author of The Twilight of the Presidency. *He is now (1973) Dean of the College of Journalism at Marquette University, Milwaukee, Wisconsin.*

Brian: I spoke with Hugh Sidey and he anticipated what you might say to explain President Johnson's fast driving. [I then quoted Sidey.]

Reedy: There were two cases of fast driving and in neither case do I know what happened because I wasn't there. I think on the one hand you have the business about him driving down the highway and drinking beer. That's one story. The press car episode was later on when he'd gone to church. All I can say is that that's fairly normal conduct for Texas. Every automobile drives about seventy, eighty, ninety miles an hour down the road. It's not regarded as anything out of the way down there. And I think I was slightly amused at the time the story came out, because I thought, "What's happening is being covered by people that are not accustomed to the way they drive out in the rural parts of Texas."

Brian: Another thing I discussed with Sidey was the occasion when Robert Kennedy was reported to have called President Johnson an s.o.b. And Sidey said that people often were horrified on first meeting Johnson. D'you agree?

Reedy: When people ran into his temper they'd quite frequently be horrified, yes.

Brian: D'you think Sidey was right in saying President

Johnson would be subjective in reporting his version of the stormy meeting he had with Robert Kennedy?

Reedy: I've never known a politician who wouldn't be subjective about a meeting like that.

Brian: I know you say in your book that there's a great danger of the President being completely detached from criticism . . .

Reedy: From face-to-face criticism.

Brian: Yes, criticism that has more impact, in fact. Don't you think that tape-recorded meetings of the Johnson-Kennedy sort would be a minor safeguard to prevent the President from taking a Napoleonic attitude?

Reedy: No, because a man has too many ways of interpreting it in his own mind. He can always rationalize it the way he wants to. It would straighten out the record. But, you know, when politicians talk to each other, more things are understood than are ever said. This is one of the rules of the game. And I don't think you'd find very many recordings of what very sophisticated politicians said to each other that would throw much light on the thing.

Brian: D'you agree that most top politicians conceal rather than reveal?

Reedy: They're accustomed to communicating with each other by sort of an extrasensory perception, in which there's a lot of shorthand talk and a lot of things understood that are never said.

Brian: Did you encounter J.F.K. much?

Reedy: I knew him quite a long time.

Brian: Sidey thought that President Kennedy was, of all the politicians, exceptionally frank, outspoken, and confident in speaking like that.

Reedy: No, I don't really. I think he was capable of creating that impression that he was being quite frank and candid. But essentially he had all the political instincts, and the political instincts are against putting too many things on the record.

The Lasky-Longworth Affair

In the foreword to his book Robert F. Kennedy: The Myth and the Man, *Victor Lasky wrote: "This book seeks to portray Robert Kennedy as he actually was—an earthy, colorful figure to whom little mattered but victory. . ."*

On page 15 of his book Lasky wrote:

"Mrs. Alice Roosevelt Longworth, who has seen them come and go on the Washington scene for many decades, once kidded Bobby about one of his great mountaineering exploits. His face turned red with rage. 'What arrangements have you made for your funeral?' he snarled.

"Mrs. Longworth, who was then nearly eighty and had undergone a serious operation, was taken aback: 'Why I haven't thought about it,' she replied. 'I haven't made any arrangements.'

"'You mean,' Kennedy went on in his heartless way, 'you haven't even designated the pallbearers?'

"'No, but I do know one thing—you and Dick Nixon will be seated in the front pew.'

"'Why?' asked Bobby.

"'Because you are my two greatest disappointments.'

"Later, Mrs. Longworth said that though she was unhappy with Nixon's 1960 campaign performance—and had frequently told him so—the former Vice President had never been unkind to her. They are still friends."

Following the publication and review of his book, this letter from Victor Lasky appeared in The New York Times Book Review, *April 20, 1969:*

"To the Editor:

"In his review of my book Robert Kennedy: The Myth and the Man *(March 2), Larry L. King* declares that 'many of the anecdotes are indecent or obscene.'

"As a 'particularly vicious story,' your reviewer cites the one 'in which the late Senator is alleged to have snarled at Alice Roosevelt Longworth, as she neared 80, "What arrangements have you made for your funeral?"' And he doubts its authenticity.

"My source for the story is other than The New York Times. But in the Aug. 6, 1967, issue of The Times Magazine *there was a published interview with Mrs. Longworth, in which she quoted Robert Kennedy as having asked her 'What arrangements have you made for your funeral?'"*

I wondered why Victor Lasky hadn't asked Mrs. Longworth herself. She was—and still is—a very active, outgoing woman, living in Washington, D.C.

I had previously interviewed her for a book about Tallulah Bankhead.

Brian: I'm interviewing the outstanding interviewers in the United States.

Mrs. Longworth: That sounds amusing.

Brian: I wondered if you had any strong views about interviewers and interviewing?

Mrs. Longworth: No, I don't think so. [Chuckles.] Some of them are rather too mean of other people.

Brian: Did you ever feel that anyone had interviewed you splendidly?

Mrs. Longworth: I'm never interviewed, you know. I never have real interviews. I was thinking more of the program on television. A friend of mine did something about me in *American Heritage.*

Brian: Did they ever ask you to speak for the oral history program at Columbia?

Mrs. Longworth: Oh yes, I did that a long time ago. I did it with reluctance [chuckles]. I was talking the whole time with my ears laid back. I didn't like it at all. And I don't know what it would be like now. I've done so many other things since that time, that I'm now more at ease with them. I don't care. I hardly ever do them. Jonathan Aiken did a thing on television with me: that's the only thing I ever did of that sort. But I'll be interested to see your things about Tallulah: that will be great fun.

Brian: Did Allan Nevins interview you for the oral history?

Mrs. Longworth: Yes, and a man named Jack Kennedy—not the Irish Jack Kennedy, not the President. We had a rather stilted talk.

Brian: A very good friend of Robert Kennedy's, Jack Newfield, has published a book about him. And Newfield thinks that the newspaper myths about Robert Kennedy are entirely wrong, that the ruthless Robert Kennedy didn't exist, or that it was only a small part of him. Well, you know Robert Kennedy is said to have been very ruthless to you.

Mrs. Longworth: That's what I took great pains to see that they wouldn't do. Because I was perfectly sure someone ill-disposed to the Kennedys, Democrats or Republicans, would say: "Ah, this cruel man. Poor old woman, he was mean to her!" Perfect nonsense! I goaded him, deliberately, teased him, and he responded splendidly, with fury. [Chuckles.] It couldn't have been more fun.

Brian: There's a man called Victor Lasky who wrote a very anti-Kennedy book. He quoted Robert Kennedy as saying to you, "What arrangements have you made for your funeral?"

Mrs. Longworth: I had an interview with Henry Brandon (Washington correspondent for the British *Sunday Times*). So all of that is in an interview with Henry

Brandon, where I said I began by teasing Robert Kennedy about something and then I went a step further and then I went too far. Because when I teased him about Teddy, saying he'd climbed a higher mountain and it didn't take the Canadian Mounted Police to get him up.... And then he became rather savage. And then I got on hallowed ground. I said I only hoped that he wouldn't feel it necessary to walk in record time around Kennedy Airport [laughs]. It had exactly the effect that I expected. And then he said, "What arrangements have you made for your funeral?" And I said, "None." [Chuckles.] "I always thought it would be rather nice to be tossed into a burning mountain." Whereupon Bobby said, "You would say that when you know [chuckles] cremation is against my faith." And then we went on from that and he said, "Who would you count on for pallbearers?" And I said, "I know who's going to sit in the front pew. It's going to be you and Dick Nixon." And that was the end of it.

Brian: I think this is the chief problem with interviews. People forget to put in that something was said as a joke.

Mrs. Longworth: Yes, it was a tease. It was a big tease.

Brian: So you don't think he was ruthless at all?

Mrs. Longworth: Well, I could perfectly well see that I made him lose his temper. [Chuckles.] We laughed about it. I was doing what I've just said to you—I was sitting between Bobby and Teddy White—and Bobby was saying to Teddy White, "What do you think, Teddy?" So he said, "I was back in my grandfather's saloon." [Chuckles.] And I said, "Indeed you were there. That's just where you were." And he said, "I was the face on the barroom floor, to be trampled on." So you see ... I'm so sorry Lasky did that. How tiresome of him.

Brian: The lightheartedness was missing in Lasky's account. In fact you were delighted with Robert Kennedy's response.

Mrs. Longworth: Enchanted with his response. I was making him just as angry as I hoped to. I was always afraid that someone would do exactly what Lasky did, evidently. So that's why I took great trouble to tell Henry Brandon, so he had it all.

Brian: A reviewer of Lasky's book said it wasn't true about Kennedy saying this to you. And Lasky responded in a letter to *The Times Book Review,* quoting one of the sources as the *Times Magazine* section, and saying that Robert Kennedy *had* said it. But Lasky didn't point out that when Kennedy said it, you found it amusing and that you had goaded him into it.

Mrs. Longworth: No, of course he didn't. They leave things like that out.

I spoke with Victor Lasky the next day.

Brian: There was a letter from you in the press about the comment that Robert Kennedy had made to Mrs. Roosevelt Longworth.

Lasky: Yes, it was in *The New York Times* a year or so ago.

Brian: How was that resolved eventually?

Lasky: The reviewer sort of doubted that Mrs. Roosevelt Longworth ever uttered those words and I pointed out that *The Times* itself had quoted something to that effect.

Brian: I spoke with Mrs. Longworth about this. Did you know that she said that the thing was done very much in jest, that she had deliberately aroused Robert Kennedy to say this and that she was delighted with his response, because that was exactly the sort of thing she wanted to hear from him?

Lasky: Well, I want to tell you frankly it's been so long that I can't really recall the circumstances. I know she's a wonderful human being. I haven't seen her in some time.

Brian: She said she feared she would be misquoted when she had the interview with Henry Brandon.

Lasky: She said it to several other people besides Brandon, let's put it that way. She made no secret of the thing.

Brian: You never confirmed with her that it was done in a lighthearted way?

Lasky: I frankly, in all honesty, don't even recall the situation or anything like that. I'd rather forget it.

Brian: Right. Okay Mr. Lasky.

Lasky: Okay?

Brian: Okay, fine.

Lasky: Thank you.

The interview with Mrs. Roosevelt Longworth in The New York Times Magazine, *August 6, 1967, contains this exchange:*

Brandon: You had quite an argument with Bobby the other day.

Longworth: You mean the argument about my funeral? That was just fun. (And later:) I'm really fond of Bobby and I know that Bobby's fond of me. He's like a favorite great-nephew. I like him, as I like all the Kennedys—I have a real feeling for them.

After transcribing my interview with Mrs. Longworth, I called her again on July 3, 1971, to make sure I'd got it quite clear.

Brian: Mrs. Longworth, when you were talking about Robert Kennedy you said: "I teased him about Teddy, saying he'd climbed a higher mountain and it didn't take the Canadian Mounted Police to get him up . . ." Which Teddy were you referring to?

Mrs. Longworth: Teddy Kennedy, his brother.

Brian: And then you said: "I was sitting between Bobby and Teddy White." Is that the author Teddy White?

Mrs. Longworth: That's the author, yes.

Brian: And here's another of your lines. "And Bobby

was saying to Teddy White, 'I was back in my grandfather's saloon.'"

Mrs. Longworth: How marvelous that you've got all that. Did you have it on tape?

Brian: Yes.

Mrs. Longworth: That's the difference. You've got it on tape.

Brian: Now this was Robert Kennedy referring to being in *his* grandfather's saloon?

Mrs. Longworth: Yes, he said that to Teddy White. Then I said I was the face on the barroom floor to be trampled on—because Bobby was cross about what I'd been saying. [Laughs.] It's a bit complicated.

Brian: The difficulty was that there were three of you talking.

Mrs. Longworth: I know, "you, I, him," and another Teddy there too, you see.

Brian: Right. And I didn't know whether you might be referring to your father as Teddy.

Mrs. Longworth: The funny thing is he never was called Teddy in the family. I never heard a friend of his call him Teddy. As far as I can remember it was entirely newspapers: he just became Teddy.

Brian: Because he did the famous charge up the hill and I thought perhaps that was what you meant about climbing a higher mountain.

Mrs. Longworth: No, no, no, no, no. And the Teddy thing: naturally you didn't realize but he would never have been Teddy. Some of the children called him "Uncle Ted" and others called him Theodore.

Brian: You see how confused a writer can get unless he asks questions.

Mrs. Longworth: Oh, absolutely! Praise be for tape recorders!

Brian: I'm glad you said that. I'll ask the publisher to send you a copy of the book. It's called *Murderers and Other Friendly People.*

Mrs. Longworth: How nice!

Brian: It's called that because two famous interviewers have made friends of murderers.

Mrs. Longworth: Wait a moment. Who's that? . . . Truman Capote.

Brian: Right. And William Buckley, Jr., with Edgar Smith.

Mrs. Longworth: Edgar Smith is the one who got out of prison for a few hours and then suddenly they put him back.

Brian: That's right. And he expects to face another trial.

Mrs. Longworth: I expect he has to. It must have been perfectly horrifying. (Edgar Smith has since been freed, thanks partly to William F. Buckley, Jr.)

Brian: What's your reaction to the no-longer-secret Pentagon Papers, Mrs. Longworth?

Mrs. Longworth: Oh, I've had such a good time. Just the reaction of one who enjoys things like that. I'm delighted with the press.

Brian: Are you glad that they have triumphed?

Mrs. Longworth: Oh yes. Very decidedly. Aren't you? [Laughs.]

Brian: Of course I am, 100 percent. I think it could only happen in America, you know.

Mrs. Longworth: Under our constitution. I don't see how it could happen anywhere else.

Arthur Schlesinger, Jr.

BORN IN COLUMBUS, OHIO, OCTOBER 15, 1917

A former professor of history at Harvard, Special Assistant to President Kennedy, and author of A Thousand Days: John F. Kennedy in the White House *(1965), Schlesinger is now Albert Schweitzer Professor of Humanities at the City University of New York.*

Brian: You're reported as saying to the Overseas Press Club in 1965: "Democracy is based on full information. Unless there's a critical reason, a reason of national security, for withholding information, it should be made available to the public. And national security is not the same as the reputation of people. There's nothing in a democracy that exempts people in high office from public comment." Do you disagree then with those who think there is a side of a man's life that should not be revealed to the public?

Schlesinger: I think it's a matter of time. I think so long as what happens in the private life of a public man does not affect his attitude on public issues, or some decision, there's no urgent need that that be disclosed. But again it's a matter of time. There are things about, say, the relationship between Abraham Lincoln and his wife, which there was absolutely no point in writing about or disclosing in the 1860s. But Carl Sandburg could write about these things with no problem a century later.

Brian: You think if one took a century later as the figure . . . ?

Schlesinger: A century or half a century—when everyone's dead. I think there's no point in gratuitously wounding people, so long as it doesn't bear on questions of public policy.

Brian: But then, you think, everything should be told that is known, that is relevant?

Schlesinger: That bears on public policy, yes.

Brian: And, for example, portrays the whole man?

Schlesinger: Well, as I say, I think that portraying the whole man—there are matters of private lives of people that don't bear on public policy, which, I think, there are good reasons for not ventilating at once. But, in time, I think, historians should write about everything.

Brian: Your comment on Robert Kennedy and the ruthless tag which stuck to him through his life: "I do not know of any case in contemporary politics where there seems to have been a greater discrepancy between the myth and the man." Did you ever have any theory why so many of his enemies, anyway, would call him ruthless?

Schlesinger: I think that's because of the public role he played in his early years. First in connection with Congressional investigating committees and then in the 1960 campaign. The image of the prosecutor which came out very strongly in Senate Rackets Committee Hearings is not necessarily an appealing one. And in 1960 his job was to make his brother President of the United States, and he became, in effect, the man who was the repository of discipline and denial in that campaign. And that's what people who just read the newspapers know about him. It was quite understandable that that was a misconception people might have had.

Brian: You feel he was playing a role, then, that it wasn't really true to his nature?

Schlesinger: I think he was doing a job for his brother. I think it was a very minor part of his total personality, as became evident later.

Brian: Edwin Newman said he thought Robert Kennedy displayed ruthlessness during the Eugene McCarthy bid for the Democratic nomination.

Schlesinger: Well, I don't agree with that. It seems to me this whole conception that, because McCarthy had announced his candidacy, that gave him a moral title and that it was unfair for anyone else to do so is ridiculous. I went through the 1952 campaign where Estes Kefauver not only won in New Hampshire but won in a whole series of primaries, and he was a good, admirable liberal. Adlai Stevenson did not even enter a primary and ran behind Kefauver in the first ballot in Chicago, but I don't remember people then thinking that what Adlai Stevenson did was ruthless, to take the nomination away from Estes Kefauver. It seems to me—you know politics is a rough game—the fact that McCarthy went in in New Hampshire didn't mean that everyone else should stay out.

Brian: Your account of President Kennedy weeping in his wife's arms after the Bay of Pigs fiasco that appeared in *Life* magazine but not in your book, *A Thousand Days*—because you said it sounded like a sob-sister and violated the tone of the book—couldn't you have merely written "that night he wept"?

Schlesinger: What happened was that *Life* was serializing the book, because of the competition with Sorensen in *Look*, while I was writing it. So that what they really did was to take portions from what essentially was an earlier draft. And I think I made a mistake in putting that in because I didn't write it well enough. That, it seems to me, is precisely the kind of thing that Sandburg would write about Lincoln. I don't think it was appropriate.

Brian: Perhaps in twenty-five years you would have done it.

Schlesinger: Perhaps.

Brian: Who actually witnessed President Kennedy weeping?

Schlesinger: Well, obviously there's only one source for a story like that.

Brian: Oh, his wife. Did you leave a lot out in a similar vein that might have given a human picture of him?

Schlesinger: I don't think I left out anything of any consequence so far as Presidential responsibilities.

Brian: Did you like this description of you by Helen Dundar in *The New York Post*? "A sudden boyish smile, a teenager's sunshine giggle, and a pain threshold so low that ten seconds of boredom or conversational idiocy will automatically begin curling his lip."

Schlesinger: I'd forgotten that. I don't think that's very accurate. I see myself as a person of immense patience and tolerance.

Brian: Irwin Ross, also in *The New York Post*, writes: "Few people turn Schlesinger down. For, as Stevenson has also pointed out, he is a good companion, a witty and accomplished conversationalist, and also a superb gossip, with a vast storehouse of fresh anecdotes and inside dope." He goes on to say that you relish gossip because it gives an insight into people and their human frailties. Do you think this is fair comment? And fairly true?

Schlesinger: Yes, I think so. Historians, in a way . . . the kind of history I write, it's part of the effort to recreate the atmosphere and reconstruct people as they are.

PART SEVEN
Dangerous Assignments

ALEX HALEY

Alex Haley

BORN IN ITHACA, NEW YORK, 1921

Alex Haley spent hundreds of hours interviewing one man —Malcolm X—and out of it came The Autobiography of Malcolm X. *Haley, a black man, went alone to interview George Lincoln Rockwell, black-hating leader of the American Nazis, questioning him in the farmhouse headquarters in a Virginian wood. And out of that encounter came a fascinating study of Rockwell and of Haley, too. Haley can claim to have started the interview feature in* Playboy—*by accident. He was in San Francisco when I interviewed him, and although preoccupied with work on a film and on a forthcoming book,* Roots, *in which he traces his ancestors back to Africa, he was willing to talk about the art of interviewing of which he is one of the masters.*

Haley spent his childhood days in Henning, Tennessee, where his mother was a teacher. He grew up on the campuses of black colleges in the South where his father taught. At seventeen he enlisted in the U.S. Coast Guard as a messboy. The family planned for him to gain experience and see the world before returning to college to train to be a teacher. But he stayed on and served for twenty years as a cook. Haley is a direct, friendly man who admires "be-thyselfness" in others—a quality he has himself.

Brian: How did you become an interviewer?
Haley: By accident. I had written an article about Miles Davis. D'you know who Miles Davis is?

Brian: Sounds like an orchestra leader.

Haley: He's a trumpet player. He's a master. Saying Miles Davis is like saying Gabriel in some circles. Miles talks very little to the press and I had written this article for a magazine to capture whatever little he had said. I had written it mostly in direct question and answer form. And the magazine that was going to buy it was going out of business and *Playboy* bought the article and asked me if I would do it totally in question and answer. And I did it and that became the first *Playboy* interview. And that was how that feature began.

Brian: Up till then you'd been a writer for how long?

Haley: I guess maybe ten, twelve years. When I say writer, I hadn't been earning any money for that long. But I had been writing about eight years before I sold the first story. You see, I was in the service twenty years. That's where I learned to write. I was a cook and I used to write at night at sea and that was how I got into it. And literally the way I got into writing was writing love letters for other guys on the ship. Then I started trying to write for women's confession magazines. And that went on for just years and I didn't sell any of them, but I was, you know, working around with words and trying to write. Then, finally, when I did sell I used to write for the old *Coronet* Magazine, little features, and lots and lots of small magazines. And finally I wrote for *Reader's Digest* about two years. And then I went from—I guess, one of the switches of all time—I went from *Digest* to *Playboy*. You know I used to write for *Atlantic* and *Harper's* and *Saturday Evening Post*, but not a lot, and *The New York Times Magazine*. I paid the dues, I guess that's the way to say it.

Brian: Are you interested in all people or just those of achievement?

Haley: No sir, all people. The simple thing that I have found out is that all of our lives are dramas and some of the greatest dramas and some of the most fascinating people are people who never would be described as people of achievement by the usual yardstick. I mean, a guy who is down there sweeping the streets, I only wish I had more time to get to know him better; probably a fascinating person, you know.

Brian: Do you have any picture of what life will be like after death?

Haley: No, I don't. The only time I ever really talked with anyone about that was with the late Bishop Pike. I interviewed him not too long after his son had taken his life. And we were down at Santa Barbara, where he was at the time with the Center for Democratic Studies, and Bishop Pike was telling me about the experiences he had of receiving messages from his son, who had described what life after death was like. For myself, I have no images, no idea.

Brian: You haven't had any occult experiences?

Haley: Not of that nature. I have had what I would consider a very interesting experience.

Brian: You mean like telepathy?

Haley: Yes, sure. I think the thing we know least of all about is our minds. And what our minds can do. The next book I'm coming out with, a big book, is *Roots*. It's the biography of my family, but it's really the saga of us black people. And it's a book that has involved in some way, almost occult, at times, type experiences. I was able to trace my family back into Africa, literally. It took some seven years of research and some of the things that occurred seemed almost occult.

Brian: What do you think your purpose in life is?

Haley: I tell you this much. I don't know a man in the world I would swap places with, because I can't imagine anything I could enjoy more than what I do. I guess the best way I could sum up what I would like my life to be, to achieve, whatever, would be the person who is known in African history as the *griot.* The *griot* is the teller of stories. He is the man who informs and entertains the people with insight, better knowledge, better appreciation of themselves, and where they've been in terms of history. Yes, I would like to be the *griot.* That's what I'd like to think of myself as symbolizing for all African descendants.

Brian: Malcolm X had terrible tragedy in his family—his grandmother raped and several of his relatives lynched. Don't you think that this was partly responsible for what he became?

Haley: Well, indeed, this kind of thing has happened in all too many families and in all too high an incidence of black families. You see, people today really and truly cannot appreciate the degree to which or the incidence of which black people are just atrociously misused. It just seems incredible now, but in my lifetime I can remember when white men would, without a thought, walk into a black community of total strangers and walk up to a black man on the street and ask him, "Where can I get a girl?" And if he did that today he would be the worst kind of fool. But that was literally the case up until, say, World War II. I've seen people right in Harlem, New York City, do that, as I've seen people do it in the South in little towns. It was just a matter of course. And that was the nicer part. Then girls were raped almost at will. And this thing happened in many families. I've talked with a lot of my peers, other black guys, about things in our past, and there are a lot of guys around who you just wouldn't believe some of the things that they remember. A very dear friend of mine is Dr. C. Eric Lincoln. He's at the Union Theological Seminary, and Dr. Lincoln has got all kinds of richly deserved honors and kudos for the work he does, the man he is, the distinguished educator and personage that he is. Eric is my friend and I think of him telling me how in Memphis, Tennessee, he was on a streetcar when some little nothing incident happened, and a policeman came up and stuck the end of his pistol, literally, in Eric's nose and told him: "Someday, nigger, I'll blow your head off!" And when you know the man that Eric Lincoln is today, and you think of such an atrocious thing as that, it just seems incredible that a person could have lived through something like that without flipping his lid. And I bet you I would not know a black person anywhere, no matter who he is, or what high post . . . you name them, and we could sit down and name dozens of things that have happened in our growing-up life which were utterly atrocious. And if you found one of us who couldn't name one, I would show you a freak. That's just the way it is.

Brian: Was Malcolm X the most fascinating person you ever interviewed?

Haley: I would certainly say so. I interviewed him for a solid *year*, for about three to five nights a week, maybe three to five hours each of those nights. And then I spent another year putting all the information together into the book.

Brian: What I thought was incredible was that in the end he came around to being almost a mild man and a humanitarian who felt quite warmly toward whites. Am I exaggerating when I say that?

Haley: Yes, you are. I think the best way I can put that was said by Malcolm's widow, Sister Betty. And she said: "Malcolm did not hate white people. He hated what white people had done to black people." And one can interpret that however one will. And when I now tell you, "I think you're exaggerating," it is not in a pejorative way I'm saying that, but in a factual way. I don't think Malcolm felt what might be phrased as "warmth" for the whites. But he came to the point that he accepted individual white people on their own merits. And I don't really know any white people for whom I would say, at least in my observations of being somewhat close around him, I think he felt warmth.

Brian: I spoke with Irv Kupcinet who said that he had you and Malcolm X on his show several times. I asked Kupcinet about integration and he said that he was completely for it with no reservations. I wondered how you and Malcolm X felt when you met a man like that. If you said, "So what?" or whether you did like him a little more for it. I'm asking this because in your *Playboy* interview with him, Malcolm X says that he admired white men like Verwoerd and Faubus and Rockwell. Would he in fact admire—in truth, at the end—admire them more than men like Robert Kennedy and Kupcinet?

Haley: I wouldn't pin it to individuals in the sense of saying he would admire X person more than he would Kennedy or Kupcinet. I do know this much: Malcolm sincerely appreciated those whom he considered to be honest and direct and open. Now, in the area of the people that were "liberal" or whatever, it was a matter of how the individual person came off to Malcolm or to me or to whomever else might be viewing them. I know, myself, say of Kupcinet, I just intuitively feel of him that he is a sincere, across-the-board guy, who is, if he's for you, he's for you whether you're black or polka dot or pink. We haven't met very many times but it's just my intuitive feeling and it was probably shared by Malcolm. About the late Bobby Kennedy I don't know, I never met him. Without question the best of the interviews I ever did in *Playboy* was with the late Nazi, George Lincoln Rockwell, and that was my most graphic experience with the thing that Malcolm, for instance, was talking about: the person who came right out on the line and laid it right there, what he felt or thought. Of course, obviously, I didn't *agree* with Rockwell. But the point was, we had a most exhilarating experience, and this is something I would like to talk with you about in the area of interviewing, too.

Brian: When you originally arranged to interview Rockwell did you contact him by phone?

Haley: Originally by phone. In fact it was very funny. When I called him and told him we were interested in interviewing him he went into a big thing about: "Well, you know, I can't be sure ... You can't trust these magazines," and so forth. And he said, "I'll call you back." And then he did call me back. And he said he thought he'd take the chance. And then he said, "Will you be doing the interview?" And I said, "That's right." And he said, "I have to ask you a very personal question." And I said, "Go right ahead." And he said, "Are you a Jew?" And I said, "No." And I didn't go on. And then we set up the logistics for me coming there and all that and they had no dream when I arrived that I was black. And that was something that shook the Nazis quite considerably. It was tense for both of us, it really was.

Brian: When you first spoke with him on the phone, arranging the interview, you just said, "I'm a *Playboy* interviewer"?

Haley: Yes, that's right, and my name, you know. And people don't know a writer's name. I mean they don't know who he is necessarily, they don't know what color he is.

Brian: What was his first emotional reaction when he saw you?

Haley: First I went to their place in the city and they called him and told him what had happened, that I was black. And so he gave orders that I should be brought under guard to him. And he was at a farmhouse out in the woods in Virginia. I got in a station wagon between four of them, who were in uniform and what not, with the swastika and all that. They drove me out to the farmhouse in the woods and they frisked me. Then I went up some steps and I knocked at a door. And finally he jerked open the door and jerked it open sort of with his finger in my face. And he was very upset. And he said: "I see you're black, and I'm going to be very honest with you right now, that we call your kind 'niggers' and we think you should all be shipped back to Africa." And I said: "Well, sir, I've been called 'nigger' before. But this time I'm being paid very well for it, so now you go right ahead and say what you've got against us niggers." And that was the way the interview started. And we had no illusions from the beginning, from the get-go, as the saying goes, started right off from first base, you know. And it worked out to be a very, very interesting experience, working with him over a period of time.

Brian: Did you ever get the feeling that he and Malcolm X had something in common because of their extreme views?

Haley: They had in common some of the things that are characteristic of men who have and who espouse, with any degree of success, what might be termed as "extreme" views. For one thing they had charismatic charm about them. God knows Malcolm X had it in full quantity. And Rockwell also was very, personally, a magnetic kind of man. Anyone who could get people to follow them like that and particularly in something as arduous as Rockwell proposed, had to have some kind of drawing power.

Brian: Did you find them equally truthful and frank?

Haley: I found Malcolm more frank than Rockwell and I'm not saying that to try to down Rockwell. But the thing Rockwell was trying to espouse would necessitate that he be less frank. Because there were too many things that had to be shored up with semantics and covered up and made to appear something it wasn't really. The plight of the black people, the condition of the black people, and the cry of the blacks is a much more clear-cut, honest, open issue.

Brian: For Malcolm X and Rockwell had you done a lot of research and prepared questions?

Haley: No, in neither case. As a matter of fact, after I'd learned a little bit about interviewing, I would almost deliberately not become prepared in any kind of depth. I knew what the general image of the person was and I found out that you do much better as a rule to play it by ear than to get in with a set of fifty prepared questions. You have some, of course, but what I'd find was the most valuable thing about interviewing was what one might call *the ear*—you know, to hear in depth. To hear something said that tells you there's something in there: go in there and find out what it is. So you conduct kind of an exploratory.

Brian: You said that with Malcolm X, mentioning his mother opened a floodgate.

Haley: Yes indeed.

Brian: I've asked interviewers if there's one remarkable thing they remember of their childhood and very rarely do any of them have anything to say. They seem to have had rather bland childhoods.

Haley: If I might offer you a tip, when I go to interview someone I have a researcher, George Sims, who works with me. And when I get someone to interview, he goes out looking—not anything that they've done since they got to be famous—but for everything he could find about that person before they were fifteen years of age. I found time and again with the people I was interviewing, who were famous, heavily interviewed people, that their attitude almost automatically is, "Okay, buster, what are you going to ask me that fifty people haven't already asked?" So I would ask innocuous things, of no importance really. I would act as if I wasn't all that anxious to get on with the interview. And then I would drop something like, "You know, I was in contact with so-and-so who was with you in fourth grade," or "Your fourth-grade teacher mentioned you had a great passion for lemonade," or something. Something as ridiculous as that. And it immediately does a couple of things. It raises a little bit of interest and when you come back with something else in the same genre, then it piques a little curiosity. "How much does this person know about back there?" And it also serves to start moving that person into a kind of nostalgic point of mind, *before* they were famous, *before* they were controversial, *before* they were whatever they are. And it's disarming. And a person will start talking and reminiscing, hopefully, in that area. I'd try, if it was an important interview, to go to their hometown and poke around, meet people that they knew and find out little anecdotes about them. And you find some apocryphal stories. People are somehow immensely flattered to know that back home where they were in fourth, fifth, sixth grades, people have little anecdotes about them. That means more to famous people than the latest headlines about them. So I found that technique, if techniques exist, was very effective.

Brian: Is your aim in an interview always to look for material that hasn't been revealed before?

Haley: It's not literally so much what hasn't been revealed before, but you will get depth and insight and facets which compositely will give a picture of that person, hopefully, which has not previously been painted in words.

Brian: There were frightening times, weren't there, for you when you were with Malcolm X, because he feared assassination, didn't he?

Haley: Yes, he did. But somehow my fright, I guess, wasn't so much the fear of getting killed, and I say that simply because I went through World War II, was in the battle zone, and I always felt that whenever death comes it comes. I guess what I'm trying to say is that I don't fear death. And I worked around people like Malcolm X. In fact three of the people I've interviewed have been assassinated: Malcolm X, Dr. King, and Rockwell. And all of those men reacted the same way to the question of death: that they had come to grips with its potentiality, and if they were going to do their work they had to do their work every day for itself, you know.

Brian: You were a soldier?

Haley: No, I was in the Coast Guard, U.S. Coast Guard, twenty years.

Brian: When Malcolm X was talking about God— you're a Christian, are you?

Haley: Yes.

Brian: When Malcolm X was talking about God, which he did a lot in the *Playboy* interview, did you feel he was talking about the same God as you believe in?

Haley: My own feeling about God is that every man has *his* God, and I will defend mine to the last thread of me. And I will *absolutely* never mess with yours. I know that I never felt anything except he was talking about his concept of his God, whoever it be, you know.

Brian: Did you feel there was a sanctity about Malcolm X and Dr. King?

Haley: Without question. They both had upon them the thing of greatness, without any question. And you knew it in their presence.

Brian: Did you attempt to interview the men who killed Malcolm X?

Haley: I don't know who killed Malcolm X to start with.

Brian: Weren't two men sent to prison?

Haley: Yes, they were, but that's not necessarily who killed him. What I'm saying is simply that, I guess, when you said it like that it came into me out of some considerable experience—and I know that wasn't your intent—but that's the way someone loads the hell out of a question. [Chuckles.] But no, that wasn't your thing.

Brian: I wondered if your curiosity was aroused sufficiently, and your interest, to want to get to talk with them, if they would talk.

Haley: As a matter of fact no. I'll tell you what my feeling was with them. My thing was to write the book of the man. I worked with him loyally and faithfully and I brought the best I could to him as a writer. And of course when I worked with Malcolm, we had a warm relationship. And when he was gone I really felt that I had done the best I could do in the writing of that book and that somehow it just wasn't for me to go poking around to add any postcripts or add any tangential things. That was my thing with Malcolm, that book, and that's the way I feel about it. I never will do any more than that.

Brian: When you were traveling in the station wagon with the Nazis to meet Rockwell, how did they treat you?

Haley: Very, very politely.

Brian: They spoke to you?

Haley: Spoke to me, indeed. Well, they didn't at first, but later on, in guarded ways, they would. And then he and I became quite garrulous together, in time. And he and I also had a rather considerable exchange of correspondence later.

Brian: Did he change his views in any respect as a result of talking with you?

Haley: I don't think he changed his basic views. I think he altered his views somewhat about me, the individual. I mean, he found that I wasn't a baboon. And I was able to discuss things he hadn't realized that I could.

Brian: Did he realize, as I imagine is true, that you are better educated than he?

Haley: I wouldn't say I was better educated, because he finished college and I didn't.

Brian: That's a technicality, of course.

Haley: I still wouldn't say I was better educated.

Brian: He struck you as being quite a well-educated man?

Haley: Well, he was. Rockwell was the kind of man who, if he appeared in the average cocktail party, in a sophisticated setting, and people didn't know who he was, and he didn't go on with the thing he was odious about, people would have found him a charming man. He was personally a very charming fellow.

Brian: In the preface in *Playboy* it said that Malcolm X wouldn't allow any white man to interview him. This would mean that only a black interviewer would be able to get to him.

Haley: In depth, I think that's true.

Brian: And usually only a white or non-Jewish white interviewer could get to Rockwell. But you had the best of both worlds.

Haley: I guess that somewhere this is an advantage.

Brian: I think Rockwell must have admired your courage, going to see him under armed guard.

Haley: I think he did in a way. Later, after the interview, I had some very interesting letters from Rockwell.

Brian: What did he write about?

Haley: One of the things was the difficulty he had relating to me as a black person, until he made the statement, "You've got some white blood in you, haven't you?" And I responded to that: "Of course, most of us black people have white blood." And I went into the 200 years of slavery. And then he said, "I don't care about all that. What makes you intelligent is white blood in you." And he said, "I will address myself to the white blood." So it was on that basis he began to talk to me and to give me the interview. And there was another thing he said: that he and his group found it difficult after being around me for several days to continue to hate me. I thought that was interesting. And it gave one insight into the fact that when people are exposed to each other they then begin to see each other as something other than the phobia or stereotype they have held of each other.

Brian: This is what he put in his letters, was it?

Haley: Yes, things like that.

Brian: Why do you think he wrote to you?

Haley: One, he was a man who had a kind of zest in exchanging letters with me, as I found in exchanging letters with him. It was a kind of engagement of, not so much trying to put each other down, but it's not just like getting a letter from somebody when you know what he's going to say all the time. It was just an interesting exchange.

Brian: Did he shake hands with you during your meetings?

Haley: As I recall I don't think I offered to, nor did he. So I think we, by tacit agreement, did not shake hands.

Brian: Was the white-blood theme developed while you were interviewing Rockwell?

Haley: He told me that the worst thing possible was for a black man to even notice a white woman. And I went by a florist and got a corsage and had it in a little box, and when I came in I just walked over and put it on his secretary's desk. And she looked at him. And he looked at me as if I were obviously daft. And there was this little moment of silence and I just said: "You'll have to excuse me, commander. It was my white blood that had that impulse." The thing was, he had a sense of humor. And when I said that, he thought about it and he started laughing. He thought it was funny as hell.

Brian: Was he angry that you'd come to interview him without warning him that you were a black man?

Haley: He was put out about it but it worked out. And I

think he probably was as pleased about it later as I was. Because it put both of us most on guard and hopefully brought out the best of whatever we could bring out.

Brian: Did any American Nazis go in with you after they'd driven you to lunch at Howard Johnson's?

Haley: No, they waited for me to finish and then drove me back to continue the interview with Rockwell.

Brian: They didn't treat you to lunch?

Haley: They didn't have that kind of budget. Their problem was feeding themselves; it really was.

Brian: Wasn't the house fairly luxurious though, their headquarters?

Haley: No, quite the contrary. It was a big farmhouse back in the woods and far from luxurious.

Brian: How did you feel when you heard Rockwell had been killed?

Haley: I thought about what I had asked him about this. How did he feel about the potentiality that he would be killed? And he had said that when one was doing the kind of thing he was, he had to live every day for itself. And I thought about the irony that he, the head of the Nazis in America, so-called, should die in a laundromat washing his clothes. And I thought about things I have come to know: this mocking irony that attends so often a thrust toward race-supremacy type things.

Alex Haley's interview with Malcolm X appeared in the May 1963 issue of Playboy. *This is an extract.*

Haley: You say that white men are devils by nature. Was Christ a devil?

Malcolm X: Christ wasn't white. Christ was a black man.

Haley: On what Scripture do you base this assertion?

Malcolm X: Sir, Billy Graham has made the statement in public. Why not ask *him* what Scripture he found it in? When Pope Pius XII died, *Life* magazine carried a picture of him in his private study kneeling before a black Christ.

Haley: Those are hardly quotations from Scripture. Was He not reviled as "King of the Jews"—a people the Black Muslims attack?

Malcolm X: Only the poor, brainwashed American Negro has been made to believe that Christ was white, to maneuver him into worshiping the white man. After becoming a Muslim in prison, I read almost everything I could put my hands on in the prison library. I began to think back on everything I had read and especially with the histories, I realized that nearly all of them read by the general public have been made into white histories. I found out that the history-whitening process either had left out great things that black men had done, or some of the great black men had gotten whitened.

Haley: Would you list a few of these men?

Malcolm X: Well, Hannibal, the most successful general that ever lived was a black man. So was Beethoven: Beethoven's father was one of the blackamoors that hired themselves out in Europe as professional soldiers. Haydn, Beethoven's teacher, was of African descent. Columbus, the discoverer of America, was a half-black man.

Haley: According to biographies considered definitive, Beethoven's father, Johann, was a court tenor in Cologne; Haydn's parents were Croatian; Columbus's parents were Italian——

Malcolm X: Whole black empires, like the Moorish, have been whitened to hide the fact that a great black empire had conquered a white empire even before America was discovered. The Moorish civilization—black Africans—conquered and ruled Spain: they kept the light burning in Southern Europe. The word "Moor" means "black," by the way. Egyptian civilization is a classic example of how the white man stole great African cultures and made them appear today as white European. The black nation of Egypt is the only country that has a science named after its culture: Egyptology. The ancient Sumerians, a black-skinned people, occupied the Middle Eastern areas and were contemporary with the Egyptian civilization. The Incas, the Aztecs, the Mayans, all dark-skinned Indian people, had a highly developed culture here in America. These people had mastered agriculture at the time when European white people were still living in mud huts and eating weeds. But white children, or black children, or grownups here today in America don't get to read this in the average books they are exposed to.

Haley: Can you cite any authoritative historical documents for these observations?

Malcolm X: I can cite a great man, sir. You could start with Herodotus, the Greek historian. He outright described the Egyptians as "black with woolly hair." And the American archeologist and Egyptologist James Henry Breasted did the same thing.

Haley: You seem to have based your thesis on the premise that all nonwhite races are necessarily black.

Malcolm X: Mr. Muhammad says that the red, the brown, and the yellow are indeed all part of the black nation. Which means that black, brown, red, yellow are all brothers, all are one family. The white one is a stranger. He's the odd fellow.

PART EIGHT
Everybody's Favorite

STUDS TERKEL

Studs Terkel

BORN IN NEW YORK CITY, MAY 16, 1912

Studs Terkel is the interviewer's interviewer: a man who makes the end result a work of art, as in his book Division Street: America. *Of it the* Nation *reviewer said: "The gentle, rapid, cigar-chewing little radioman Chicagoans call 'Studs' has drawn seventy noncelebrated fellow citizens into the very sort of self-revelation that until very recently could be heard only from the mouths of poets. . . . We come to know the people in Terkel's book. Again and again, the life heart is shown." And author Nadine Gordimer wrote: "A city speaks uninhibitedly through this book. Reading it, one learns the night-thoughts of urban man. Studs Terkel is a wonderfully skilled interviewer, with an instinctive ability to put the question that unlocks defenses and coaxes self-revelation."*

Terkel was educated at the University of Chicago. He has been master of ceremonies at music festivals, has written Hard Times: An Oral History of the Great American Depression *and a book for young people called* Giants of Jazz, *and has appeared as an actor on stage. He won the Prix Italia in 1962 and the UNESCO award for his radio program over WFMT, Chicago's Fine Arts Station.*

When I spoke with him on August 27, 1970, he was preparing to interview three women reporters about the women's movement and was interrupted several times for discussions with his engineer.

Terkel: Shoot!

Brian: Harrison Salisbury. What was his special interest to you?

Terkel: I interviewed him when his first two books appeared. Before he did the one on *Leningrad: 900 Days,* he wrote an early book on Russia and a novel dealing with his Russian experiences. What I do is quite simple—homework. And as a result it was pretty thrilling for both of us, I guess. We knew each other and when his *Leningrad: 900 Days* was published, he was here. In reading it, things came to my mind: such as a movement of Shostakovich's Leningrad symphony. We'd open with a piece of that. Later on there's a Russian folk song, a woman whom he knew—her voice during one of the scenes where Olga's taking that long walk. Basically, to me, interviewing is equivalent to being a craftsman or being a slovenly workman. You could not conceive of a carpenter coming to the house without his toolbox, could you? You couldn't think of an electrician coming without his fusebox, you know. And yet in radio and TV interviewing we have slovenly men at work. So when someone says to me: "Gee, that's remarkable!" I say: "No, the sadness is that it's so rare. It's not remarkable at all. It should be par for the course." I mean, do you say a carpenter is remarkable when he comes with his tools? Basically I must respect the person I'm interviewing: there's no point to it otherwise, life is much too short.

Brian: But you have the pressure of time, too, don't you?

Terkel: Sure, always. It's a matter of rhythm I guess. I do a variety of things. Yesterday I tried a sort of human comedy, capturing the voices of men watching the Women's Liberation Front rally. It's sad and funny—that is, not the Women's Liberation Front rally, no not that—I mean the comments of the guys. They're sad and funny. Their fears disguised as cheap jokes. So I make it a sort of oral tapestry. When the Picasso statue was unveiled here, a similar thing.

Brian: Not unlike when you did the Freedom Ride in "This Train."

Terkel: Oh, how did you know about that?

Brian: I got *Perspective,* which I thought was a fabulous publication. (A marvelous monthly magazine once published in Chicago "on ideas and the arts.")

Terkel: Oh, you did get *Perspective*! I'll be darned!

Brian: They had your African interviews . . .

Terkel: Did they? With Luthuli and Paton and Nadine Gordimer.

Brian: The Zulu chief Luthuli, the Nobel Peace Prize-winner, was marvelous. And Fellini . . .

Terkel: Fellini, yes. Along with a variety of others.

Brian: With Harrison Salisbury did you get any surprises? I remember you said in *Division Street* that you were astonished with the responses of people. Did you find anything like that with Salisbury?

Terkel: There's a gentleness, you know. I think what most impressed me about him is his probing, his continuously searching for what he feels is truth: at times he would be almost ruthless you know, in a good way—a seeker after the truth.

Brian: You read the Gay Talese book about *The New York Times*?

Terkel: Yes, well that's Talese being a "parajournalist": that's the phrase that Dwight MacDonald used about Tom Wolfe. I'm fond of Harrison Salisbury and I got a kick out of Talese. What was haunting me continually through the reading of *The Kingdom and the Power* were two figures: Reston and Matthews: Reston honored by this old German-Jewish family (the owners of *The New York Times*); this Protestant, puritanical sort of guy, who's really an Establishment man, who is literate, who is intelligent, at the same time, safe. Whereas you have a poetic figure in Herbert Matthews, who is also an adventurous figure, who is "Spain and Cuba," and he is put aside in Coventry. So you have, in these two, the essence of the thoughts of this family, and perhaps of *The Times*; the best paper it is, of course, by far. At the same time you have this *safeness*, you see.

Brian: The safeness of Reston?

Terkel: Safeness, oh yes, of course. The other would be *risk*. The risk of life. The risk of such changes Matthews was seeing in such a poetic . . . if there was an international Lincoln Steffens it would be he, in that sense, I mean—in a poetic way. The thing that's amazing to me is that after Talese wrote that book, only one man on *The New York Times* spoke to him, took him out to lunch. Salisbury.

Brian: I asked Salisbury if Talese would be welcomed back and he said: "Yes, I'm sure he would."

Terkel: Salisbury is the one who was nicest to him: he's obviously quite a forgiving guy.

Brian: Didn't you think Talese was rather cruel to Clifton Daniel?

Terkel: I'm not up on *The New York Times* personnel. I don't go in much for "private" revelations, that's not my world.

Brian: I notice you don't ask any sex questions. That's almost unique.

Terkel: Yes. I must tell you a story. Way back when Diana Barrymore was still alive—and she had a rough life, the last several years, she committed suicide finally—she was here in Chicago in Tennessee Williams' *Suddenly Last Summer*. And she was quite good and surprised everyone. And I was interviewing her about this. It was a good interview and she was analyzing the Williams' heroines, and I'd almost finished, when she says: "I like this interview, but wait a minute, haven't you forgotten something?" And I said: "What?" This is on the air, you know. And she said: "You haven't asked me about my personal life." She had difficulties with guys at the time and drinking. I was saying: "Well, no I haven't. It's no concern of mine. I find out about you as a person through your art. That's so exciting, you see." And she started crying. Next day—I smoke cigars—next day I got a box of cigars with a little note and it says: "No one's ever said that to me before." [Chuckles.] Anyway, that's my approach. So when you ask me about these questions I don't know what to say.

Brian: Has your technique changed dramatically over the years?

Terkel: It's hard for me to tell. You know R. D. Laing, the Scottish psychiatrist? He's a very exciting guy, I think, quite controversial in psychiatric circles. A lot of guys don't like him. One of his points is that the psychiatrist has to be the fellow-traveler with the patient: that is, he must reveal his own being to the person. That opens up the person, and, in a sense, your own vulnerability. I'm vulnerable, you see. I'm pretty terrible with a portable tape-recorder. [Chuckles.] And sometimes the person, particularly if it's a noncelebrated person—an old lady in a public housing project—will see my tape-recorder isn't working. She'll say: "Hey, it's not working!" And I say: "No, I goofed." Well, you see, my own vulnerability makes her feel more kinship.

Brian: This is almost a contradiction of one view of you, which is that you stay very much out of the picture when the interview is written, in fact.

Terkel: Right. There you have it. I think that's part of the contradiction. There's a detachment, at the same time, attachment. It's both. You know what they say of Stendhal: he was objective and subjective at the same time; he was outside and inside, both. In a sense, if one could be that—I don't know if I am—but that is the [chuckles] desideratum, whatever. That would be it, that's devoutly to be wished.

Brian: This is spontaneous with you, though?

Terkel: Oh, yes, I often get lost. The word they use a lot, I notice, is my enthusiasm. Perhaps I am. But always up above, way in the back, that detachment, too. It's not deliberate, it just is. There's a risk here too—to yourself as a person; the fate of Nathanael West's *Miss Lonelyhearts* or the efficient zombiness of the "cool" observer.

Brian: Do you consciously shape the interview with the easier, more relaxing questions to begin with?

Terkel: Very often. Particularly with the nonarticulate, the noncelebrated, in say *Hard Times* or *Division Street*. Often they're the best talkers. My god, you open up a guy from Appalachia and he's *fantastic,* you know. Or an old black man. It's incredible.

Brian: They maybe have been waiting for you for years.

Terkel: Oh my god, I must tell you this one story. He's in *Division Street*. I call him Clyde Fulton in the book; his name was Mr. Faulkner. It was a housing project for old white and black people, but mostly blacks were there. He'd retired, was about eighty-five. He was ill and his wife was there and I'm sitting in the apartment talking to him and the tape machine is working and we're just talking along and he's telling about his great skill years ago as a boner in meat packing. That was a skillful job; you skin the meat from the bone, you see. And he's saying: "I could still do that." And it's very funny because his wife is looking heavenward: "Oh God, there he goes again!" He's got heart trouble, diabetes, he's got everything, eighty-five, and, "If it weren't for those darned doctors and that woman over there," he says, "I could still be a man." And she says: "God have mercy." Anyway, we're laughing and she's giving me coffee and then I'm about to finish and it's a *marvelous* conversation and he says: "Wait a minute. Did I ever tell you what were the three great surprises of my life?" And I said, "No, what were they, Mr. Faulkner?" He said: "Well, first was when they chose me, a darkie"—the word he used was "darkie," because he was an old black guy, you know—"they chose me to be the 'Man of the World's Fair' in 1934, as the boner, Swift and Company did. The second surprise, I'm down in Tampa, Florida, oh this must be forty years ago, and a white man comes along with a woman beside him and says: "This is my sidewalk, I want it." So I give it to him. I socked him and gave him the sidewalk. And I run for the train and go back," And I'm laughing, and I'm packing up and I'm about to pull the tape-recorder plug out of the wall, when he says, "Wait a minute, you haven't asked me the biggest surprise of my life." And I say, "What's that?" He said: "You coming to see me." I said, "Now wait a minute. Why should that surprise you?" He said, "You mean that I got something to *say*? You mean I got something to say that you'd come to see me about?" I said, "Oh boy, do you!" Well, there you are. There it is. That refrain, it's a recurring theme in many of these interviews: "You mean I got something to say?" This came into my mind when you said they'd been waiting for me. Some of these guys are there, there's so much inside them waiting to be told, to come out.

Brian: You mentioned you laughed a lot with him. When you write up the interview, do you put in the fact that you laughed?

Terkel: Yes, a few times, when I put myself in it. Very often I cut myself out of it. And that's a problem I have now and then with listeners, for some reason, I guess it's the subconscious, my voice is hard to hear sometimes on the radio [chuckles]. And I've been in radio and soap operas since 1934. But I still get complaints once a month from regular listeners. They say: "When the hell are you going to speak up? We hear your guests all the time so clear." I guess it's the subconscious. It's both: I'm enthusiastic, at the same time, I've got to bring this person out, you know.

Brian: What is your essential aim in interviewing?

Terkel: Aaaah, I don't know: that's a tough one. I think it's curiosity. I suppose my essential impulse is curiosity about what Mark Twain would call "the damned human race," and each one unique, as he is, each one is an individual. The name "hardhat" makes no sense to me, you see. The words liberal, conservative—these are stupid labels, because each individual on issues is so individual and complex, very complex. And I'm fascinated, drawn . . . it's almost like Queequeg, wanting to get toward the honeyed head of Moby Dick. You know, the harpooner.

Brian: I take it that you don't have a list of questions that you stick to.

Terkel: Oh no. What I do do, with a writer, let's say, I read the book fully, and I mark, I use all kinds of crazy markings only I can decipher. And I use that as a sort of catapult and from then on what he says—and also what I remember from the book. Sometimes I'll read a certain passage which is quite revealing, whether novel or nonfiction . . .

Brian: That hits you?

Terkel: Yes. And that passage certainly explodes and opens up on other things and you freely associate. There are several things involved here. There's free association and yet not. More or less like jazz. Let's put it this way: I suppose I have been influenced by jazz, since I was a jazz disk jockey for a time and wrote columns on it. Jazz has a beginning, a middle, and an end. The framework is skeletal; at the same time there is an arrangement. When Count Basie plays an Ernie Wilkins arrangement, the soloist gets up; he creates at the same time that he interprets.

Brian: Were you very close to your parents?

Terkel: I had two older brothers, I was the pet of the family. But we split up a lot, fragmented. My father was ill: mother ran the hotel. She was a tightfisted old lady, you know, and that was her life, pretty much. I was her favorite at the expense of the other two. My middle brother and I would be at the hotel a lot, but I was mostly independent—living with my family all the time, but an air of independence was there. Could go to the Loop when I was eight or nine. Our hotel was near the Loop you see. And I had money in my pocket all the time, could go to see plays and things like that.

Brian: Did you have any heroes in those days?

Terkel: Clarence Darrow, of course. I attended the University of Chicago Law School and that was a great mistake: it wasn't the fault of the good learned men, it was just mine. I put it this way: I went to law school dreaming of Clarence Darrow and woke up to see Julius Hoffman. You can imagine my astonishment. [Laughs.]

Brian: I was going to ask if you'd done anything about the law, after graduating.

Terkel: No, no. In fact, I'm willing to bet that the average ten-year-old child knows more about law than I do, because I blocked it out. The three years were so bleak, they were unhappy years. I don't know why, I wasn't treated badly, it was just that I wasn't a very good student. It was wrong but I didn't know it at the time.

Brian: How are you most like your father?

Terkel: He was a very gentle man: I don't know whether I'm gentle or not. I guess they are both in me, some of the vitality of my old lady, I hope without her ruthlessness. She was ruthless, you know, in order to survive, because the old man was ill. Women's Movement people could understand this very well.

Brian: She was ruthless for her family?

Terkel: Sure; she was also playing what would be described in archaic language—in the pre-Women's Liberation days—as the man's role. She was a businesswoman and my father was a gentle, easy, poetic sort of guy. She was very much like Eliza in *Look Homeward,*

Angel. My old man was not like old Gant, because old Gant was a lusty, brawling . . . My father was gentle, but I guess he had the spirit of Gant.

Brian: Is there any quality you most like in people?

Terkel: I guess vitality, color, some life force. I don't give a damn what a person's ideology is, really, I really don't. Of course, I'm more drawn toward what I think is enlightenment: what I think is. But I find a guy who's almost fascistic, with a drive that is sometimes almost frightening . . . I would rather argue with him, let us say, than sit and hear the tiresome clichés of the liberal guy. You see what I mean. There's this *life* and it's a *challenge.* I think passion, that's the word I'm looking for: the passion in people.

Brian: And what do you hate?

Terkel: I guess, indifference; I guess complacency. You see I much prefer Gerald L. K. Smith to William Buckley, Jr. That's the way I can put it. Gerald L. K. Smith, you see, I saw him, and of course he's an old dinosaur, but that's not it; there's a life . . . whereas there's a complacency, the smugness—I needn't say Buckley alone, I could apply it to his "liberal" opposite number, say.

Brian: This surprises me. I've interviewed Buckley and I find him very enthusiastic.

Terkel: Maybe he is, maybe I'm unjust to him. This is just an image that I have and I might be wrong. But I do think he's closer to Frank Fay than he is to Edmund Burke. Vaudevillian, yes. Thinker, no.

Brian: I think I share your political views . . .

Terkel: But that's not the important thing for me. I almost think that political ideologies, as we know them today, are going to become archaic. There's something new in the world and it has to concern itself with life against death, as simple as that. And the *passion* for life.

Brian: Who would you most like to interview, alive or dead, that you never reached?

Terkel: Aaaaah. I reached Bertrand Russell. He was interesting. I suppose, well, Gandhi. I think he would have been very interesting because of Gandhi's young manhood, too. The lustfulness of him, too. That to me would have been interesting: a sort of poetic and political sublimation, a case here. Einstein of course. Not Schweitzer, no. A very close friend of mine, a British writer, James Cameron, found him to be a horrendous old man. [Chuckles.]

Brian: Too dictatorial?

Terkel: Oh, yes—the great White Father. He was horrible to the indigenes of Lambarene.

Brian: In the case of Gandhi you would ask personal questions, then?

Terkel: Well, childhood. Let's put it this way: I think that's the key. Autobiographical. Let *him* come out with what it is. Personal, only in that it would reveal the man's philosophy and how the philosophy came to be, or the outlook. I use the phrase "the open window." When did the window open? Was there any one time, was there one teacher, one influence, or was it an accretion of events?

Brian: Do you feel there was for you?

Terkel: In my case it was an accretion of things, there wasn't any one. I imagine it is for most. In the case of Luthuli, d'you recall he was saying that the window opened for him "at the missionary school"? It showed how remarkably paradoxical... how contradiction works. The mission schools, you know, are generally trying to impose another religion and culture on a people at the expense of their own. And yet Luthuli said a crazy thing happened. He learned to read there. He learned English, the lingua franca, you see.

Brian: I remember he did say he was grateful.

Terkel: Sure. So you see the very thing that is supposed to keep people down, or impose a superior outlook on life, becomes the very thing that frees them and makes them recognize their own strength. When Frederick

Douglass was a small boy, in his autobiography he told how his mistress taught him to read the Bible and then her husband, his master, was furious. And it was too late by that time. He had learned to read. And so, you see, "the open window." I often ask, when was it? I think of Gandhi. But I would love to have interviewed somebody like William Jennings Bryan, because here's the change that occurred the other way.

Brian: The popular picture of him is of a buffoon.

Terkel: I know, but that's not the point. In the beginning one of the Populist heroes, the boy orator of North Platte, and then bit by bit how religion took hold. You see, many Populists have become—not in Bryan's case—racists, like Tom Watson of the South. Or why does a certain man who's voted for Bob La Follette then switch to Father Coughlin? That's why the state of Wisconsin is so exciting to me. It's probably the most paradoxical state in the country, more than California.

Brian: Have you ever tried to interview J. D. Salinger or Garbo?

Terkel: I haven't tried: they'd be difficult. I imagine I wouldn't succeed. Chaplin. I did try Chaplin years ago—maybe I could succeed now, I don't know—this was years ago when he'd just moved to Switzerland, the pressures were on, you know? I wrote him a note and somehow it got to him in Vevey. And I said, "I have an idea; I'd love to interview you." And got this marvelous letter back that evidently he'd typed himself. Said: "Listen, you sound like a nice guy and I don't want you to get hurt." This was when he was still under attack. He says, "My name is anathema there and you sound like a nice person. I suggest you keep quiet about it." [Chuckles.] My idea was to name a Chaplin Theater. There was a Loew's Theater, a Warner's, a Fox—all entrepreneurs—and no theater named after the greatest artist in the history of the cinema.

Brian: Did you get into interviewing accidentally?

Terkel: Wholly accidentally. I was a gangster in soap operas, and I was with the WPA writers' project, and I was sportscasting for a while. And then one day it was just about the war's ending and one of these Agency guys who liked me, this hoodlum beer company had some money [chuckles] and they wanted to spend it on *anything*. I said, "I'd like to do a program of old records." And that's how it began—*The Wax Museum*. And that wasn't interviewing: just that. And then there were the TV days, a show called Studs' Place; it was early Chicago television for a couple of years: little greasy spoon, it was, and the four of us, that was kind of nice. It had a jazz approach, a beginning, middle, and end. And the dialogue was written by the cast, but it worked out sort of. And then I came to the station WFMT: it fascinated me, you know, the station: because once I heard Woody Guthrie on the radio, a record, and no one in Chicago played Woody Guthrie except *me*. So I called up and I said: "Who's playing Woody? I want to come down there." And they said, "We haven't any money." And I said, "I don't care." And I wasn't working then, anyway. So I started with the station and then bit by bit, interviews. They were just gradual: originally folk singers, Big Bill Broonzy and Pete Seeger together, and combinations, because I was interested in that.

Brian: Did you ever interview anyone you would call evil?

Terkel: Evil? Jeez, I don't know. That's a tough one. That's a tough word—evil.

Brian: How about saintly?

Terkel: Saintly? Yah, a woman named Jane Kennedy. She's a nurse, the head resident nurse at Billings Hospital in Chicago. And Jane—at the age of forty-four, upper-middle class, Roman Catholic background, single—joined these kids to burn the Dow Chemical files and she's been in jail up in Michigan. And I was interviewing her and she was absolutely incredible, describing her experiences and her sympathy for the matrons. And the matrons were of course, terribly moved by her. Oh, A. J. Muste probably came pretty close, too. He wasn't saintly. He had a marvelous raffish quality. You know, A. J. Muste, the old pacifist. He was pretty close up there I'd say.

Brian: I suppose you'd call Bertrand Russell a genius.

Terkel: Oh, Russell, my God, how else can he be described? Malcolm Barnes—the British editor who worked for Allen & Unwin—Barnes had known Russell and Unwin. He said, "You think of Russell now. Russell's life span—that is of his mind—is perhaps longer than that of any man in the history of mankind. That is, he lived with his grandfather and his grandfather knew Napoleon. And Russell led the kids in the Aldermaston march against the bomb. Now you think of the span of his handshake, you know—there's an old vaudeville song, 'I'm the man who shook the hand of the man who shook the hand of John L. Sullivan,' so he's the man who shook the hand of the guy who shook the hand of Napoleon."

Brian: Did anything about Russell astonish you?

Terkel: Oh yes. His clarity. *His* life force. [Chuckles.] I must tell you, my wife and a friend of ours, Phyllis Evans—her husband is the Welsh folksinger, she's American and Meredyd Evans' wife—she drove us from Anglesey where they lived, to see Russell. We had this appointment. And when Russell came to the door—he was close to ninety then, he's little, china-doll-like in features—and he shook hands and both the women said to me later on "Wow!" I said, "What d'you mean, 'wow'?" "Well, can you *imagine.* He shook our hands, he looked into our eyes." I said, "But he's ninety!" They said, "Can you imagine him at seventy!" [Chuckles.] His life, his vitality, even then at that moment, ill and everything, wow! And he would do everything himself, that was the important thing: physically that is. He wanted to rise from the chair by himself, even though I tried to help him, he just gently brushed my hand away. He would open the bay window himself, to let the little dog in. Or he'd pick up the andiron and rake the coal himself, you see.

Brian: What do you think of Mike Wallace?

Terkel: Mike probes; his approach is a wholly different one than mine. But he's okay. I think he's mellowed a great deal.

Brian: Edwin Newman?

Terkel: Okay.

Brian: David Susskind?

Terkel: [Chuckles.] No, not very good.

Brian: What's your complaint?

Terkel: Ah ... silly ... I find it ... Oh God, I don't know what to say. *Comic.* I find it amusing. He's serious but I find it amusing. I find TV commercials very amusing, you know, those that are serious. He's like a comic. A deadpan comic.

Brian: Rex Reed?

Terkel: I liked his piece on Carson McCullers.

Brian: David Frost?

Terkel: Um. I think much overrated. I feel very strongly about that. The thing I told you about at the very beginning: mediocrity has become so much the order of our day, when somebody is pretty good we say he's great. And you'd have to name an interviewer for me to say he's great: I couldn't think of one right now.

Brian: Gay Talese?

Terkel: I like him. I get a kick out of him. I like him and Tom Wolfe. I like Tom Wolfe a lot.

Brian: William Buckley, Jr.?

Terkel: I don't like his put-downs. If he's a gracious host, why is he so gauche with the obvious put-down of his guests? He has the guest ill at ease rather than at ease. He reminds me of my high school debating days: out to make points. Why do you ask me about an entertainer?

Ask me about James Agee and Henry Mayhew and Oscar Lewis and Robert Coles. Seekers I admire. If I have a model, it's Mayhew. He was a contemporary of Dickens who was great as a chronicler of the lives of the anonymous. They say he was the prototype for Micawber. I'm afraid I resemble him only in that respect—figuring something will turn up.

Brian: One of the things that specially interested me in *Division Street* was your interview with the sympathetic cop, Tom Kearney, and you printed it next to the interview with Carlos Alvarez, whose arm was badly broken by the sadistic cops. Did you ever find out what happened to Alvarez?

Terkel: He left town. I called, I don't know where he went, I called the institute where he worked. Tom Kearney is an old friend of mine. Retired now, living in California, and he's a very good man. And there again, that's what I'm talking about. The thing that disturbs me most in the world is stereotyping people. That to me is the most *horrible* thing. Because people in uniform do behave like beasts, that doesn't mean they *are* beasts. The word pigs I found so horrendous . . . It does something to the person doing the calling, too. What I'm interested in is the man stripped of the uniform.

Brian: To your question, "How would Jesus be treated if he returned to earth?" most people seemed convinced he'd be crucified again. And it was very funny that con man suggesting Jesus was also a con artist who practiced hypnotism.

Terkel: [Laughs.] Kid Pharaoh, yeh!

Brian: Are you a Christian?

Terkel: No, I'm nothing really.

Brian: Does he interest you?

Terkel: Oh yes, in that sense I'm a Christian, I suppose. I'm not, I'm an agnostic, probably an atheist. Of course, Christ interests me.

Brian: My question is, what would you ask Christ if he came back to earth?

Terkel: What would I ask Christ? Oh god, what would I ask Christ? I suppose I would start going back to his boyhood, you know. There are so many spirituals and carols that come to my mind. The one called, *Little Boy, How Old Are You?* "I'm only twelve years old." The wise men came and he answered all the questions. Talking to Jesus I suppose I'd go back, oh god [chuckles] to beginnings. Well, I wouldn't ask him who his father was. There, again, it's a private matter. But probably childhood. When did he feel he was different? Not when did he feel he was different, because he'd say, "I'm not different." When did he feel that the world could be altered? When did he feel that man is better than he is behaving? Something like that. What was it—his mother? Or was it some old man that he met?

Brian: Would you speak with him as you would with Bertrand Russell? I mean you wouldn't take him as divine?

Terkel: No, no. I would take him as a man. I would speak to him as I would Bertrand Russell, yah. Oh, of course, sure. And what it is, the vision that he has? But the big thing: what has given him the feeling that man is better than he is behaving? And does he feel that in man both strains are there, as I believe they are, you know.

Brian: Do you feel you have a purpose?

Terkel: Oh god, I don't know. Just to scrounge around, I guess. My purpose is to scrounge around, scuffle around and to enjoy life and cigars and whisky and good company and to find out. To *find out* about this damned human race.

Brian: I know you said you were an agnostic and that cuts out any belief in heaven or hell, I presume.

Terkel: Well, I would say there is immortality in this

sense: whatever man does has a piece of immortality to it. Continuity is a better word.

Brian: Are you easily moved to tears?

Terkel: I suppose I am.

Brian: What frightens you?

Terkel: As a kid, dogs did, I don't know why. But now man does. I think what frightens me now is the banality. What frightens me is this iron cage. At first it's amusing, I think, I can't take it seriously, Agnew and Reagan and Nixon. And all of a sudden I realize it is serious. And that's what frightens me. The power of, not the power of evil, the power of banality. Remember Hannah Arendt's book *Eichmann in Jerusalem*, which she subtitled *The Banality of Evil?* I like to switch that: it's the evil of banality. You see the banality itself is the evil, because it's nonimaginative, it cuts off imagination. The thing that cuts off imagination—which is what we most need today, is new imagination and the use of it—and if that cuts it off, that frightens me.

Brian: Here's one for your imagination. If you had no need of money what would you do?

Terkel: I would do what I'm doing, probably. I think. I like what I'm doing, it's a freewheeling sort of life. I like to talk, I'm curious about people, I like to hear music, I like to drink, and so I live relatively freely within a world in which no one is really free.

Brian: Do you ever get very angry at anything?

Terkel: Oh yes. I get angry at stupidities and ignorance and what I call brutality. Others might not. Angry when I see there's a fire and it's page seventy in the newspaper, you know, and it's in the ghetto and the housing authorities just go along. And then Mylai: not at Calley or Medina, you know. Just the goddam thing that led to Mylai and we still go on and suddenly I believe I'm part of this thing.

Brian: In your preface to *Division Street* you say that "interviews conventionally conducted were meaningless. Conditioned clichés were certain to come. The question-and answer technique may be of value in determining favored detergents, toothpaste, and deodorants, but not in the discovery of men and women. It was simply a case of making conversation. And listening." This is just referring to unsophisticated subjects, is it?

Terkel: Yes, I was talking of the idea of interviews conventionally conducted: "What do you think of . . . ? Who's your favorite politician? Wallace." And Wallace is, it so happens, the favorite politician among a *great many*, far more than Nixon. And that's rather interesting. I'm seeing a guy, he works as a steel laborer, a very disturbing and very interesting guy, full of violence and passion and quite disturbing: he could go either way. He likes Wallace far more than he does Nixon: he associates with him more. Anyway a conventional interview is just that: "What do you think of the riots that occurred last night?" Stuff like that, that tells us *nothing*. I'm interested in what I call "the hidden hurts."

Brian: As the subject of interviews, when you yourself are asked questions—I presume you get a lot of the same questions—do you try to avoid boring yourself by not saying the same thing, by trying to give different answers?

Terkel: I vary; I try to. That's an interesting point you raise. No one is ever quite the same. Each day I'm older . . . Right now talking with you, there is an engineer here, we're going to work something out—that by its very nature altered our conversation, you see. It made me conscious of his being there. I might have answered the question the same way—that is, substantially the same way—but in style somewhat different perhaps.

Brian: He's still waiting, is he?

Terkel: Oh no, he's okay.

Brian: My reaction to your *Division Street* was that life is generally sad or poignant for most of the people. There seemed a poverty of spirit and financial and intellectual poverty in a lot of cases.

Terkel: Yes. At the same time, in so many cases, the possibility. That's what frightens me, the fact that we might not be able—the human race—to realize its potential, with technology what it is and stupidity what it is. And even the people in the book, the poverty and nameless fears—each one is saying, "Look at me," though, each one. I use the phrase "fear and face." Each one looking for recognition as *somebody*, you know. That's the other part, the possibilities. I'm not egalitarian in the sense that all men are the same; of course they're not, but each should have the *right* to fulfill whatever there is inside him.

Brian: What shocks you?

Terkel: Gee, it's hard to be shocked these days. People's acceptance of the daily debasements and demeanings, whether it's on the CTA bus with forty-five-cent fare now, being shoved into service worse than ever, Nixon's daily affront to our intelligence, the garbage men making an infernal noise . . . Nobody objects. I did one day; I ran with my pajamas. I woke at six-thirty or so . . . I said to the man right down the alley . . . This was like a dream, but it's true . . . I was in my bare feet and pajamas and there are high rises around and all the windows were shut: nobody opened a window. And I said to this big guy: "What the hell are you doing?" "Whazzamatter?" Then a young guy comes along: he's the boss, "Is something wrong?" I said: "Why at this hour?" He said: "You don't like it at this . . . ? I said: "No. For Christ's sake I went to sleep at two." He said: "I'll come back at nine." I said: "Okay." And so for a whole week he came at nine. Then later on they went back. The point I'm making is somebody at the office said: "We'll knock off at two o'clock today." But no one questions. My point is I was the only one. And that's what shocks me, the passivity. And this also frightens me—that people will accept more and more and more.

Brian: And you could only change it for a week, anyway.

Terkel: Yes. It was a pretty good week.

Brian: Are there any mysteries that intrigue you— Judge Crater, *Marie Celeste*?

Terkel: "Where did all the yellow go?" I'll think of Chicago mysteries. Tommy O'Connor disappeared, he was supposed to be electrocuted or hanged in Chicago way back in the days of Hecht and MacArthur, and no one knows where he went.

Brian: I take it you're against capital punishment?

Terkel: Of course. To me, you see, there again someone says why don't I have two sides on my program? I say, "It's too late." How can we discuss capital punishment? I want to go a step beyond that. "What is it about a society that is so vindictive? Somebody says: "Why don't you have someone in favor of capital punishment?" I say: "No. I just haven't any time. I just haven't any time." So somebody says: "Why don't you have someone in favor of our Vietnamese adventure?" I say: "No, just haven't any time." As simple as that: "Have no time, I'm sorry." Capital punishment is worse than the crime that was originally committed, because it's planned, it's legal, it's ritual, and it's vengeful and it's approved of.

Brian: And I take it you're 100 percent for integration?

Terkel: Yes, but there again we come to something. Of course, I'm for integration in the full sense of the word, yet I can understand some of the blacks and their feelings [sighs]; it's so long. It's got to be integration on terms of person-to-person, not on terms of entering a white community. What's so great about a white community? Separatism is crazy, but I can understand the feelings about it.

Brian: Could I have your quick reaction to these names, almost as if it's a psychological test? President Nixon.

Terkel: Oh . . . god. Just a package of cigarettes or detergent. Joe McGinniss' book is right (*The Selling of the President 1968*): cipher. Who'd think a cipher would have *so much* power?

Brian: Castro.

Terkel: Colorful. I'd like to meet him.

Brian: Mayor Daley.

Terkel: Overrated hack. Neighborhood bully.

Brian: Ted Kennedy.

Terkel: Sad. I don't know enough . . .

Brian: Would you like to interview him?

Terkel: If he'd talk. I feel he'd have too many inhibitions. He's been too long in public, political life, I think. So . . . vague feelings.

Brian: Norman Mailer.

Terkel: Colorful. I would like to see more where that came from. Tremendous, an almost embarrassment of riches. At the same time wasting, horsing about. Horsing about is good, but *too much* horsing about . . . I like what Nelson Algren wrote about him several years ago. He referred to Norman Manlifellow, who was standing on his head. A trouser leg slips down, a stocking is revealed. On it reads: "Look at me." The other trouser leg slips; the other stocking says: "Keep looking." Too bad. So much waste of talent. He has a giftedness of a Nobel Laureate. It's time he quit standing on his head.

Brian: Charles Lindbergh.

Terkel: That's an interesting one. Jesus. I think about him as living on an island. You know his father was a great, progressive congressman. Split. Not his father's son.

Brian: Clare Booth Luce.

Terkel: No. Boring, I'd say.

Brian: Jacqueline Kennedy.

Terkel: Boring.

Brian: Lestor Maddox.

Terkel: Horrifying. I would say clownish. He's one of the clowns of the day. Not a Bert Lahr or Bobby Clark—he's a cheap burlesque comic.

Brian: What was your reaction when Dennis Hart said to you in *Hard Times*: "A conservative feels pain for other people because a conservative is closer to God"?

Terkel: Oh, the young John Birch kid, yeh. Well, I feel sad. You see, he to me was perhaps the saddest figure in the whole book. This kid was full of so much hurt and so many fears. I felt the most sympathy for him, and he was a John Birch member.

Brian: Was there ever a most exciting or remarkable period or moment of your life?

Terkel: I think it may be now without my realizing it. Every moment has been for me, for some time, depressing and exhilarating both. I describe myself as an emotional yo-yo.

Brian: Do you have any strong feeling about the Bay of Pigs and the press coverage beforehand?

Terkel: Yes, I sure do. It's horrendous and shocking. I think *The New York Times*, Reston's role was pretty horrendous. I think the whorishness, I call it whorishness in a way—it's not just whorishness, it's stupidity as well. Because the world is changing, we have to recognize the nature of the change and how to make that change toward the benefit of man, all men. That's why I loathe these labels, whatever they may be.

Brian: One reporter was told by his editor that the role of a newspaperman is to go down the middle of the street and shoot the windows out of both sides. Perhaps that's what should have happened there.

Terkel: Yes. The Chicago Convention made the young newspaperman aware that there is no such thing as objective journalism: there is advocate journalism. And the question: advocate what? To cover the facts as much as one possibly can, but one has a point of view and to deny it is to deny oneself. I think that Richard J. Daley and Julius Hoffman are the two greatest teachers the young have had since Socrates, because they made them know themselves. What was greater teaching to a newspaperman than a club on the head by Daley's boys? And Hoffman's incredible behavior in the courtroom, you see.

Brian: But don't you think the Chicago Seven also behaved badly?

Terkel: Oh yes, there was a bizarre quality to the whole thing, sure. They made it theater. But still I can't judge the two forces equally because there is a thing called law. There is a thing called justice. And no matter what theatrics are involved, the important thing is justice ... It came out in the new issue of *Evergreen Review.* It has a piece involving four of the jurors who said the judge kept them in. He sent them back each time they came back with a hung jury. This calls for impeachment. He didn't tell them what the rights of jurors were. So I can't equate an individual crime with institutional crime. This is the horror of the "law and order" cry. It's as phony as a $3 bill.

Brian: In *Hard Times* James Farley said of F.D.R., "He saved our free enterprise system, he saved the banks, he saved the insurance companies." Why then was he hated by so many conservatives?

Terkel: Ah, that's the question. Why does someone hate the man, sometimes, who saved his life? That's psychologically so, you know. The guy whose life is saved often hates the guy who saved his life. The old Wobbly in the book, there's an old IWW guy, Fred Thompson, who says an old friend of his wrote an obituary: "F.D.R. was loved by those he helped the least hated by those whom he helped the most." I happen to admire F.D.R. He was an astute politician. Of course he pulled fast ones, horrible things. But the one thing he had that none of his successors have had, to me it seems, is a sense of history. I think of him fondly, naturally.

Brian: Did you ever interview Robert Kennedy?

Terkel: No, I never did. I wish I did, in depth. That would have been a very interesting one, if he had been open. I think he would have been fascinating, because of the changes that were happening to him—or so I have been told by journalists I respect. I'd be curious to know why he expressed so much compassion for Joe McCarthy and so little for his victims. Would he acknowledge error? It was quite a leap from McCarthy to Martin Luther King. I do believe people can change, can grow. Bobby Kennedy may have been a classic case in point.

Brian: What are your faults or weaknesses?

Terkel: Oh god, I don't know. Repeating myself a lot, and impatience. I talk to myself a lot, swear a great deal. and, oh god, I don't know.

Brian: Are you easily bored?

Terkel: No, when I'm bored, I walk out, disappear.

Brian: What does your wife say are your best qualities?

Terkel: Oh god, I don't know. [Chuckles.] God knows what. I think she'd like my enthusiasm. But she'd [chuckles] point out many of my horrendous qualities. I have been having some wild moments of bitterness lately. I think I am getting more so as I grow older. I hope not, but I'm afraid so. I sense it.

Brian: Do you feel strongly about censorship?

Terkel: Yes. I don't think there should be any at all. It all depends upon the whole attitude toward life, toward what we think is morality. Here we have the brutish killings that demean people so. A man and woman in bed does not involve morality; but man's attitude toward man involves morality.

Brian: Do you think America is the freest of the countries for a writer?

Terkel: I would imagine England might be freer.

There's so much self-censorship here to make it. There's hidden censorship which is self-censorship, to make out. The self-censorship, to me, is the most subtle form.

Brian: The final question is a big one. Do you have any solutions to the world or national problems, the Middle East?

Terkel: Oh Jesus. Oh god. Well, I think there has to be . . . Oh, Christ. I think there has to be a new and as yet untried use of the imagination. We have to overcome all these hang-ups. I think there has to be an end to these blocks, you know. There has to be a complete reevaluation of what the hell life is all about, particularly in this age of technology, and the computer. I think all these liberation movements are connected. I think all are related in some way to the split atom, which offers two possibilities: the end of the world or the possibility of new energy, new life forces. We have splits in our species as well. This is a separatism that is healthy. It's terribly important: each one is finding his own autonomy. This is the stage now we're in. Once man—whether it's the homosexual, or whether it's the black, or whether it's the WASP, or the Chicano or the Indian, or the Mozambique rebel, or whoever the hell it is—finds his independence, his being, out of all this may emerge the possibility for all in this world. You know, something like that. Of course, none of this can happen unless the empty bellies of two-thirds of the world are fed pretty god damn soon. Now, for instance.

Brian: Mr. Terkel, you're great to interview.

Terkel: Hah! Thank you.